KNIGHT-CAPRON LIBRARY
LYNCHBURG COLLEGE
LYNCHBURG, VIRGINIA 24501

WITHDRAWN

Dorothy Livesay

Twayne's World Authors Series
Canadian Literature

Robert Lecker, Editor
McGill University

TWAS 784

DOROTHY LIVESAY
(1909–   )
Photograph by A. Lawrence Eddy.

Dorothy Livesay

By Lee Briscoe Thompson

University of Vermont

Twayne Publishers
A Division of G. K. Hall & Co. • *Boston*

Dorothy Livesay

Lee Briscoe Thompson

Copyright © 1987 by G. K. Hall & Co.
All rights reserved.
Published by Twayne Publishers
A Division of G. K. Hall & Co.
70 Lincoln Street
Boston, Massachusetts 02111

Copyediting supervised by Lewis DeSimone
Book production by Janet Zietowski
Book design by Barbara Anderson

Typeset in 11 pt. Garamond
by Compset, Inc., of Beverly, Massachusetts

Printed on permanent/durable acid-free paper
and bound in the United States of America

Library of Congress Cataloging in Publication Data

Thompson, Lee Briscoe.
  Dorothy Livesay.

  (Twayne's world authors series ; TWAS 784)
  Bibliography: p.
  Includes index.
  1. Livesay, Dorothy, 1909–   . 2. Authors,
Canadian—20th century—Biography. I. Title.
II. Series.
PR9199.3.L56Z894 1987   818'.5209   [B]   87-8553
ISBN 0-8057-6631-6 (alk. paper)

Contents

About the Author
Preface
Acknowledgments
Chronology

    Chapter One
    A Writer's Life   1

    Chapter Two
    Songs of Innocence   16

    Chapter Three
    Songs of Humanity   33

    Chapter Four
    More Poems for People   63

    Chapter Five
    Songs of Experience: Flesh Made Word   82

    Chapter Six
    A Poet's Prose   114

    Chapter Seven
    A Woman's I: *Right Hand Left Hand*   134

    Chapter Eight
    Conclusion: Measure of a Writer   143

Notes and References   149
Selected Bibliography   161
Index   171

About the Author

Born in Montreal and reared there, in Quebec City, and in Winnipeg, Lee Thompson has given each of her academic degrees a Canadian orientation. Her B.A. (Honors) thesis at the University of Winnipeg (1968) was on prairie novelist Frederick Philip Grove's *Settlers of the Marsh;* her M.A. thesis at the University of Manitoba (1969) studied the structures in Grove's entire canon; her Ph.D. dissertation at Queen's University, Kingston (1975), explored the responses of Canadian poetry to the Great Depression. Since that time she has taught English-Canadian literature in the large Canadian Studies Program at the University of Vermont and has served as associate director of that program. A member of the executive council of the Association for Canadian Studies in the United States, Thompson is the associate editor of the *American Review of Canadian Studies.* She has published articles and reviews on Canadian, British, Australian, and New Zealand literature—with several on Dorothy Livesay in particular—and has given conference papers and lectures in North America, Europe, Asia, and the South Pacific on Canadian and Australian literature.

Dr. Thompson first met Dorothy Livesay in 1970 at a Commonwealth literature conference in the West Indies. Nine years later they renewed their acquaintance at another Commonwealth literature conference, this time in their native Canada. Thompson had by then already decided to do a book-length study of Livesay's writings, attracted not only by the quality of her poetry but also by their shared experience of prairie life in Winnipeg, the link of gender, and their mutual interest in the 1930s. Livesay has been encouraging, helpful, and candid from the start, making immediately and fully accessible her home, her private papers, and her personal world.

Preface

In November 1929 Dorothy Livesay wrote in her diary: "If ever I could write one thought that would comfort some one, lift them into light, then I could surely turn to the earth content. But it is much to hope for." Nearly half a century later, her ambition had not changed:

> The validity of my life
> is whether you read this poem
> or not
> and whether it speeds
> your arrow.
> ("A Catechism," *Nine Poems of Farewell, 1972–1973*)

It is an aspiration that has been amply fulfilled. Readers in Canada and abroad have been comforted, lifted to light, moved—and more—by her songs of self, society, and life. Livesay may reasonably be evaluated by several criteria as one of Canada's most distinguished writers, and indeed a ranking figure in modern world literature.

A first gauge of her stature is the high caliber of her writing, confirmed by numerous awards and signal honors from 1928 to 1985. These include two Governor-General's Awards for Poetry and the Governor-General's Persons Award (given to outstanding Canadian women); the Lorne Pierce Medal of the Royal Society of Canada for her significant contribution to Canadian literature; the Queen's Canada Medal; the University of Western Ontario President's Medal; honorary doctorates from the Universities of Waterloo and McGill; designation as Fellow of St. John's College (University of Manitoba) and of Trinity College (University of Toronto); a Canada Council Fellowship and a Senior Arts Grant; invitations from foreign governments (e.g., Bulgaria) and universities (e.g., Aarhus); writer-in-residenceships at universities across Canada; almost six decades of largely praising reviews; accolades from fellow poets and ordinary readers, cutting across class and age lines; spotlighting on Canadian radio and television, in many published interviews, on various audio recordings, and as the subject of a documentary film, *The Woman I Am;* and translation of her poetry into not only foreign languages but also music and dance.

Then there is that impressive versatility: poetry, fiction, essays, literary criticism, journalism, drama, anthologizing, editing, and founding of periodicals. Add to this the rich abundance of her canon: as of August 1985, 22 published volumes of verse or prose; 3 edited books; easily 460 poems and reprints in periodicals and anthologies; over 120 articles, reviews, and open letters; 20 short stories; 80 journalistic pieces; 5 plays/docudramas, 5 poetry broadsides; 4 librettos or texts for interpretive dance; and new work in preparation. And finally there is the fact of her extremely active participation in, attendance upon, and nurturing of Canadian literature over close to six decades of this century.

Oddly, considering the breadth and depth of her literary career, no study of Dorothy Livesay's life and writing has ever been published. This book seeks to fill that gap, tracing the literary career and analyzing the work of a Canadian woman who is one of the most important, most remarkable, most innovative writers Canada has ever produced.

The introductory chapter of this book provides a chronological overview of Livesay's life, personal as well as literary, which is necessary to the appreciation of an artist who has for over threescore years responded intensely to her place and time.

In the second chapter, Livesay's early lyric verse is considered, with attention paid to not only her published works of the late 1920s and early 1930s but also the youthful poems that lay unpublished, many until fifty or sixty years later.

Chapter 3 is concerned with Livesay's socially committed writings in the 1930s and 1940s, and chapter 4 pursues this social orientation as it modulates into a more general humanism from the 1950s through to the present.

The fifth chapter is devoted to Livesay's sexual poetry, with particular attention to the period from the 1960s through the early 1980s. The multiple intersections of flesh, love, time's flight, and female experience are explored in detail.

Chapter 6 studies other faces altogether of Livesay's literary achievement: various types of prose. A brief investigation of family influences upon her desire to excel in prose introduces a consideration of her fiction, both published and unpublished. As well, Livesay's substantial career in journalism in the 1940s and 1950s is examined with an eye to the kinship of this public voice with her poetic voice. And her contributions as literary critic are documented.

Preface

Chapter 7 continues the attention to prose in looking at Livesay's multigenre retrospective of the 1930s, *Right Hand Left Hand,* emphasizing its innovations in the realm of female autobiography.

Finally, the eighth chapter concludes with a speculative inquiry into the reasons for the neglect by literary critics of a writer as powerful, productive, and excellent as Dorothy Livesay.

Lee Briscoe Thompson

University of Vermont

Acknowledgments

To Dorothy Livesay for her generous cooperation and encouragement; for her hospitality at her homes at Winnipeg Beach, Manitoba, and Galiano Island, British Columbia; for her permission to quote from her letters, diaries, and published and unpublished poetry and prose.

To Richard Bennett and his staff at the University of Manitoba Special Collections and to Anne MacDermaid of the Queen's University Archives for their extended and energetic assistance in exploring their voluminous Livesay holdings; to the staff of the Bruce Peel Special Collections Library at the University of Alberta.

To the Canadian Government and the Social Sciences and Humanities Research Council for a research fellowship in 1979–80 to do my initial research.

To the Canadian Government and the Canadian Embassy for a senior fellowship to complete the manuscript in 1984–85.

To the University of Vermont for sabbatical leave in 1979–80, a summer fellowship from the Graduate College in 1984, a leave of absence in 1984–85, and a scholarly grant from Dean John J. Jewett in the summer of 1985.

To Dr. E. J. Miles, director of the Canadian Studies Program, and Dr. Virginia Clark, chair of the English Department at the University of Vermont, for their unstinting support of my work, for their aid in bringing Dorothy Livesay to our campus in 1981, and for their assistance in obtaining funding for my travel and research.

To my editor, Robert Lecker, for his astute, detailed, and patient advice despite his own crushing schedule; to Judith Webster for reading the manuscript at a crucial phase; to family and friends for standing by.

Frontispiece photograph, used with his permission, is by A. Lawrence Eddy of Renaissance Books, Victoria, B.C.

Permission for general quotation from her work has been granted by Dorothy Livesay. I gratefully acknowledge the permission of the following publishers to quote extensively from copyrighted material:

Collected Poems: The Two Seasons, by Dorothy Livesay, © Dorothy Livesay by permission of McGraw-Hill Ryerson Ltd.

Feeling the Worlds, by Dorothy Livesay, © Dorothy Livesay by permission of Fiddlehead Poetry Books & Goose Lane Editions Ltd.

Beginnings: A Winnipeg Childhood, by Dorothy Livesay, © Dorothy Livesay by permission of Peguis Publishers Ltd.

Right Hand Left Hand, by Dorothy Livesay, © Dorothy Livesay by permission of Press Porcépic.

The following universities have also kindly given permission to quote from their unpublished Livesay materials: the Bruce Peel Special Collections Library, University of Alberta; the Queen's University Archives; the Archives and Special Collections, Elizabeth Dafoe Library, University of Manitoba. The University of Manitoba Livesay Collection has recently been entirely reorganized; a lengthy finding aid was published in the spring of 1986. I wish to acknowledge as well the kind permission of the estate of Lorne Pierce to quote from one of his letters.

Chronology

1909	Dorothy Kathleen May Livesay born 12 October in Winnipeg, Manitoba, Canada, to Florence Hamilton Randal Livesay and John Frederick Bligh Livesay.
1920	Moves to Toronto, when father joins Canadian Press.
1927	Senior matriculation, Glen Mawr School, Toronto.
1927–1931	B.A. (Honors) studies in modern languages, Trinity College, University of Toronto; third year (1929–30) abroad at University of Aix-en-Provence; degree granted 1931.
1928	*Green Pitcher* (poetry). First of several prizes over the years for individual poems; here, MacDougall Prize, Canadian Authors Assoc., Montreal, for poem "Impuissance." First literary articles, *St. Hilda's Chronicle* (Trinity).
1930	First article for commercial magazine, *Saturday Night*.
1932	*Signpost* (poetry); Diplôme d'études supérieures, Sorbonne.
1932–1934	School of Social Work, University of Toronto, fieldwork with Family Service Bureau, Montreal; diploma granted 1934. Progressive Arts Club. Writing for *Masses*. Illness; convalescence in Toronto, spring and summer 1934.
1934–1935	Case worker, Englewood, N.J. Summer 1935, nervous collapse; long convalescence at country home "Woodlot."
1936–1937	Regional editor, *New Frontier*. Readings, talks across Canada on modern verse; poetry, articles for *New Frontier*.
1936–1939	Case worker, Vancouver. Marriage to Duncan Cameron Macnair, 14 August 1937.
1940	Birth of son Peter on 19 April.

1942	Birth of daughter Marcia on 10 July.
1944	*Day and Night* (poetry); Governor-General's Award for Poetry. Death of father on 15 June.
1945–1947	Regional editor (West Coast), *Northern Review*.
1946	Postwar correspondent for *Toronto Daily Star* in England, France, and Germany, September–December.
1947–1953	Free-lance journalist and radio script writer, Canadian Broadcasting Corporation.
1947	*Poems for People;* Governor-General's Award for Poetry. Lorne Pierce Medal for literature, Royal Society of Canada.
1949	Editing, memoir: *The Collected Poems of Raymond Knister*.
1950	*Call My People Home* (poetry).
1951–1953	First of many university appointments: lecturer in creative writing, University of British Columbia (U.B.C.)
1953	Death of mother on 28 July.
1953–1955	Program director, Vancouver Y.M.C.A.
1955	*New Poems*.
1956–1958	Diploma in Secondary Level Teaching of English (1966). High School English teaching and counselling, Vancouver.
1957	*Selected Poems of Dorothy Livesay, 1926–1956*.
1958–1959	Canada Council fellowship: Institute of Education, University of London (England), research in creative methods of teaching English at the secondary level.
1959	Death of husband on 12 February; summer travels to France.
1959–1960	Program assistant, UNESCO, Paris; Department of Education working papers: adult education for women, education of African girls.
1960	Supply teaching, Birmingham (England), September, October.
1960–1963	Specialist in teacher training in Northern Rhodesia (now Zambia) at Chalimbana Teachers' College. Return

	to Vancouver, summer 1963. Graduate work in education (U.B.C.)
1964	*The Colour of God's Face* (poetry).
1965–1966	Lecturer in poetry, Department of Creative Writing, U.B.C.
1966	M.Ed. degree (U.B.C.)
1966–1968	Writer-in-residence, University of New Brunswick.
1967	*The Unquiet Bed* (poetry).
1968	*The Documentaries* (poetry). Surgery for lung cancer.
1968–1971	Associate professor of English, University of Alberta.
1969	*Plainsongs* (poetry).
1971	*Plainsongs* (revised, expanded). *40 Women Poets of Canada.*
1972	*Collected Poems: The Two Seasons.* First of several honorary degrees: D.Litt., University of Waterloo.
1972–1974	Visiting lecturer in English, University of Victoria.
1973	*A Winnipeg Childhood* (short stories), retitled *Beginnings: A Winnipeg Childhood* (1975). *Nine Poems of Farewell.*
1974	Guest editor, *White Pelican,* issue on Canadian North.
1974–1976	Writer-in-residence and professor, University of Manitoba.
1975	*Ice Age* (poetry).
1975–1977	*CV/II* founder-editor.
1977	*The Woman I Am* (poetry). *Right Hand Left Hand* (multigenre). Queen's Canada Medal.
1978	Editing, foreword to *Woman's Eye: 12 B.C. Poets.*
1979	*Room of One's Own* Livesay double issue, by/about Livesay.
1980–1981	Writer-in-residence, Simon Fraser University.
1981	*The Raw Edges: Voices from Our Time* (poetry).
1981–1982	Seminar, Creative Writing, Simon Fraser University.
1983	*The Phases of Love* (poetry). "The Evolution of Canadian

	Poetry, A Conference on Dorothy Livesay." 4–5 March 1983.
1983–1984	Writer-in-residence, New College, University of Toronto.
1984	*Feeling the Worlds* (poetry). Governor-General's "Persons" Award.
1985	*Beyond War: The Poetry* (poetry).

Chapter One
A Writer's Life

Dorothy Livesay has often described herself as growing up "in a garden," in the sense that both of her parents were writers, voracious readers, nurturers of Livesay's literary interests, providers of fertile soil for the blossoming of their daughter's talents. J. F. B. Livesay and Florence Randal, who met as journalists at the Winnipeg *Telegram* and married in 1908, would go on to make their marks in Canadian culture: the father as manager of the Canadian Press, essayist, and war historian; the mother as poet, novelist, and translator of Ukrainian literature; the couple as parents to one of Canada's finest poets. Born into middle-class circumstances, Livesay and her younger sister, Sophie, were encouraged artistically from childhood. The texture of those prairie years would be captured in poetry and in short fiction entitled *Beginnings: A Winnipeg Childhood*.

When, around 1920, the family shifted to Toronto and also acquired property at Clarkson, Livesay became acquainted with new aspects of the Canadian landscape: the lushness of Ontario, the brilliance of its autumns, and the conservative traditions and ceremonies of the eastern establishment. Livesay attended first a private girls' school, Glen Mawr, and then a four-year honors course in modern languages at the University of Toronto. A bespectacled "bluestocking," she and her best friend, Eugenia "Jim" Watts, at first took little interest in the opposite sex but enormous interest in such writers as Emily Dickinson, Katherine Mansfield, D. H. Lawrence, and later G. B. Shaw, Walt Whitman, Virginia Woolf, and Emma Goldman. The sophistication of even her earliest juvenilia may be attributed in part to the enriching influence in the Livesay household of everything from *Poetry* (Chicago) to the verse of Siegfried Sassoon. Throughout her youth Livesay's parents supported all her educational ambitions and discreetly promoted publication of her adolescent writings.

In 1928, encouraged by two poetry awards, Livesay published with Macmillan of Canada a slim sixteen-paged volume of poetry, *Green Pitcher*. For a university sophomore, she was remarkably well received, reviewed in the *Times Literary Supplement*[1] and by such critics as Charles Bruce[2] and Raymond Knister[3], who noted her skill with both free and traditional verse forms; the musicality of her lines; a lyrical love of nature; and the recurrence of images of wind and rain, flowers, sun, and night. Clarity of image and control of strong emotion impressed several commentators enough to predict great things of the young poet.

After a "junior year abroad" in Aix-en-Provence, soaking up French culture and sunshine and attempting to capture the experience in articles for the Toronto *Daily Star* and a still-unpublished novel, Livesay returned to her senior year at Toronto, where she had her first encounter, via a colorful professor named Otto Van der Sprenkel, with theoretical Marxism. Graduating in French and Italian in 1931, Livesay went to Paris to do a Thèse d'études supérieures at the Sorbonne. In a Canadian circle that included future historian Stanley Ryerson and Henry James critic Leon Edel, Livesay acquired some familiarity with Marx, Engels, and Barbusse. More immediate in impact, however, was her witnessing of police brutality, workers' parades, and civil disobedience. At the same time, a tempestuous love affair prompted poems that would wait forty years to be published, and Livesay dutifully completed an excellent study of the influence of the French symbolists and metaphysicals on contemporary British poets—the Sitwells, Aldous Huxley, and T. S. Eliot. In the process she found herself increasingly alienated from the elitism and obscurantism of such poets as Eliot and the sort of imagist poetry she had practiced as an undergraduate. By her return in 1932 to Canada and her first recognition of the Great Depression, social concerns ruled her thinking.

Livesay's father was hoping she would try journalism, language teaching, or diplomacy; but certain critics and writer-friends like Raymond Knister urged her to perfect her lyric poetry. To the newly radicalized young poet, these suggestions were incredibly anachronistic. When her second book of poetry appeared months after her return to Toronto, critics noted her succinctness of language, sure hand with an image, beautiful lyricism, modernist experimentation with form, and avoidance of sentimental mush. To Livesay, however, it was no longer appropriate to be writing, as she had done in *Signpost,* of rural Ontario scenes or the agonies of a private love. One reviewer who agreed with her put it this way: "Dorothy Livesay's poetry . . . has not enough contact with life."[4]

Determined to make "contact with life," Livesay enrolled in a social work course that called for a first year of study in Toronto and a second year of apprenticeship in an agency. Assignment to the Family Service Bureau in Montreal was a rapid lesson in poverty and repression. Livesay turned abruptly away from Georgian and imagist poetry and began to write proletarian verse, agitprop drama, and Marxist leaflets. Her activism in the Young Communist League, the Progressive Arts Club, and the League Against War and Fascism, as well as samples of the literature produced in those causes, are major elements of Livesay's brilliant retrospective of the 1930s, *Right Hand Left Hand*.

Critical assessment of Livesay's writing of this period has tended to be cool and dismissive, arguing that she deliberately and disastrously sacrificed her lyrical gifts and innate subtlety to what she regarded as higher causes—proletarian literature and social revolution. Certainly, such poems as "Pink Ballad" have little more than enthusiasm and sincerity to commend them, but Livesay was feeling her way toward a new style of expression that would culminate splendidly in such pieces as her famous industrial poem, "Day and Night," or the anguished and triumphant "Lorca." And the mass chants for labor halls, albeit crude, were obviously rhythmic, in accord with her lifelong principle that music underlies all poetry.

In the fall of 1934 social work took Livesay to Englewood, New Jersey, as case worker for families on relief. While dismayed by her first encounter with racial prejudice against blacks, Livesay was positively stimulated by the diversity of her friendships, the countercultural experience of being Marxist and "colorblind," and the cultural energies of Roosevelt's New Deal. In New Jersey bookshops she discovered exciting new literary models in Britain's C. Day Lewis, Stephen Spender, and W. H. Auden—poets who managed to fuse revolutionary vision with lyricism and passion. At last she could see a way to reconcile the personal and the public/political; the way was open to the dramatic jazz rhythms of the 1944 collection, *Day and Night*.

Illness, possibly a nervous breakdown, forced Livesay to return to Clarkson, Ontario, in 1935. Months spent recuperating in bed allowed her time to write of American steel mills, discrimination, and other social realities. E. J. Pratt accepted "Day and Night" for his first issue of *Canadian Poetry Magazine* (1936), declaring it "one of the best things I have ever seen you do."[5] *New Frontier,* a leftist monthly, not only published her poetry, fiction, and reviews, but also invited her to become western editor. Selling subscriptions to the periodical, speaking about modern poetry, writing articles about the places she visited, and learning about such aspects of Canadian labor history as the On to Ottawa Trek, the Regina Riots, and company towns like Corbin in British Columbia, Livesay in 1936 moved westward toward Vancouver and a new phase—geographical, literary, and private—of her life.

In Vancouver, Livesay quickly landed a family welfare job, which meshed nicely with her social activism and left-wing companionship. She married Duncan Macnair, a Scot of similar political and literary interests, who was also selling *New Frontier*. A writers' group that they formed convinced the city to let them convert an old bath house on English Bay into the West End Community Centre. Domestic, political, and cultural activities cut to a trickle the number of poems and articles Livesay was able to complete and publish in this period. The birth of a son, Peter, and a daughter, Marcia, increased for a time the difficulties of full concentration on creative writing. In addition, Livesay became an editor of Alan Crawley's journal, *Contemporary Verse*, which kept her in touch with a lively West-Coast group of writers but was an added responsibility. All of these commitments, of course, were valuable material and instruction for a volume of poetry that would win Livesay one of her country's highest literary awards.

When *Day and Night* appeared in 1944, all but the most conservative Canadian critics greeted it with high praise. The collection of verse from 1934 to 1943 was arranged chronologically, from the most urgent of social indictments through personal and pastoral poems to a concluding portrait of the unexpected vitality that World War II had given a shipyard town. The majority of reviewers perceived and lauded the intense expression, innovative driving rhythms, and overt bitterness of the social commentaries as much as or more than the lyrics of nature and the personal themes. Particularly appreciated was Livesay's clarity throughout: the crystalline imagery, the refreshing intelligibility, the precise control of sound, and the purity of tone. "Lorca," "The Child Looks Out," "The Outrider," "The Fallow Mind," "Prelude for Spring," "West Coast," and the title poem were repeatedly cited at the time and often reprinted since. And nobody was much surprised at *Day and Night*'s carrying off the 1944 Governor-General's Award for Poetry.

After the war, the Toronto *Daily Star* sent Livesay to Europe for three months to report on conditions in Britain, Germany, and France. Some thirty articles rapidly returned to Canada, tackling everything from the United Kingdom's shortage of milk to perceptions of UNESCO—Livesay's customary micro-/macrocosmic range. Despite this, her most concentrated journalistic period, Livesay also managed to draft a lengthy verse drama about Métis hero Louis Riel, eventually revised and published as "Prophet of the New World" in the 1970s.

More remarkably, Livesay also wrote and brought together the poems for a second Governor-General's Award winner: *Poems for People* (1947). She divided the collection in three: "Poems of Childhood," "Poems for People," and "Poems as Pictures." The first section demonstrated, more freely perhaps than ever before, her celebration of sound; the second spoke with great sensitivity of war and its aftermath; the third sketched vignettes from British Columbia to Wales. Once again there was the richly restrained diction, the energy and sensitivity, the humanitarianism; more than ever before, Livesay showed her ability to see wholly through the eyes of others—the child's, the war veteran's.

Also in 1947 Livesay was awarded the Lorne Pierce Gold Medal of the Royal Society of Canada "in recognition of work of outstanding distinction throughout the years." The accompanying citation by W. O. Raymond applies as accurately to her subsequent writing as it did then:

Whether she deals with Nature or Man, her art is never static or merely photographic. Professor E. K. Brown has written that her special power is energy, fiery and [some]times smoky energy. Her individual quality is revealed in the dash and originality of her poetic imagery. Sharpness of outline, vivid colouring, impressionistic flashes of lyricism, are characteristics of her work. Yet her intuitive flare does not run into romantic extravagance, but is disciplined by careful and conscientious artistry. Her poetry is aesthetically as well as ethically sincere; and the dedication of her imaginative gifts to popular causes does not impair that beauty of pattern and rhythm which is one of the most attractive qualities of her verse.[6]

From her childhood intimacy with her Ukrainian nannies and her firsthand experience of the cultural patchwork quilt of the prairies, through her ethnically diverse friendships in university, abroad, and in social work, Livesay had always been drawn to those different from herself and her white, Anglo-Saxon origins. That factor, combined with her instinct to defend underdogs (immigrants, blacks, native peoples, workers, veterans, women), made almost inevitable her writing next a poetic exposé of injustices to Canada's Japanese in World War II. Encouraged by Malcolm Lowry and others, and inspired by the

Nisei (second-generation) student who boarded with her one winter, Livesay conceived of *Call My People Home* as a documentary poem to be read on radio. A restrained and balanced plea for reconciliation and brotherhood, the poem chronicled from multiple angles the evacuation and internment of Japanese fisher families from the Pacific coast. Reviews were mixed. The control, irony, imagery, and compassion were admired; some criticism was directed specifically to the more prosaic narrative parts and more generally to problems of cadence in poetry especially created for radio. If the critics were uneasy with her innovation, not so her audience. The poem was performed, when partly complete, on Vancouver radio; repeated in Montreal; printed in full in *Contemporary Verse;* and then reprinted in Ryerson Chapbook form, together with ten shorter poems full of sun and darkness, trees and fire. There have been several Canadian Broadcasting Corporation (CBC) repetitions since then and additional reprintings in Livesay's 1968 *Documentaries* and 1972 *Collected Poems.* The title poem of *Call My People Home* continues to be a frequent request at college and high school readings.

During the early years of the 1950s Livesay put considerable effort into trying to make her mark in fiction. Encouraged by interest expressed in a story called "The Glass House" (*Northern Review,* 1950; reprinted in Martha Foley's *The Best American Short Stories,* 1951), she made numerous fiction submissions to magazines but rarely was successful. Having been taught young by her father to honor fiction above verse, Livesay has always seemed ruefully puzzled by the insistence of the majority of her readers that her poetry is her great gift, her prose a minor talent in comparison.

Correspondence of this period shows Livesay increasingly restive under family obligations and anxious to establish a more satisfying career, preferably in teaching. A short stint leading a creative writing class at the University of British Columbia Extension Department was followed by an appointment in 1953 as director of the Young Adult Department of YMCA Vancouver. While she set up adult education classes and such popular programs as Housewife's Holiday, she also continued to find time for verse. In 1955 Jay Macpherson edited a small chapbook of ten of Livesay's *New Poems,* considered by some her best work to that point. "Bartok and the Geranium," an exciting and ambiguous juxtaposition of perfectly sustained images, has certainly provoked more anthologizing and requests at readings than almost any other of her poems. The only notable competitor from *New Poems* might be "Lament," a moving poem about her father's death, recognized by the University of Western Ontario President's Medal the previous year.

From 1956 to 1958 Livesay wrestled with the teaching of difficult adolescents and left with relief when a bursary for overseas study in educational methods became available. Her son Peter was planning to work a year with a land survey crew before starting university, and his sister Marcia had won a scholarship to a progressive school in Colorado. With arrangements made for her husband's board and comfort in her absence, Livesay eagerly set off in the autumn of 1958 for studies at the Institute of Education, University of London. Nobody could have guessed that, back in Canada, Duncan would collapse and die less than six months later.

Livesay has been candid about the cycles of grief, relief, and guilt that came with widowhood. Poems from this period, published largely in periodicals and later in the "Poems from Exile" section of the *Collected Poems,* are sharp with images of death, mortality, dismemberment. There is, however, a counterpoint of bright excitement about the new freedom open to the poet no longer bound by family responsibilities. With a strong sense of putting a gray, largely frustrating decade behind her, Livesay headed for Paris and a research position with UNESCO. In 1960 she accepted a UNESCO teaching post in Northern Rhodesia.

The African experience, of three years' duration, had an enormous impact upon Livesay. She immediately achieved a rapport with her black, adult students that contrasted strikingly with the condescension of her British colleagues toward their classes. After years of focus primarily upon the personal, her eyes were once again turned to the larger scene: the transition from tribal to industrial, from Northern Rhodesia to the new nation of Zambia—a gigantic, complex, and vital proceeding. As well, Livesay threw herself into her exploration of the texture, color, taste of life in an alien world, characteristically scorning any ethnocentrism that would dismiss Zambian culture as inferior to or less attractive than the European or North American. Her letters, essays, and diaries from this period are rich with detailed description, anecdote, humanistic concern, and a rejoicing both in the warmth of her social contact and in the exhilaration of attending a country's birth.

Most important from a literary viewpoint was the fact that Africa brought Livesay into exultant contact with song and dance. In an essay by that name, "Song and Dance," Livesay tells of common-room jitterbugging by students and their delight when she participated. "And so Africa set me dancing again!"[7] Her use of the word "again" reminds us that response to music had been part of Livesay's thought and work from the earliest years. She was daughter to a translator of Ukrainian songs and was attended as a youngster by Slavic girls who sang as they moved rhythmically through their housework. Anglicanism in childhood and adolescence had introduced her to the Psalms, the Song of Songs, and the aural pleasures of the liturgy. Whitman, free verse, and the ancient dance of sex were all part of her young adult pursuit of uninhibited rhythm. Even throughout the most radicalized and prosaic period of her writing career, her assaults on mechanized madness had been repeatedly cast in industrial rhythms. In personal poetry of the 1940s and 1950s, natural rhythms did not abate. An increasing sense of stricture and confinement, however, weighted her feet, saddened her song. It was a predictable condition in one who was mother of two; wife to an authoritarian and flinty older man; working woman beset by financial and professional anxieties; western Canadian female writer in a national culture dominated by an eastern male elite; and citizen of a nation with a self-image of reserve and caution. Autonomous at last in the bright light of the "dark continent," she gave free rein to a sensuous appreciation of Africa's colors, sounds, and movements. The section "To Speak With Tongues" in *Collected Poems* and the 1964 publication, *The Colour of God's Face* (reprinted in *The Unquiet Bed* and *Collected Poems* as the "Zambia" sequence), demonstrate this new emphasis: the beating of drums, the drumming of rain, the circles of sun and moon, dance and ritual, life and love.

Returning to Canada in 1963, Livesay suffered severe doubts. The country seemed dull, complacent, crass; few fully appreciated her African writings or had much interest in events beyond their frontiers; out of the public eye for so long, she felt shy about her poetic abilities, uncertain where she would fit in with such new poetry as the American Black Mountain movement. Gradually put at ease by attending outdoor readings, teaching creative writing at UBC, and coming to know the major faces and trends on the Canadian literary scene, Livesay found herself perfectly in tune with many elements of the 1960s. The hippie celebration of love, peace, and self-expression, the interest in artifacts of native peoples and natural lifestyles, and the experiments in expansion of consciousness and of language were all intensely compatible with the new openness to life that she felt and wished to embody in her art.

Small surprise that she should at this juncture fall in love with a much younger man and at last discover with him over the next five years all the fullness possible in male-female relationships. The impact on her writing was direct: *The Unquiet Bed* (1967). Fresh, frank, spare, utterly vulnerable in its honesty, this book abandoned structured meter and conventional rhyme almost entirely but stayed taut and close to the bone, never sloppy or vague. It flowed and ebbed, shouted and whispered, was altogether (as so many noticed) a book to be read aloud. The treatment of sex and love was very beautiful, with no blinking from pain, ecstasy, contradiction, or weakness, eager for communication whatever the personal price. The title poem anticipated feminist themes of today and gave fine illustration to Livesay's many decades of expressing a woman's perspectives. The last of the four lean stanzas warns simply:

> The woman I am
> is not what you see
> move over love
> make room for me

Reviewers of *The Unquiet Bed* praised its wit, maturity, candor, and wisdom, announcing that Livesay had outstripped the work of younger poets in sensitivity, erotic intensity, and directness.

Hard on the heels of this triumph, Livesay published *The Documentaries*, six poems reflecting Canadian historical events: "Ontario Story," "The Outrider," "Day and Night," "West Coast," "Call My People Home," and "Roots." Her intent was primarily to inform young Canadians about their past and the similarities between the concerns of the 1960s and those of the 1930s and 1940s. Critics, although approving, were contradictory in their reasons: some thought them excellent poems but only incidentally appealing as history; others considered them weak art but perceptive social documents. It must be said that Livesay has always and with some justification resented certain reviewers' dismissal of her political and public writing as less worthy than her apolitical material, and she makes no apology for that or any other phase of her writing. That some still consider the social impulse an immature stage in her development, however, is clear from such incidents as the near dismissal of her 1930s activism in the 1980 film about Livesay, *The Woman I Am*.

Yet another product of this poet's reemergence in Canada was *Plain-

songs, published in 1969 and again in revised, expanded form in 1971. The collection's blend of objective description, pacifist and socially aware verse, and poems both passionate and specifically erotic was considered equal in quality to and of a piece with *The Unquiet Bed.*

Back in 1957, Desmond Pacey had edited and helpfully introduced a volume of the *Selected Poems of Dorothy Livesay,* covering 1926 through 1956. While much of his analysis is as valid today, Pacey wisely made plain that it was "impossible to predict just what turn" Livesay's poetry would take, that her track record, "constantly experimenting and growing in skill and power," guaranteed new directions. How true that was is seen at a glance in 1972's *Collected Poems: The Two Seasons.* No better commentary on this collection has been written than Livesay's own foreword, which explains in part:

These poems . . . create an autobiography: a psychic if not a literal autobiography. All the people I have known intimately, loving or hating, are here. . . . Even within the space of one year I may write formally or informally; in a structured, almost classical style, or in a free arrangement of associations. . . . always, I believe, I hear music behind the rhythm of the words. And always one or more of these symbols occur: the seasons, day and night; sun, wind and snow; the garden with its flowers and birds; the house, the door, the bed. Especially do I note the dichotomy that exists here between town and country—that pull between community and private identity that is characteristic of being a woman; and characteristic, for that matter, of life "north," life in Canada. Perhaps we are a country more feminine than we like to admit, because the unifying, regenerative principle is a passion with us. We make a synthesis of those two seasons, innocence and experience.

This book demonstrated what readers of poetry had known for several decades: that Livesay is one of Canada's best modern poets and entirely able to stand up to rigorous international criteria.

But the *Collected Poems* were no funereal signal. Nor were *Nine Poems of Farewell 1972–1973.* In 1975 Livesay brought out *Ice Age,* a book of verses that drew on the accumulated past but zeroed in on the feminine psyche and on aging, often in combination. Grandmother, old lady, elderly artist, underestimated silverhead, experienced explorer, wise individual contemplating extinctions personal and global—the facets glittered separately, then overlapped. As one critic noted, she was "still taking chances. That is the work of a great poet. That is class."[8] Free verse and street slang, contemporaneous references, vulgar humor, confessions, tenderness and defiance, irony and unabashed loneliness showed Livesay unconcerned with promoting any late-life image of the serene senior bard. Tough, compassionate, straightforward yet subtle, offering warm hope simultaneously with a chilling glimpse of apocalypse, personal and ever political, Livesay's *Ice Age* testified not to any glacial retreat but rather to her continuing profound balance of innocence and experience.

Wanting to reach new readers, in 1977 Livesay authorized the printing of an inexpensive paperback, *The Woman I Am,* providing a spectrum of poems from 1926 to 1977. In accord with her oft-voiced complaint that anthologists kept passing over her recent work for old favorites like "The Three Emilys," "Green Rain," and "Bartok and the Geranium," she allowed only thirty-three selections to come from the first forty-five years; thirty-nine poems dated from the seven years thereafter, several seeing print for the first time. The newest verses typically tackled mistreatment of native peoples and of children, Canadian disunity, abuse of the media, a recently murdered poet. Increasingly prosaic, rather like "found" conversational poems, many of these selections reinforced Livesay's pronouncements that she wishes in her final years to concentrate upon prose.

Indeed, in the midst of all this poetry, Livesay had already returned to her first literary love: prose. In 1973 she drew together short stories that had been in the making since at least the 1950s and possibly the 1920s. Entitled *A Winnipeg Childhood,* with *Beginnings* prefixed to the 1975 edition, the stories followed a lightly disguised Dorothy ("Elizabeth") through her early years in Winnipeg, before the family's move to Ontario. The rendering of a child's universe was startlingly authentic, her prairie world sharply real. The descriptive simplicity, a magic-realist dwelling upon the commonplace, the strong empathy of the stories and a lucid, fluid, rhythmic prose all charmed reviewers. Only a few saw no connection with her poetry and argued she should stick to verse.

In a format now widely imitated, Livesay in 1977 published *Right Hand Left Hand,* subtitled somewhat volubly *A True Life of the Thirties: Paris, Toronto, Montreal, the West and Vancouver. Love, Politics, the Depression and Feminism.* A remarkable account of the 1930s from a highly individual and intelligent point of view, the book was a collage of poems, letters, stories, plays, diary entries, photographs, clippings, theater programs, and articles, all linked by explanatory authorial notes. Beyond the inevitable editorial hand, Livesay resisted the natural temptation to trim and delete, to clean up and remove foolishness.

Ever one to refuse to call a spade a garden implement, Livesay has often alarmed family and friends by her insistence on telling things the way they were, undoctored. It seems to be unrelated to exhibitionism, no matter how much Livesay admits to an artist's ego. Rather it appears to derive from a passionate commitment to truth and an irrepressible optimism that directness, candor, and veracity are always preferable in the long haul. The artist is not there to prettify but to document in the most sensitive way s/he can. Thus in *Right Hand Left Hand* Livesay was prepared to term herself "duped" by communism and to print some of her pretentious juvenile letters. Generously, she included important work of other Canadians of that era, in the same impulse that has so often moved her to promote the work of others (Raymond Knister, Milton Acorn, Pat Lowther, Isabella Valancy Crawford, Anne Marriott, Peter Trower, etc.).

Readers applauded her benevolence and dedication, the integrity of the collage, and the fascinating testimony both of a time of national trauma and of a developing talent. Feminists, the young, political and intellectual historians, nostalgists, social scientists, the literati, veterans of the period—all mined *Right Hand Left Hand* for what most interested them. A few, however, complained of a randomness, partialness, or unevenness in the overall effect, failing to see any deliberate artistic purpose in the format.

Fascinated by her parents' role in the cultural history of Canada, Livesay has since labored long on prose memoirs of her family, and particularly her first thirty years with them. To date, only snippets have appeared in print, entirely in periodicals, for editors and publishers have continued to prefer her poetry. In the last decade there have been numerous individual poems in journals; several poetry broadsides, such as *Collared, Winter Ascending,* and *Beyond War: The Poetry;* and two full volumes of verse: *The Phases of Love* (1983) and *Feeling the Worlds* (1984). One verse drama, *The Raw Edges: A Script for Voices,* has had at least three incarnations: as a poem sequence in a British periodical called *Aquarius;* as a six-page pamphlet intended for school readings, with half of its profits earmarked for the Peace Tax Fund; and as a slightly altered, softbound volume called *The Raw Edges: Voices from Our Time.*

The Phases of Love might as easily have been called *The Faces of Love,* for it concerns itself with many different facets of that complicated emotion. Published in 1983 after several years of painstaking winnowing through her published and unpublished poetry, the book is carefully arranged in three chronological parts. First, there are the romantic, breathless 1920s poems of "Adolescence"; then the "Fire and Frost" of Livesay's profound sexual experiences in middle age; and finally the mature, humanist, all-embracing late-life poems of "Voices of Women." Although (as has been the case with several of Livesay's books) publication with one of the smaller presses, Coach House, has meant reduced promotion, circulation, and public awareness of this beautiful collection, critical reaction has been highly favorable and the poems generally hailed as intense, honest, finely crafted, and timeless.

Livesay's most recent[9] book of poetry, *Feeling the Worlds* (1984), takes its title from Richard Wilbur's view that "Poetry is feeling the world."[10] After considerable deliberation, Livesay pluralized "world" to capture her unabated sense of the multiple levels, aspects, and marvels of life. She has divided the volume in four, beginning with "Family Tree: A Suite," whose emphases are the generations, aging, and death. In part 2, called "Voices of Women" as was a section of *The Phases of Love,* Livesay explores female perspectives, celebrating women artists, deploring the barriers to female fulfillment, venturing some sapphic songs of love. Part 3 is a smorgasbord entitled "The Found Poems"; it ranges from the flimsily anecdotal "Fable: The Bare Necessities" through the paradoxically prosaic lyricism of "Bread and Circuses" to the emphatically poetic rhymes and cadences of "The Dialectics of Acupuncture" and "The Panic Syndrome." Then the closing section, "Nature Studies," offers a wide range of approaches to the position of humankind on this planet, with special attention to the integrity of other species and the cycles human beings so foolishly resist.

Of the four parts of *Feeling the Worlds,* the sequence of topics and moods in "Nature Studies" seems at first the least artistic, indeed downright chaotic. It starts with antiwar statements, shifts to a humorous denunciation of the Canadian beaver, thence to a declaration of utter autonomy ("Inter Rim") soon to be contradicted by a statement of absolute need to share ("Two"); the sensual appreciation of the sun on old bones ("September Equinox") strikes one as light years away from the claustrophobic, bleak vision of the subsequent "Letter from Prison." It is startling to have a psychological preparation for death ("Partings") followed by a chatty mockery of local traffic and noise, which in turn gives way to a serious ecological plea, an urgent political appeal, and the utterly serene concluding "Epitaph." But, upon reflection, the disorder seems deliberate, for Livesay has no interest in declining into predictability. The flash and swirl of theme and mood betoken an extremely active mind and heart still noticing and questioning and caring. Too tidy a format might please the logician but would be antithetical to a higher commitment: continuing, as a poet, to feel the worlds.

In overview, the years 1965–1985—Livesay's "old age"—have been from a professional angle almost crushingly busy. Shuttling from one end of Canada to the other, with countless speaking engagements scattered from local libraries to the most prestigious universities, Livesay has thrown her energies into university teaching and writer-in-residenceships in British Columbia, Alberta, Manitoba, Ontario, and New Brunswick. In Winnipeg she founded, subsidized, and edited a journal dedicated to poetry and its criticism, named *CV/II* in remembrance of Alan Crawley's *Contemporary Verse* of the 1940s. Under her editorial hand two anthologies of Canadian women's writing have come forth: *40 Women Poets of Canada* in 1971 and *Woman's Eye: 12 B.C. Poets* in 1978. She has been active in a vast range of organizations united only by the larger links of humanism, social concern, and a caring about knowledge—for example, the Committee for an Independent Canada, the League of Canadian Poets, the Association of Canadian University Teachers of English, World Federalists, Amnesty International, the Unitarian Church, and so forth. A list of her correspondents over these years reads like a *Who's Who* of Canadian letters, politics, and history, but she has also devoted much time to counselling unknown writers, journalists, and graduate students, and to encouraging fledgling periodicals. Add to this numerous literary articles; reviews; concerned letters to Members of Parliament, the CBC, and dozens of other authorities; and feisty theoretical disputes with fellow writers. Nor can the student of Livesay—or Canadiana—ignore her prodigious personal correspondence, which has never slackened in volume or liveliness from the 1920s to the present. Housed variously at the Universities of Manitoba, Queen's, and Alberta, its range and sheer bulk attest to her centrality in modern Canadian culture.

Now "retired" on Galiano Island, B.C., Livesay continues to keep abreast of national and international events, give readings, write articles, prod the young out of complacency and inertia, and work on a book about her parents and the 1920s. As her mother labored so hard for Livesay's recognition, so now "Dee," as her friends call her, has helped in the perpetuation of Florence's ("FRL's") literary memory, assisting in the preparation of a doctoral dissertation on FRL, coediting a book of FRL's Ukrainian translations, and providing Sandra Gwyn with FRL's Boer War diaries for an entire chapter on FRL in Gwyn's acclaimed new book, *The Private Capital*. Livesay would like as well to do justice to her African years, to write more short stories, to continue expanding her knowledge of the poets of other nations, and to lend continuing support to women artists in Canada. The impressive diversity of her interests, the unabated honesty of her observations, and the sparkling clarity of her sensibilities are evident in the sampling of poetry, essays, and other items assembled in the double issue of *Room of One's Own* (vol. 5, 1979) devoted to Livesay. Plagued over the years by physical ailments and emotional turmoil, Livesay has long craved synthesis but has more often been left with polarities and contradictions; these she has wisely accepted as the inherent dialectic of life. Dorothy Livesay continues to be intellectually and artistically energetic, still dispensing the advice that is at the center of her art:

> Give credence to the heart!
> Those who proceed
> by logic and good sense
> are withered at the start—
> never achieve
> old age's innocence[11]

Chapter Two
Songs of Innocence

As a frail child, Dorothy Livesay often spent long days home from school in the care of servant girls, whom she remembers as cheerful, patient, hardworking, and musical. Singing as they worked, the servants made music a natural, inevitable part of expression, the daily round, and living.[1] This had an influence on Livesay's life-long sensitivity to song, her oft-repeated theory that "Behind all poetry is the song: what Ezra Pound called *melopoeia*—melody."[2]

Contrary, however, to the conventional assumption that poetry is the highest form of human utterance, Livesay's father had taught her from the start that prose was the sublime genre. The conflict between impulse (poetry) and aspiration (prose) thus arrived early and has stayed late in Livesay's career. Despite an obvious gift for poetry, Livesay has always shared her father's preference for fiction and has never ceased to wish her talent lay in prose. Throughout the decades she has made intermittent, largely unsuccessful forays into fiction, and now, in her seventies, she has announced a return to prose, her first love. But poems continue to leap, unbidden, into her mind, and so it was sixty years ago. At the age of fifteen she entered in her diary an abstract discussion of the qualities of music and prose, concluding with sudden passion:

> I love prose—it seems akin to God. At times I long to spend my life making prose,—prose,—beautiful prose. But alas! There is music in my soul as well. Nothing will daunt my music; it swells and swells, sometimes leaving me glad—more often, leaving me sad. I wish the music would go away and let me have prose—and yet—I love my music![3]

Music prevailed, and it amuses Livesay today to tell how her mother sent off one of Dorothy's poems to the Vancouver *Province,* the result being her poetic debut and a handsome payment of two dollars. From 1926 through 1928, with guidance from her father and mother, the teen-age author placed nearly two dozen poems with reputable magazines, literary yearbooks, newspapers, and university journals. Parental ambition was almost certainly a prime mover behind the assembling of Livesay's first chapbook of verse, under the title of *Green Pitcher*. The verse in that collection was drawn from at least 250 poems young Livesay had written by the spring of 1928; some of those rejected for *Green Pitcher* would show up in subsequent books right into the 1980s, usually justifying the resurrection.

The appearance of *Green Pitcher* in September 1928 was greeted with rather more interest than the average eighteen-year-old literary debutante could expect. Poet Charles Bruce went beyond the polite praise one might anticipate from a friend of Livesay's father to commend the book's clarity and unexpected punch.[4] Writer Raymond Knister admired the capacity of its "magic of wording" to capture "an almost impalpable experience."[5] Other less prestigious reviewers extolled the spontaneity, piquancy, and lyricism of her verses. And avuncular Lorne Pierce, editor of the Ryerson Press, wrote encouragingly to her:

You have the gift of real song. I may be a little old fashioned, but I warm to poetry that sings to me as yours does. Then you have ideas, and very beautiful word-pictures to paint them with. Sometimes, as in "The Invincible," "Impuissance," "Explanation," "Chinese," and others you approach almost to magic, certainly to the memorable. So go on and up and out and over and crown the promise of your first book.[6]

Green Pitcher was, as is so often said of first books of poetry, a "slim" volume of verse: twenty-five poems printed attractively on sixteen pages, bound in an appropriately green cover, and available from the Macmillan Company of Canada for only fifty cents. The epigraph, translated from the Spanish, read: "In a pitcher I have my songs in store; / When I uncalk it, out they pour." Livesay has since remarked on the aptness of that couplet: "That was how I felt about poetry, that it was there locked up inside me and all one had to do was pull the cork and out the poems would come."[7] Examination of the initial drafts of these poems (and indeed all of Livesay's worksheets over seven decades) corroborates Livesay's sense of the spontaneity of her poetry. Most of the time what spilled onto the first blank page was almost exactly what ultimately appeared in print. An adjective or article might be dropped here, a long line made into two short ones there; a more vivid or more direct word might be substituted; deletions and changes—but virtually never additions—paring rather than expansion.

Occasionally one sees a notation, "bad," beside a line to be changed, but frequently the alteration is eventually struck out in favor of the original version.

Impatient of the constraints of regular verse forms, then as now, Livesay poured out eighteen of the twenty-five poems as free verse. Even a poem like "Wraith," which adheres to an *abcb abdb* rhyme scheme, throws over the traces to some degree with irregular meter, and the one line of "Reality" that is not pentameter is deliberately truncated to simulate the abrupt waking up from the protection of dream to the realization of "Myself alone, within a narrow bed." Livesay has often commented on her distaste for sacrificing sense for sound, on her concern that what is to be said should flow freely without being hobbled by considerations of end rhyme and formal meter. Instead devices such as repetition give a musicality to "Song from a Sequence," "The Forsaken," "Widow-Woman," and "The Lake." Livesay skillfully employed sibilance in "The Forsaken" to link stone and self. The four free-verse quatrains of "Fireweed" alternate between consonantal diction (stanzas 1 and 3) in speaking of the charred and rocky origins of the flower and an emphasis on vowels and latterly the fluidity of "f" alliteration in singing about the exhilarating results, the flower and its function as correlative for the poet's own fire. "Chinese" uses a powerful combination of pounding dimeter stresses and strong verbals ("Bellowing," "harpooned," "writhing," "pierces," etc.) to create that horrific comparison of waves with slaughtered whales that will then contrast so dramatically with the serenity of the poet's contemplativeness. The title "Chinese" reinforces the Zen effect of the polysyllabic one-word final line, "Meditation," versus the mono- or disyllabic word choice of all the rest, in fine reinforcement of the way the artist's mind has the power to conjure something up (the violent simile) and then use that as a springboard to further creativity. A final example of Livesay's technical instinct even in this first volume is "The Invincible," whose two- and three-stress compactness is combined with resonant aural effects: the internal repetitions of "dark garden," of "elms" to "delve" and "helpless" and of "elms" also to "arms"; the glancing alliteration of "suck" to "spring" to "stronger" and "bolder" to "blinded," and even, slanted, of "elms" to "men." No one effect is indispensable, of course, but the accumulation of such linkages works closely with the metric form to realize the content fully.

Almost every poem in *Green Pitcher* touches in some important respect upon that eternal theme, nature, from the opening notion of the silent eloquence of mountains and birds ("Sympathy") to the concluding statement of nature's superiority to man ("Fire and Reason"). Country mice know fairy mysteries the city mouse will never comprehend; nature can offer a perfect silence for which the spirit yearns; compared with autumnal "snatches of wonder" the poet is a "colourless wraith"; appreciation of the loveliness of natural details (bird wings, leaves) makes it possible to "hear / How silence sings"; hot sun and stubbled fields mirror sexual longings. Tulips teach joy; trees teach strength; a stone teaches the self about itself. Images of wind and rain, of flowers and trees and grasses, of sun and night and the seasons (especially autumn) predominate in *Green Pitcher,* setting a pattern for Livesay's work that is muted at times but never disappears in six subsequent decades.

The publication in 1972 of Livesay's *Collected Poems: The Two Seasons* permitted a return to some of this earliest material. In a section entitled "The Garden of Childhood" Livesay chose four free-verse and ten rhymed or blank-verse poems, almost all concerned with nature and showing the same range of moods from celebratory to fearful as did *Green Pitcher*. The effect is reinforced of a young poet awed by natural forces and by life itself, tentative and eager simultaneously, aware of the contradictions within. In "The Shrouding" she is frightened by the sun and wishes to lie dormant, "safe on lonely northern ground / Safe in the snow," the reluctant virgin "unready still to yield to loosening sap." Even the gentle breeze of "Indian Summer" is deceptive, for winter is conspiring with November "To raise its tower of swords." Summer heat, winter chill, stormy youth, and bleak old age—all are daunting. But "Experience" has already taught her something of "How the heart is fed." And a blank-verse narrative, "Hermit," delivers a reassuring message perceptive beyond Livesay's years. Declaring the wisdom of simple ways and the follies of civilization, the hermit claims that a renewal of man's forgotten kinship with nature will free him from fear, loneliness, aging, and death. In the perpetual renewal of nature's cycles, he argues, "life is a constant sun." Of course, these poems are the choices of maturity—not by accident is the final line of "The Garden of Childhood" section "From morning into darkness are we sent"—but they are also the voice of youth and the hallmark of a remarkable precocity.

The Canadian Authors Association, which had been including

individual Livesay poems in their *Yearbooks* since 1926, selected *Green Pitcher*'s "Impuissance" as joint winner of their Montreal chapter's MacDougall Prize in 1928. The next January a poem called "City Wife" won the Jardine Memorial Prize, the University of Toronto's most prestigious literary award. At the formal presentation, particular attention was drawn to Livesay's "mastery of word values rarely found in the work of so young a poet."[8] The poem thus lauded was a lengthy blank-verse first-person narrative, interspersed with rhyming quatrains, about a spring day in the life of a city girl transplanted to the country. Comparison of first with final draft shows remarkably little revision, another instance of Livesay's capacity to strike a poem out intuitively at one blow, to say it right the first time. The poem captures the mixed feelings of the young wife, enchanted by the beauty of nature, tremulous about the passing of such beauty, resentful of the land's firm claim on her husband's attentions. The elements of wind and sun, song and silence, house and flower loom large. There are intricate counterpoints of plodding man and soaring crows, delicate golden dreams and iron hands on heavy gates, flaming maples and pale cherry trees, harsh cawing and sighing wind, within the frames of morning and evening, departure and return.

When the proofs of *Green Pitcher* arrived, Livesay had already become bored with the project. She dreaded being dismissed as a merely "charming" versifier and confided to her diary that she longed for "power, fire."[9] More crucially, she lamented, "How little poetry matters to me!"[10] It was probably in part a case of disparaging what she could do so effortlessly and instinctively and wishing to master what did not come easily. (Even today, Livesay often bemoans the way poetry seems to flow from her unasked, while every page of fiction is a struggle.) The winter of 1929–30, spent in Aix-en-Provence studying French and Italian as the equivalent of third or junior year at the University of Toronto, was a long indulgence in prose—short stories, a novel, letters—but even the intercession of her father did not manage a publisher for the fiction. Spurred by the far greater recognition accorded her poetic efforts, Livesay began putting together a second volume of poetry. To her mother, who did much of the work of culling through masses of new and old poems eventually numbering some six hundred, Livesay wrote from France, "You are an angel to bother with my stuff."[11] Other letters show tempers becoming hot, as FRL attempted to edit out parts of poems and Dorothy charged that such "hacked up excerpts" were "utterly incoherent."[12] But the irritated poet eventually pondered and accepted many of her mother's detailed suggestions and acknowledged her debt in dedicating the new book "To FRL."

Signpost, presented to its public in a handsome maroon and gold cover, contained forty-six poems ranging in length from a couplet to a five-page blank-verse narrative. Livesay had atypically fretted long over the title poem, "Signpost," massively revising it several times. Her indecision seemed an echo of the indecision the poem discusses.

> Spring is forever a question
> And no one really knows
> Whether to dig in his garden
> Or follow the flight of the crows
> Led by a veering signpost—
> The old wind's nose!

Even more than the epigram at the beginning of *Green Pitcher,* this little verse serves as a sort of key to the poetry that follows. First there is the prominent presence of nature. All but perhaps three of *Signpost*'s poems either are about nature itself or use a natural metaphor or simile. The old wind and the crows presage a frequent recurrence of birds (from crows to canaries, twenty-two references) and wind (over thirty-five mentions), varying in their associations but, like the crows in *Signpost,* having most often to do with a spirit of escape or freedom. The dilemma of whether to choose to work in the garden—safe, known, productive, conservative—or fly away with the crows—risky, alien, exciting, daring—is also a signpost to the numerous doubts, questions, fears, longings, and uncertainties of the poems that follow. Pausing in her early twenties on a "Threshold," "Balanced for this brief time between the thought / Of what the heart has known, and yet must know," Livesay ends many stanzas with question marks and constantly queries her motives, her stratagems, her goals, her responses. The signpost is a "veering," changeable one. She wants to trust it:

> Lest I be hurt
> I put this armour on:
> Faith in the trees,
> And in the living wind.
>   ("Weapons")

But that image of the old wind's nose is an unsettling, irreverent one, reminiscent of Edith Sitwell. It is thus a reminder of Livesay's 1932 thesis on the metaphysical tradition in modern English poetry, with its chapters on the Sitwells and T. S. Eliot. The old wind's nose becomes a signpost both to Livesay's vacillation between old and new directions in her own verse and to *Signpost* as a marker of new tendencies in Canadian poetry.

What's so new about more nature poetry? Well, first of all, there is form. Livesay was hardly the first Canadian to write in free verse but she *was* a young poet writing at a time when *vers libre* was still viewed with a certain amount of displeasure. Her choice in *Signpost* of exactly half traditional verse and half free or innovative verse forms represented a declaration of some independence from received models, including the highly structured preferences of her own mother. Practicing such combinations as the blank-verse sonnet, written in iambic pentameter with no end rhyme, was a guarantee of some adverse criticism; one critic, especially piqued by her "mock-sonnet," declared it "disrespectful to the art."[13] Yet that "mock-sonnet," permitted the satisfying regularity and encouraged the demanding terseness of the sonnet, without obliging Livesay to skew her content to the arbitrary difficulties of end rhyme. A good illustration of the misunderstanding of readers about both the formal model and Livesay's deliberate deviation is Peter Grant's remark in his review of *Signpost* that " 'Sonnet for Ontario' is fair considering its brevity and would doubtless be much better if it were more sustained and lengthened to, say, 'City Wife' [length],"[14] a proposed extension of a sonnet from 14 to 135 lines!

It should not be thought that Livesay avoided end rhyme because of a lack of technical skill. The unpublished, unedited worksheets of her poetry demonstrate a thousand times over her rhyming facility and also the musicality that made those rhymes effortless. What seems to be the key is the subtlety afforded by flexible use of rhyme. "Climax" is a case in point. Eloquent, desperate, the free verse is counterpointed by rhyming dimeter, creating a perfect accord between the tensions of form and of content:

> My heart is stretched on wires,
> Tight, tight.
> Even the smallest wind,
> However light,
> Can set it quivering—

> And simply a word of yours,
> However slight,
> Could make it snap.

Fortunately, most reviewers gave credit to the evident artistry of the *Signpost* poems and applauded her inventiveness.[15] In addition, these might be age-old nature references, but they were being done in a newly bare, stark, spare way, each word and image sharp-edged and precise. Instead of a vague pastoral wash of cattle in a field, for instance, one could actually hear

> the slow moving of hooves,
> The soft breathings of friendly cows
> Or the sudden thunder of a young calf.
> ("Prince Edward Island")

The imagist precision of "long veils of green rain / Feathered like the shawl of my grandmother" tightly contained a nostalgia only implied by an alliance of equally exact images:

> green carpets,
> Geraniums, a trilling canary
> And shining horse-hair chairs.
> ("Green Rain")

Wind, "caressing" and comforting in one moment ("City Wife"), elsewhere becomes "the March wind's arrow," "relentless," identified directly with the lover's "sharp coldness" that "retards my spring"; then it is a fumbling, mumbling, talking, cackling parrot pecking at Livesay's bedroom blind ("Staccato"). These varied and often startling incarnations of natural forces meant that recurrence in her poetry was not merely repetition.

Not only is there a moving away from the dream landscapes favored by such nineteenth-century Canadian poets as Sir Charles G. D. Roberts, Bliss Carman, Archibald Lampman, and Duncan Campbell Scott, but there is also in *Signpost* and all of Livesay's poetry thereafter a resistance to the identifying of nature in any one stance—ally or foe or convenient metaphor for psychological states. Nature in Livesay's verse has too much life, too many ambiguous nuances, and too accurate a rendering to be simply a metaphoric vehicle. Even in those poems where nature serves as a way to understand human responses and relationships, it is a substantial third party with a vitality all its own. In that excellent sonnet "The Difference," for example, an interesting comparison is made between the lover's sober caution and the poet's spontaneity. Intellectually all is said in the first line: "Your way of loving is too slow for me." And the rest of the poem proceeds as a vivid gloss on that judgment. But the moral and aesthetic edge are ceded in the last line to nature, which can produce (whether appreciated by dull human beings or not) "A falling flame, a flower's brevity."

Most reviewers were well pleased with *Signpost* and rhapsodized on its "careful singing" (T. G. Roberts), its "curious and rather beautiful fatalism" (Charles Bruce), and the "mystic wistfulness" of its lyrics (J. P. C.). They admired Livesay's "dazzling clarity"[16] and generally were indulgent of her "Whitmanesque" songs that sported occasional modern ornaments like motorcars.[17] Nobody raged that he had been shortchanged in spending the princely sum of $1.50 for poems that made absolutely no mention of the Great Depression that had been blighting Canada and the world for three long years. Nor would they have faulted the then unpublished poems of "Findings" and "The Garden of Love" on those grounds.

One critic only, W. E. Collin, mildly observed that imagism was a limited approach, that modern poetry with hopes of becoming "important" would have to "make increasing contacts with life in the intimate present. Dorothy Livesay's poetry is poetry of herself, her own mind, and is still romantic in that sense. It has not enough contact with life."[18] But he continued, approvingly, that

Canadian poetry is coming to closer grips with life as the primary facts make themselves felt more and more insistently day in day out. This is more noticeable in Montreal than in Toronto. Dorothy Livesay's work is important as introductory to a poetry which is coming in; a poetry of vital emotion which has passed through the mind's alembic and comes out rich in images and allusions but impassioned, strong like steel.

When Collin so gently criticized *Signpost* for lacking "enough contact with life," he was voicing a reservation strongly held by the author herself. During the winter of 1931–32 Livesay had pursued advanced studies at the Sorbonne that increasingly diverged from her most immediate interests. Fired by exposure to Marxist principles and French student activism but academically committed to a dissertation on metaphysical and symbolist poetry, Livesay found it difficult to muster the enthusiasm necessary to write her thesis on what seemed to her such socially irrelevant verse. Characteristically thorough and intelligent, she produced a study of sufficiently high caliber for her thesis advisor, Louis Cazamian, to urge its expansion for publication as well as her continuation to the doctorate. But it was time to return to what the newly radicalized Livesay felt to be the real world, in which the nature and love lyrics of *Signpost* seemed for a time to be anachronisms.

From *Green Pitcher* to *Signpost* what shifts perceptibly is the poet's consciousness of intimate relationships. *Green Pitcher* had been marked by a certain adolescent preoccupation with the self; the nearest approach to explicit romantic involvement was in "Impuissance," where, as the title suggest, the bronzed farmboy was oblivious to the poet's "mute desires." Her lovers then are the sun, the wind—and those, it must be stressed, are life-long affairs. But by *Signpost* the lover acquires body and blood and an often distressing amount of power over young Livesay. A brief romance before she left for the Sorbonne had been a sweet introduction to the pleasures of the flesh and prelude to a full-scale passion in Paris. Not surprisingly, then, thirty of the forty-six poems in *Signpost* investigate aspects of romantic love, its ecstasies but also its tyrannies.

The anxieties that were veiled and expressed metaphorically in *Green Pitcher* (stones "In quivering, jagged piles," a panting greyhound, the "Defeat of sun," "The terrible animal / Pain" about to spring, the loneliness of the "narrow bed," harpoons) have in *Signpost* become much more explicit. "Weapons" repeats thrice "Lest I be hurt," trying to take refuge in nature but wondering "what shields, what swords / Can save me" if the lover decides to enter that sanctuary, "invade my skies." Although car tires on wet pavement make "A sound I have come to love," the poet waiting for her man feels inexplicably startled and then genuinely frightened by the "soft silken rush":

> Oh the low cat-coming
> Of a motor-car!
> It is as terrible
> As Fear—surging—pounding.
> ("Monition")

So vulnerable: "Your look, if not your word, / Starts me quivering like a bird." One day's heartache, although only a fraction of the sorrow life holds,

> Drops a stone
> That plunges deep
> Through flesh, through bone.
> ("Song for Solomon")

And Livesay's experience of love lost is palpable. Thinking she has

> brushed
> Your cobweb image
> From my heart

she turns abruptly and sees "Along my path / Your shadow dart" ("Dust"). In "Time" the mere mention of his name is so like sudden searing flame in her face that she is stunned to realize "that after breach of time / I could not love you less." It is interesting to note, however, that the "searing" awareness is part of a first stanza retained in Livesay's *Selected Poems* (1957) but finally deleted from "Time" in the *Collected Poems* (1972). What *has* been kept is the far more affirmative image of the former second stanza, composed some two months after the first:

> The thought of you is like a glove
> That I had hidden in a drawer:
> But when I take it out again
> It fits; as close as years before.[19]

Grief, she cynically suggests, can even be banal. "Neighbourhood" grimly explains that the stabbing memories the sight of the beloved's house used to engender have gradually lost their force; since she now passes that house daily, "Pain has a too familiar look / To need the averted head."

Livesay has said that freedom is a major interest in her writing, and her early musings on its paradoxes in love are pronounced in *Signpost*. "The Unbeliever" listens for her potential lover's voice "in these lonely places," questioning her decision to forego emotional commitment in favor of independence.

> Could I have thought there was something greater
> For my heart to gain
> By running away untouched, unshackled,
> Friends only with sun and rain?

Songs of Innocence

To be "unshackled" is sadly to be "untouched," yet to surrender is to "tremble and falter / With the first crocus" before the beloved's "breath of winter" (" 'Ask of the Winds' ") or to have one's heart "stretched on wires," about to "snap" ("Climax"). Sometimes nature resolves or at least reconciles the paradox:

> This sunlight spills the answer, and is swift
> To magnetize my passion . . .
> . . . .
> I am as bound as earth, yet wholly free
> . . . .
> I may escape—you hold my body still
> In stretching out your hand to feel the wind.
>   ("Sun")

And always there is the ambivalence—wanting the rattling at the bedroom blind to be "You" but trying to dismiss it as the wind or humorize it as a chattering parrot.

With a background of British reserve, Livesay, especially in the pride of youth, predictably often hates the exposed feeling of strong emotion. Rain compassionately cloaks her tears, while "I dread the sun / For his fierce honesty" ("In the Street"). "Interrogation" tries self-protectively to scout out the receptiveness of the beloved to her overtures:

> If I come unasked
> Will you be kind,
> Your look fair,
> Steady?

"Blindness" is shyly glad that her dancing goes unnoticed, convinced that it is somehow shameful that an elated "fluttering breath of me / Flashed with the sunlight on the wall" and relieved in her notion that "Your blindness saves my self's integrity." But there is an antithetical longing, not for self-concealment but for self-revelation, wherein the lover's obtuseness and misunderstanding can be infuriating. In "Perversity" her red gown, worn to alert him to her fire within, is taken as a sign of pride; when she switches to black to suggest humbleness, he assumes it signifies bitterness.

> I dare not wear a white gown,
> My honesty to show:

> You'd take it for a shroud, no doubt—
> Uncomforting as snow.

The division of *Signpost* into three parts—1. Sober Songs; 2. Pastorals; 3. Variations—seems primarily a concession to the fashions of poetry publication, for almost every poem could be justifiably reassigned to one of the other sections. Virtually all are sober songs; nearly all use nature imagery; and among "Variations" only "Journey" (about a streetcar trip) is neither nature linked nor particularly sober. The fifteen *Signpost* poems that survive into the *Selected Poems* in the 1950s are inverted, those of sections 2 and 3 going into the new section 1 and those of *Signpost*'s section 1 being placed in section 2 of the *Selected Poems*. Finally, when all but five of the original *Signpost* poems make it into the *Collected Poems* in the 1970s, the practice of subdivision is abandoned altogether. Later in her career Livesay plays a far more aggressive part in the physical arrangement of her work. Indeed, in the cases of *The Unquiet Bed*, *Collected Poems: The Two Seasons,* and *Left Hand Right Hand,* the organizing principle of each is a significant aspect of the book.

Once again, as with *Green Pitcher* and its sister series "The Garden of Childhood," it is instructive to look at the contemporaneous poems that were published only in journals or not at all until 1972. Thirteen poems from about 1929 to 1931 were gathered together in the *Collected Poems* under the title "Findings," followed by another sixteen from 1931 to 1932 as "The Garden of Love." There is a roughly even choosing of free verse and metrically regular poems (from a body of unpublished work similarly balanced). All the now-familiar elements return: wind, flowers, and birds; the sun and fire; silence and fascinated fear; love and pain.

The dominant mood in "Findings" is disquietude. The "strange song" of a loon, "lonely," awakening man and beast with its "laughter splintered into grief," proclaims in nature as in human life "The marriage never long delayed / Of pain with singing ecstasy" ("Northern Loon"). "White Fingers" of snow ominously invade a young girl's room. Enormous feet and "the fierce blast of burning sun" stomp on "ants / And other such small, determined creatures" in a disturbing allegory of the human condition ("Old Man Dozing"). A pioneer, appalled by "progress," repents that his struggle has made roaring cities out of wilderness and

> ravaged earth
> Of her last stone,

> Her last, most stubborn tree.
> ("Pioneer")

The poet worries about someday becoming as rigid as the parents she has just triumphantly escaped ("Now, I Am Free"). Even lovely amethyst summer days "Slip past as my arms rise vainly," unable to fly with the meadowlark ("The Prisoner") and in another season, spring, unable "to whirr / Through the air" with the sassy old crow ("Caw"). Savoring a winter fireside, she nonetheless wishes it were as easy "To creep close up to love / And gather strength." If she could,

> There would be none of these
> Cold heavy evenings
> Storm-bound, outside the door.
> ("If It Were Easy")

"Storm-bound": the participle may mean either "besieged by storm" or "headed toward storm"—and may mean both. And, as so often with Livesay's syntax, the ambiguous placement of the preposition "outside" permits us to apply it with equal ease and gloomy resonance to the storm and to the poet herself, longing for love. Elsewhere, an inexplicit pain tortures her on sleepless nights ("If I Awake"), and ironically, while childhood goblins pursue her still ("And Even Now"), she feels guilt at banishing her guardian angel in favor of her new "worship [of] earth and sky" ("The Great Divide"). Finally, in "Song from The Multitude," a sort of companion piece to "City Wife," a "country wife" is "starved for sun" and desperate to be free of factories and noise. But, "enchained" by her deep love for her husband and thus crucified by "the warring of two selves," she is dismayed to discover that love emphatically does not conquer all. Among these "Findings," then, only the brief poem "Moments" openly and unreservedly celebrates epiphanies of boundless joy, times when the poet is flawlesly attuned to the earth.

In *The Collected Poems* the second retrospective grouping of Livesay's early 1930s poetry, "The Garden of Love," shows both the blossoms and the thorns of loving. All are untitled, Livesay having even removed one title, perhaps with an eye to creating an informality, a diary effect well suited to the intimacy of the poems. Exclamation points, question marks, parentheses, and italics compound the atmosphere of immediacy, candor, and confidentiality, and are to become frequent technical devices for Livesay.

Freed from the prudish editorial hand of her mother, Livesay gives a glimpse in "The Garden of Love" of an explicitly sexual self that stays almost entirely underground until the 1960s and *The Unquiet Bed.*

> . . . O my lover
> Joy, joy with you.
> Lovely bed and lovely blankets—
> Quickly, love me too!
> ("Again the fever")

Livesay thought that nature had taught her about silence but now she admits,

> I never knew much about silence
> Until I knew
> Your silence over mine
> Your breath blowing mine out.
> ("I never knew much about silence")

In another poem, terrified by more of those visits of Lucifer, the Cat, the Wind, "the fingers at my blind," she finds that "You, sleeping by my side" afford her "safety" ("This day takes hold of me and lifts me up—"). Even in tougher competition, with the allure of the distant moon, the lover's "soft warmth" and "green countries" win hands down ("Hola! the moon"). On the darker side, images of penetration and throbbing often are tied with those of pain and entombment, being "encased within the dark" ("I am merry; till I lie alone").

Even in her euphoria there are touches of apprehensiveness. Her lover's "honesty / Is a search-light" that cruelly makes small creatures "cower and run / Before it" ("Your honesty"), and the "revolving doors" of his moods cause both fascination with and "breathless fear" of being "caught" ("Amazement"). In " 'Meet me at noon.' 'All right,' " this ardent young woman is stunned by her sweetheart's casual postponement of their rendezvous and the sudden exasperating reality this gives to her previously abstract knowledge that

> Men need to be alone—
> (Why am I not the same?
> Is love a single game?)

Fear of the loss of love then becomes overt in "Let not our love grow mildewed, out of use," where domestic images of furniture and closets precede the passionate plea: "Love, do not seek / The letting go."

The picture becomes bleaker. Livesay sees love as a dark cloud, making her "tremble for the sun's old grace"; castigates love as a disease, which "enfeebles me"; mourns love as a fleeting eden before "evil crept / A twisted thing, between us" and "Shattered the laughter."

> I found the good was evil, light grew dark.
> I found my love deformed against the wind:
> A broken thing, it gives no shelter now
> ("Shape me to your will")

Inversions, failures, betrayals: the loss of love is thus only one burden; expulsion from the realm of innocence is another, perhaps greater. What she wants most, in the unhappy aftermath, is to have learned from this "terrible, beautiful loving" a purer concept of "Love / By itself" ("I think I have not learned").

Tucked away among all these roses and weeds of "The Garden of Love" are two poems that surprise by having nothing to do with affairs of the heart. One, "These things are patient out of time," devotes three quatrains to the vigils and frustrations of writing, an early instance of the many hundreds of times Livesay will turn her attention directly to what she sweepingly calls "The Writing Game." Her use here of rhymed tetrameter to make these observances seems an amusingly deliberate demonstration of some degree of control in that difficult art of poetry.

The other aberration, "It's true, philosophies," also uses traditional verse patterning to declare Livesay an intuitive rather than a cerebral poet:

> philosophies
> Have never darkened me
> I live in what I feel and hear
> And see.

Certainly that quality of direct response to stimuli is one of the reasons Livesay is so good at sharply accurate imagery. She has always been able to hear, feel, see extraordinarily clearly and to transfer that clarity into words. But, as she jotted down this poem on 30 November 1931, the assertion that she was untouched by "philosophies" was fast becoming literary history. Watching committed activists in Paris, she wrote, "My mouth is washed with silence— / I ache; but can do nothing much." Not for long. With her return the next summer from Paris to Toronto and the taking up of social work in highly politicized defiance of her parents, Livesay embarked upon what she now terms without hesitation the most exciting phase of her career, the Dirty Thirties.

Chapter Three
Songs of Humanity

Literary critics have tended in their comparisons of her poetry to see a polarity between Livesay's "imagist" and "socialist" voices, feeling a pressure to swear allegiance to one and denounce the other. It has not been fashionable to acknowledge any affinities between the two, and yet at least one surely lies in that which unites all poetry: our starting point, music. While it was true that song had begun by as early as 1932 to underlie Livesay's public rather than her private poetry, the result was still intensity propelled by rhythm. As well, the spare directness of lyrics on love and nature became the lean bluntness of songs on the common man, a shift of message more than medium. Finally, Livesay's gift for crystallizing a moment, a sensation, an insight continued into her revolutionary verse. What did change was intent: image now served an ideological rather than an aesthetic master. The lyrical and imagist early work of Dorothy Livesay is demonstrably neither simply a derivative and socially irresponsible apprenticeship nor a golden path from which she foolishly strayed for a decade; it is a solid foundation on which the many stories of her next half century have been raised.

Livesay has often spoken and written of her political consciousness as dating from her undergraduate years at the University of Toronto. Encouraged by her father to be informed, independent, and creative, Livesay and her closest friend, Jean "Jim" Watts, attended lectures by revolutionary Emma Goldman, pored over George Bernard Shaw, devoured Frederick Engels' *Family, Property and the State*. In her fourth year at Trinity, she and her circle fell under the influence of economics professor Otto Van der Sprenkel, who brought alive for them the theories of communism. This ideology became an inspiring social vision to a comparatively pampered young woman who had written in her diary only the previous spring, "I am a traditionalist . . . individualism is liberty. There is no liberty in a communist state."[1] In the eternal sunlight and static society of Aix-en-Provence it had seemed to her unlikely "that there can be equality on earth. Even a hasty look at 'nature' shows nothing but inequality."[2]

When most of this newly aware but unquestionably privileged group shifted to Paris for advanced studies, Livesay felt a widening gap between her art and her worldview. An exciting affair of the heart and all the obvious stimulations of student life in gay Paree were amply reflected in the lyric, personal poetry discussed in chapter 2. Antiseptic Marxist theory about "proletarian struggle" was, however, being played out in the city of lights. Livesay reminisces in *Right Hand Left Hand:*

The depression and the Nazi movement and the feeling of war was all abroad in Paris in 1931 and 32. We spent all our time associating with what was going on politically, that is to say we spent the day in the Bibliothèque Nationale and evenings went to meetings or watched parades. There was a great deal of pressure against the unemployed and the factory workers. I remember coming out of one meeting and the police were there waiting. Everyone coming out of the building was forced to go right down into the Métro. We weren't allowed to wander around the streets. They just took their sticks and whacked us until we went the right way. Oh, but we saw the brutality of the French police—there were workers killed and wounded who had been demonstrating and parading in March, celebrating the Paris Commune, at the cemetery of Père-la-chaise. (36)

Returning to Toronto, Livesay ignored her parents' hints about journalism or the foreign service and registered instead in the University of Toronto School of Social Work. She quickly became involved in the Toronto chapter of the Progressive Arts Club, the goal of which was to foster militant proletarian art and to protest Depression conditions. Livesay has brilliantly captured the texture and detail of this time and indeed the entire decade in her retrospective volume, *Right Hand Left Hand,* which shows its kaleidoscopic approach in its subtitle: *A True Life of the Thirties: Paris, Toronto, Montreal, the West and Vancouver. Love, Politics, the Depression, and Feminism.*

In her eagerness to embrace the cause of the working class, Livesay found her singing voice temporarily stilled. Her poetry worksheets provide stunning confirmation of the impact of Depression Canada on Livesay's lyric impulse. After having produced an average of nearly one hundred poems every year from 1926 through 1931, she drafted a total of barely two dozen poems in the pre–New Jersey phase of 1932, 1933, and 1934. The literary output of these years was almost exclusively political and largely prosaic: leaflets, articles, agitation-propaganda ("agitprop") plays, and mass chants. Only four of her poems made it into print in those three years, the depths of the Depression, and all in the Marxist periodical *Masses:* "Pink Ballad," "A Girl Sees It!" (later "In Green Solariums"), "Broadcast from Berlin," and "Canada to the Soviet Union." They were passionate and exhortatory, perhaps deliberately unpolished to convey urgency and involvement and a working-class sensibility. Livesay was not unaware of the incongruity of the child of culture trying romantically to identify with the struggling masses. As a 1930s poem finally published in *Right Hand Left Hand* (1977) explains:

> So damn little I knew
> Wanting, since fifteen, to work in a shirt factory.
> Terrible longing to *understand*.
> And it was stifled, so many years stifled,
> With leisure, literature, learning.
> ("Growing Up," 69)

The result was an earnest, fervent, awkward poetry, an uneasy union of Marxist slogans, "Hot stuff baby!" slang, and grammatically impeccable polysyllables. Most readers have felt uncomfortable with the apparent distance between the poet's experience and her material, just as they had done with the "common man" poetry of earlier reformists like Wilson Macdonald and Robert Stead.

Alert to the need for informed articles that would press social issues in an interesting and readily accessible prose style, Livesay diverted her poetic energies almost entirely into pragmatic essays on Canadian social inequities and the responsibility of Canadian artists to react to the real world. In articles such as "Proletarianitis in Canada" she argued strongly that "until we look to the people, and the industries, the economics of our social set-up, we will have no original [literary] contribution to make. Until our writers are social realists (proletarian writers if you will) we will have no Canadian literature."[3] She tackled head-on the problem of the writers' inexperience, the fact that "All of our writers today come from an educated, middle-class group" whose orientation was "almost wholly confined to . . . the consumer's" and whose fictional range therefore had to be very consciously stretched to include the producer class if their literature were to offer a balanced and complete life view. This was all the more necessary to the health of the national literature in that the working classes had not yet found their voice and depended upon the articulate to speak for them.

The next step was to practice what she was preaching. One result was articles like "Fascism in Quebec,"[4] wherein she exposed the anti-Semitism rampant in Quebec, as well as the fascist nature of governmental programs and ruling-class policies. Beginning with a mention of the bluebird emblem used by working-class merchants to signal that their goods had not been bought from Jews, Livesay traced the historic roots of such biases and demolished the Canadian self-image of a people of sweet reason. With revolutionary optimism, she managed to conclude hopefully that democracy was gradually gaining ground, that the unemployed were finally putting aside prejudice to fight together in their common cause. As with such other articles as "Indians at Caughnawaugha,"[5] Livesay used powerful vignettes, vivid images, striking quotations, and sharply plain prose to paint a compelling social picture.

As Livesay has recounted in *The Documentaries* and elsewhere, it was in a random browse through a New Jersey bookstore that she found a way of reconciling her lyricism with her new social concerns, of meshing art with message, the private with the public self. The model was offered by three leftist English poets in particular: Wystan H. Auden, Stephen Spender, and Cecil Day Lewis. To her astonishment and joy, Livesay found that they

> were writing a poetry freed from dogmatism. It was revolutionary, true, but full of lyricism and personal passion! There was nothing like it in Canada nor even America. Here was a movement in literature that met my own inclinations, for it discarded the pessimism of T. S. Eliot and reclaimed a brave new world—that of Blake and Whitman. (*The Documentaries*, 16f)

Especially illuminating for her was Day Lewis's book *A Hope for Poetry* (1934), which did not require of the artist any elaborate or difficult ideology but simply the capacity to hold a mirror up to reality, to show a society to itself. For Livesay, whose general approach has always been intuitive and heartfelt rather than theoretical and intellectual, this exemption from an alien role as philosophical leader must have been a relief.

While Livesay has often footnoted her 1930s poetry with grateful reference to Spender, Auden, and Day Lewis, it is clear upon comparison that she also shared some of their weaknesses. Longing to document social renewal, she occasionally fell, like them, into cant phrases

Songs of Humanity 37

of revolution, clichéed imagery of dawn, mountains, and harvests, and vague visions of revitalization and universal brotherhood. Conversely, where Livesay and other *Masses* and *New Frontier* poets would have done well to take a leaf from the Britishers' book, they did not: unlike their mother-country models, the Canadians seem not to have made concerted efforts to appear in print in the places the common man would have been likely to see them. Partly at the mercy of editorial preferences, of course, Livesay had published almost exclusively in journals of limited and educated readership such as the *Canadian Poetry Magazine*, the *Canadian Forum*, the *Canadian Bookman*, *Masses*, and *New Frontier*. Of twenty-three social poems that she published during the 1930s, only three appeared in popular venues such as *Saturday Night* or the Vancouver *Province*,[6] all at a very late stage of the decade, from March 1938 through November 1939, when even poetasters were trying their hand at a little social commentary.

"Joe Derry," a dramatic piece published in *Masses*, illustrates the dilemma of reaching the common person. It was intended, as the subtitle says, "for children's groups." A child spokesman explains in simple poetry what a children's mime group acts out. At the end all shout together,

ANSWER THE BOSSES' ATTACK! THE RIGHT TO ORGANIZE IS OURS! PROTEST THE ATTACK ON THE Y[oung] C[ommunist] L[eague]! DEFEND JOE DERRY![7]

The children, excited by the choreography, moved by the energy of the slogans, borne along by the swinging rhythms, would not just learn but also feel the workers' plight and the workers' potential power. Choral work would reinforce the group identification and the sense not merely of injustice but of class injustice. The mass chant, after all, was a time-honored mainstay of agitprop drama, for

In the struggle for socialism, a central role of a revolutionary movement is to make the working class consciously aware of its collective strength. The mass recitation, which joins disparate voices into a united chant, is an aesthetic process which parallels and recreates this phenomenon.[8]

But the child narrator speaks of the working class as "us," identifies the managerial class ("the bosses") as "them," and predicts "victory" of the have-nots over the haves. So the audience is an obviously proscribed one; there would not be many bankers' tots interested in denouncing their daddies. And the real worker's child—not the offspring of the radicalized teacher or disaffected artist, but the trade unionist's kid—would be unlikely to run across *Masses,* as would the parent. It meant that one aware and politicized group was trying to promote its consciousness in another group, the most victimized group but ironically the least receptive group. Revolutionary zeal, like wisdom, works only when it comes from within, and further, in a country as entrenchedly conservative as Canada, the likelihood of the lessons sticking was slight. It was an example of the perennial problem of preaching in journals bought exclusively by the already converted.

In the specific instance of "Joe Derry," there were also technical and artistic difficulties. One thing a mass chant must do is flow, and many of Livesay's lines scanned badly. She shifted without warning among iambs, dactyls, anapests, and spondees when one metric foot needed to dominate. The regular tetrameter beat was hard to maintain naturally in any of the following examples:

> Nineteen years ago he was born
> Bread and milk wasn't [*sic*] much, but it [*sic*] tasted good.
> What has happened since? Children, pay attention!
> Then he was layed [*sic*] off. The boss said he was sorry
> When they layed [*sic*] the man off, then it was bread
>   He got only, and shabbier clothes

Further, as this last example shows, the syntax was often tortured to accommodate the masses' decided preference for end rhyme. As the *sic*s above indicate, grammar and spelling also took a small beating without any artistic justification. It is not surprising, then, that Livesay declined to reprint this particular piece in *Right Hand Left Hand* even as an historio-cultural document. Art had paid too high a price to ideology.

What Livesay *has* chosen to bring again to light in the genre of agitprop drama are "Struggle" and " 'The Times Were Different'?" No confirmation has yet been unearthed of performance of "Struggle" or of audience response to either of these pieces, but Livesay's membership in the Progressive Arts Club meant that they were part of the repertoire at the disposal of workers' theater groups performing in labor temples, church halls, parks, and other highly public settings. As the socialists knew well, the oral tradition and visual presentation had more impact on the common man than the literate media. That the authorities genuinely feared the power of these dramatic public performances is shown by the repressive measures taken against them, as documented in *Right Hand Left Hand* (pp. 74-83).

"Struggle," a mass chant, positions two groups, one of five and the other of four, on opposite sides of a stage, vigorously comparing notes on the German and Canadian working classes. Sensitized by letters from her sister, Sophie, who was in Munich in 1934 and full of observations on the Nazi movement, Livesay had Group 1 spell out the horrors of life under "the threat of the swastika."[9] Then Group 2, the voice of Canadian workers, pointed out fascist incidents in Canada, equated "Hitler's bloody arm" with Prime Minister R. B. "Bennet's [*sic*] iron heel," and drove home the universality of both worker oppression and worker collective strength. The language is vigorous, plain, strongly choral and repetitive, predictable, full of generalized references to labor camps and factories but also to specific Canadian events that were revolutionary rallying cries: the murder of striking Estevan miners; the shooting of an immigrant worker, Nick Zynchuk, during a Montreal eviction proceeding; the imprisonment of Communist Party leader Tim Buck; the arrest of the jobless in Saskatoon and Calgary.

A full-fledged radio play, " 'The Times were Different' ?" came directly out of Livesay's stay in the United States in 1934 and 1935. Opening with the innocent musicality of nursery and skipping songs, the action is shaped by the narration of "Margaret," a barely disguised Dorothy. She moves from childhood and adolescent memories through to adulthood as a social worker, encountering in New Jersey a racial variant of the bigotry against Jews and Catholics with which Livesay had grown up in Canada. The content of the play follows closely the issues of racism, capitalism, socialism, and feminism, which were challenging aspects of Livesay's American experience. These ambitious abstractions are embodied in a series of very credible characterizations— a naive/novice social worker, her protective and repressive mother, her male chauvinist suitor, her genteelly racist social agency director, a cynical black victim of considerable discrimination—all based closely on actual acquaintances. Believable monologue and dialogue are counterpointed by all manner of sound effect: montages of children's rhymes, play songs, and conversational games; bouncing balls and skipping ropes; mood and theme music; train bells, engines, and whistles; negro spirituals; blues ballads; saxophones and juke boxes; scraping chairs and closing doors. A memorable student version of this play at the University of St. Jerome's College in 1983, although by no means as dependent on sound as a radio production would be, retained and made effective use of all these aural elements. Comparison of "'The Times Were Different'?" with "Struggle" shows how crucial the flesh and blood of characterization and variety of artistic effects are to the persuasiveness of a didactic piece. Where simplistic writing like "Struggle" is unlikely to move any but those already committed, " 'The Times Were Different'?" proposes complex questions draped in human form and meets demands of both propaganda and art.

Once Livesay had found a methodology to merge her lyric and political voices, poetry became again a comfortable genre for her. True, it would be thirty years before she would match the poetic profusion of her adolescence and early twenties; in her midfifties, having returned to Canada from Africa, Livesay would again draft as many as sixty poems in a single year. But the more than one hundred poems she created in the late 1930s represented a significant breaking of her poetic silence, betokening her sense of success in singing songs of the times.

The section of the *Collected Poems* entitled "The Thirties" presents seventeen poems or poem "suites" almost exclusively on social and political themes. While five had appeared in whole or in part in primarily leftist journals, none had survived the winnowing for Livesay's 1957 *Selected Poems,* a suppression unsurprising in the face of the social apathy of the 1950s. In her 1972 *Collected Poems* Livesay was addressing recent veterans of the dynamic, protest-oriented 1960s and could feel assured at last of a receptive audience.

With the exception of a romantic little free-verse lyric called "I Never Hear," the poems of "The Thirties" concentrate entirely on urban blight, social injustice, and visions of the human capacity for dignity, compassion, and creativity. Abstractions like unemployment or worker oppression are always given living shape: in the young man ashamed of being dependent on bread tickets; in the hungry scavenger pretending he's rifling garbage cans to get food for the birds rather than himself; in the terrified typist hammering out grotesque "melodies" on her machine; in the couple unable to marry without forfeiting badly needed government relief. While the forms chosen are extremely varied, from pentameter quatrains to completely free verse, most of the poems show some attention to rhyme or regularity of meter. Zooming in cinematically on specific vignettes of human suffering and hope, and speaking of them in striking image and compelling language, Livesay repeatedly achieves a union of idea and emotion, making her audience both think and feel.

Although Livesay's intention of capturing the speech of the common man is evident, her predilection for song shows up in these social poems in imagery, diction, and prosody. Often the poor have little to cheer them apart from song and dance. Nick Zynchuk, fated to be shot by eviction police, is rhythmically advised by comrades:

> "What do you say, Nick? There's a fine girl,
> Catch her and snatch her and give her a whirl;
> If we can't be millionaires, let's be men!
> It's a hell of a country—till you kiss her again!"
> ("An Immigrant")

In another instance of using song to invoke song, Livesay shows again how beleaguered male and female workers take comfort in the music and dance of bodies;

> Sing and dance now,
> Lover, shake
> The fear out from me
> Or I'll break—
> ("Queen City," pt. 4)

When the unemployed drifter sings "Hallelujah, I'm a bum / Heading now for kingdom come," Livesay is making sardonic use of a form of musical praise to underscore the plight of this man, as well as echoing a popular lyric of the day. But she is simultaneously genuinely celebrating the remarkable ability to sing at all in such circumstances, the unquenchable human spirit that makes feasible one's hope for a better world. In the exultation that such hope makes possible, the poet draws on the militant musical image of the bugle to describe how:

> Shaped like a bugle
> My thoughts split the framework
> Of silence and weeping,
> Arise, and send singing
> This song to the sleeping.
> ("Queen City," Pt. 1)

One poem series in the "The Thirties" fuses in its title the micro/macrocosmic condition of "Depression" and the musical term "Suite." Under the unnatural and inhuman pressures of capitalism and social decay, as we can see in the verses that follow, even the elementary pleasures of song and dance are perverted. In the toilet that society has become,

> If there are girls who still have left a song
> The midnight scrubber does not heed
> But mops it up like dirt.
> ("Depression Suite," pt. 1: "If there are prayers")

Confronted by "stupendous" squalor and injustice, the individual has a cowardly option: "I can sing down deep within / And not let anybody in" (pt. 2: "I can be a vagabond"). Then, in staccato rhythms, Livesay renders a grotesque dance parody of a frantic stenographer at work, her "snappy tunes" paralleling a snapping boss and her own snapped composure.

> And faster faster, Sir, we have
> Your letter of the fifteenth instant
> How do you like my harmonies
> Better than jazz dear Sir, click click.
>
> Better than jazz and kisses are
> The pounding minutes, nickels, dimes
> The dancing whirling hours, the fear
> The keys, quick quick, the fear!
>   (pt. 3: "I sit and hammer melodies")

And a jobless man (pt. 4: "You have no heart—") is despondent over his mercenary sweetheart's rejection because he cannot afford to take her to a dance; as he explains with powerful simplicity, the thwarted hunger for the normal dance of men with women is ultimately more excruciating than the hunger for food or sleep. In the Depression even nature's songs became tainted: the eager lumbermill hand who works as "Fast as the mill hum / I, a revolving bee," is shown to be a fool for thinking that would earn him the friendship of Management (pt. 5: "The boss was a friend of mine"). In fact the bees' hum and the thrush's song become downright subversive in that they treacherously lull us

Songs of Humanity

into disastrous inertia, "Inveigling us to peace" when the times insist upon collective action ("Deep Cove: Vancouver").

Although Livesay's innate lyric gifts meant that most poems did not change from first to final draft, those that did can offer insights into Livesay's thought and craft. An instance is "Dominion Day at Regina," five dimeter quatrains about the famous "riots" in Saskatchewan's capital city. A sixth quatrain was dropped,[10] probably because it was vague and repetitive, diluting the impact of the unemployeds' resolve. The order of the fourth and fifth stanzas was reversed, to build from the plea for bread to the assertion of dignity and determination: "Give us the work / and it shall be done!" In the middle stanza, important shifts of meaning are effected when:

> We from a mining town
> choking with dust
> suckled on bosses' oath
> schooled in his lust

becomes

> We from a mining town
> seared with black dust
> suckled on bosses' oath
> schooled by our struggles

First, the alliterative value of "seared"—"suckled"—"schooled" is created, and an awkward proximity of "choking" and "suckled" is avoided. Then what might be thought to be ordinary prairie dust becomes specifically the black and sinister coal dust that both sears and grimly sustains these miners. Fourth, the workers are now elevated by the education of struggle rather than debased by indoctrination to appease the bosses' lust. Finally, the end rhyme of "dust" and "lust" is deliberately dropped in favor of the more subtle sound value of the repeated "u" in "dust" and "struggle"; the alteration not only sidesteps singsonginess but completes the sibilance of "seared"—"suckled"—"schooled"—"struggles."

Another stanza with provocative revisions now reads:

> Give us no uniforms—
> warm walls instead;

> pierce with no bayonets
> we ask for bread.

Interestingly, "warm walls" is an escalation of demands from the original "blankets," and the anguished bottom-line quality of the petition for "bread" gives a concrete acuity lacking in the requests previously entertained by Livesay: for "shelter" or "labor." Here end rhyme has been restored after the conscious avoidance of it in the preceding stanza; presumably, having broken the chain of predictability, Livesay could again indulge in the pleasures of rhyme and aurally prepare the reader for her declamatory conclusion: "it shall be done!"

The latter poems of the *Collected Poems*' "The Thirties" pay considerable attention to the Spanish Civil War and the onset of World War II. "At English Bay: December, 1937, " "Spain," "Catalonia," "Words Before Battle," "Autumn: 1939," and "The Lizard: October, 1939" deliver unequivocal messages of our international involvement, our global peril. Proper-name references abound, from the murdered Spanish poet Federico Lorca to the doomed heroes of ancient Thermopylae, from Shanghai to Vienna, from Yeats to Freud, in Livesay's multifaceted call upon us to learn from history and preserve our humanity. She despairs at times of our chances and characteristically frequently expresses that negativity as sound—senseless sound, lack of song. "Autumn: 1939" explains:

> In our time no great ones live
> For ears are censored from their singing—
> No surgeon of the mind can touch
> Pillar of salt, idiot stare,
> Bell-tongues meaninglessly swinging.

Mechanical voices sing our trivial, escapist modern songs for us:

> Radios blare the censored version of our living:
> Wrestlers rage, baseball bouncers rant,
> the words of a recipe tinkle on the ear.
> ("The Lizard: October, 1939")

She concludes, however, on a typically hopeful note, both in this poem and in "The Thirties" as a whole. Like the lizard slipping "hesitant into sunlight" to tune "himself / To the wind's message," we are prepared to take risks in our longing to break out of our complacent and unnatural cocoons, to "hear real voices again, to uphold the song / Of one coming from Madrid, Shanghai or Yenan." The natural touchstones of hope and healing here—lizard, sunlight, wind—become mountains in the concluding poem, "Speak Through Me," granite teachers of wisdom and patience and wonder. The violation of chronology is deliberate: Livesay places this poem of approximately 1936 after seven of a later date in order to end with a vision of eternal rebirth:

> Speak through me, mountains
> Till the other voices be silent
> Till the sirens cease and the guns muffle their thunder
> Till the monstrous voice of man is sheltered by quiet—
> Speak through me, speak till I remember
> Movement in the womb and green renewal
> Sundrenched maples in September
> And the sweep of time as a gull's wing slanting.

As was the case for so many of Canada's best poets, the Great Depression delayed book-length publication of Livesay's socially conscious work until the ironic prosperity of the Second World War. In 1944 *Day and Night* provided a selection of Livesay's verse from the preceding eleven years, its title giving a hint of the wide spectrum of its themes and techniques. Simultaneously brought out by Bruce Humphries in Boston and Ryerson in Toronto, the collection was to secure for its Canadian publisher a literary hat trick, the winning by a Ryerson book for the third year in a row of Canada's highest poetic recognition: the Governor-General's Award.[11]

The slim volume pleased critics enormously in its breadth and technical virtuosity, wooing favorable reviews even from analysts who confessed themselves normally unhappy with modernist poets. Of eighteen reviews still fairly accessible to the researcher, one alone, "L. M. S." of the Halifax *Star,* found little to praise, thinking *Day and Night* an unintelligible "maze of words."[12] This reviewer rather reduced his credibility, however, by describing himself as having "stumbled through the book in a daze, generally," by unbelievably describing the title poem as "drab," and by admitting that the significance "evaded" him of a reference, in a factory poem, to Shadrach, Meshach, and Abednego burning in the furnace. Only five reviewers of the nineteen offered mixed evaluations, usually falling on one or the other side of the fence as to whether the public themes were superior or inferior to the personal subjects.[13] Ruth Stephan, for example, plumped for the social material as "more honest and more convincing" than the "wispy pronouncement[s]" and "pale dreams" of the personal lyrics.[14] E. K. Brown, on the other hand, felt that Livesay's "preoccupation with radical conceptions of social reform has narrowed her vision as a poet," and he identified her "excellence" as lying in the sensibility of "wind and sun and rain."[15] Margaret Avison, herself an accomplished poet, argued a "dangerous dichotomy" in Livesay's poetry between an intellectual, "determined optimism" and an artistic sense of the dark underbelly of things,[16] but the point says more of interest about Avison's philosophy and dislike of directness than about the inherent polarity, the day and night if you will, of poetic social protest. Indeed, the subjectivity of literary criticism is exposed once again in the way one person will use as an illustration of flawed verse the very lines another chooses to demonstrate brilliance; compare Avison and Stephan on the virtues of "From the husk of the old world" or "Fantasia." For critical assessment Livesay obviously had the last word: the 1944 Governor-General's Award.

While several of the poems from *Day and Night* have been enduringly admired and repeatedly anthologized, no single poem has been more frequently identified with Livesay's social voice—indeed, her most successful social singing—than the title poem. Considered by master poet E. J. Pratt one of the most important poems ever published by the *Canadian Poetry Magazine,* "Day and Night" is a scathing indictment of capitalist dehumanization. The poem applies industrial images to the human condition, fusing machine tempos to a diction of factory cacophony to drive home her passionate message.

The opening section, a single pentameter octave, is staccato with consonance, full of "whistles" and "scream after scream." Far from a rosy-fingered Homeric or pastoral dawn, this industrial dawn is from the first line a "red and angry" one, calling men not to epic roles or bucolic satisfactions but to their subhuman function as a "bolt" in "a moving human belt." The poet sardonically tells us that "The fun begins" when the workers start their grotesque parody of dancing "in time to the machines." All the major elements of the five ensuing sections—dance, robotic debasement, nightmare, parody, compulsion—make an appearance in that tight, grim beginning.

Although Livesay has been heard to claim for "Day and Night" the status of Canada's first industrial poem, the pounding dimeter stresses

Songs of Humanity 47

in sections 2, 3, 5, and 6 may well remind one of a much earlier Canadian poet, Archibald Lampman, whose "City of the End of Things" (1899) also looked into the heart of industrial darkness and listened long to the thunder of mindless machines. Livesay's treatment differs, however, above all in its alliance not with a tradition of apocalyptic vision but with the popular culture of her times. Where Lampman writes ambiguously and open-endedly of fire and darkness and the grim idiot at the gate, Livesay goes beyond that to refer plainly to the steel roller room, to wage cuts and overtime, to prejudice against "niggers," to landlords and foremen, to storerooms and sockets.

The title reverses the then-popular Cole Porter song "Night and Day," which warbles of individual, romantic love, stapling it to a portrait of the diametric opposite: collective, realistic hate. Rhythms of jazz, foxtrot, and Charleston two-step mimic in scansion the danse macabre of man with machine, man as machine. The swing of Negro spirituals is also replicated to combine the connotations of slavery with the image of the fiery factory furnace. Again parody is at work: in the subversion of biblical material and evangelical mode, in the displacement of God by the Boss, in the reference about black flesh that goes beyond the soot of coal-stoking and the one doomed Negro worker to the charring of body and spirit in those satanic mills. Broken bodies and lack of bread mock the Christian sacraments, as does the sacrifice of the worshipper rather than the God—a God/Boss who does not blow the merciful breath of life upon his children in the pit. The religious mockery is completed at last in a paraphrase of Christ's surrender to his heavenly father on the cross: "Into thy maw I commend my body" (section 6). But the poem does not end with crucifixion. Believing in social resurrection, the poet sees the diurnal wheel eventually reversing itself. There will be a still point and crumpled men, but then life will be "turned / The other way!"

Depression and progress, world war for ill but also good, childbirth and children, industrial madness and productivity, the martyred Lorca, rural-urban shifts, myth and the imagination: the roster of subjects in *Day and Night* suggests Livesay's ease in ranging between the intensely individual and the universal. The best of these poems incorporate both, give immediacy and a face to the larger issues, capture abstractions in original images.

A brilliant example of this synthesis is "The child looks out," sixth in the sequence entitled "Seven Poems."

> The child looks out from doors too high and wide for him
> On words spun large as suns, huge meanings sprayed on tree
> And roadway, spreading fields, not to be caught and clapped
> Together in a rosy nave, the sun no coin
> For fingers to indent.
>   The child runs out to stare
> At masterful young men who bat a tennis ball
> At giants in kilt skirts whose march is purposeful
> At mothers in cool gowns who move about like moons
> Upon the eternal lawns, low laughter shimmering
> About their curving mouths.
>   The child leans on the future,
> Slender tree ungainly rooted there by private worlds
> Who knew a private ecstasy unshared by him
> But let the memory slip and reared a hedge
> Of bristling phrases, last year's bills, and week-ends snatched
> In secret hate; his room laid waste when radios
> Are tuned, when rumour's blatant voice hits nerve,
> Drives tissue, brittles down
> The new unmoulded bone.
>   The child in cities toddling up
> A stifling reach of stair, gains window-seat:
> How consternation puckers up his eyes—at space
> Unplanted, seed unwanted, wars unwarranted
> Consuming his small, thankless growing place!

Livesay's rendering of the child's confusion in the jerky rhythms and consonance of the first five erratic lines is followed by a fluidly alliterative dream landscape in which adults appear to the child as gods and goddesses, their perfection elaborated in languid vowels. Consonance returns to the diction with a vengeance as the child's estranged parents act out the microcosmic version of global conflict, laying waste his little world with their ugly and unnecessary battles. This leads naturally to the poignant final image of the urban child, bewildered by a phalanx of powerful negatives: "Space / Unplanted, seed unwanted, wars unwarranted." Touched by a picture of the toddler struggling up to the window-seat, moved by the rare opportunity to see ourselves from the child's devastating perspective, readers are prepared to proceed from these "private worlds" to appreciate the concluding indictment of our world's collision course with disaster. It is startling to reflect how pertinent "The child looks out" continues to be nearly half a century later.

The light of day and the dark of night play weft and woof in Livesay's tapestry of optimistic and pessimistic views, from poem to poem, within a poem series, and even within a single poem. Day-light-affirmation have the last word in all instances; when, for example, part 3 of "Five Poems for Marcia" laments our being "late sleepers, drugged in dark / Aliens all, to morning" ("Early I lifted the oars of day"), part 4 offers "one light" in "Imagination's going forth!" ("Night's soft armour welds me into thought") and in part 5 "Leaps the self to light" ("Your words beat out in space"). The volume begins and ends with social affirmation, from the collectivist plans for a "new race" in 1934's "A shell burst in my mind" to the shipbuilders' energetic transformation of a shabby town into the arena of "new life" and a "new day" in "West Coast: 1943." This last poem is particularly interesting not only in its mature control of form and content but in the fact that its narration concerns a young, farm-born "outsider" who moves from "dreaming to be word-welder" to singing with his comrades the "song from the hearts of men at labour / welding their words into the ship's side," Livesay's own agenda.

Two lengthy poems of social import flank the roughly central "Day and Night": "The Outrider" (1935) and "Lorca" (1938). The former, dedicated to drowned poet-novelist Raymond Knister, both pays homage to him as an insufficiently recognized rural realist and offers him a posthumous answer to his argument against social verse by making use of his own types of clarity and imagery in the service of social revolution. "The Outrider" takes as epigram a line from Cecil Day Lewis's *The Magnetic Mountain:* "Swift outrider of lumbering earth." Lewis was referring to a kestrel, an English bird that, as forerunner of human settlement, represented to him a freedom closely associated with the wind, and a soaring into new territories of unlimited possibility. The application in Livesay's narrative is to a young man who returns to his country home to teach the communist wisdom he has acquired in city stockyards. "The Outrider" is a substantial accomplishment by virtue of the inherent interest of the story, the strongly rhetorical substructuring into multiple tales, and the variety of metric forms. There is also a complex and original interweaving of industrial, socialist, and agrarian terminology upon the symbolic loom of wind and flight; for example, the young social convert advises his farm friends:

> Employ your summertime, at union rate:
> Conveying energy on this green belt

> Of earth assembled, swiftly known and felt.
> Faster! Speed-up is here legitimate:
> Employ your summertime, before the thrust
> Of winter wind would harden down the dust.

The poem testifies to Livesay's increasing confidence in this lyrical-narrative approach as a most effective way of merging her two voices, reaching the mind by speaking to the heart and senses.

Among numerous marvelous figures of speech, such as the one about the racing clouds "Rumpled like sheets after a night of joy," there is a small autobiographical treat at the beginning of section 3. The stanza uses the idea of signpost, having the young zealot exhort his rural neighbors against "veering with the crow" in favor of steady, unglamorous productivity. "There's a time for flying," but not yet, he cautions. Before "air delight" there must be earth work. One thinks at once of Livesay's previous volume of poetry, *Signpost* (1932), with its title poem torn between sober gardening and heady flight with the crows. Then, the veering wind and crows seemed to win out by sheer line count—of the four lines that pinpointed the options, the one stodgy line considering digging in the garden seemed dismissed by the three exhilarating freedom-fighters that followed. Now, in "The Outrider" one sees what changes the years have wrought in Livesay's priorities. No longer the whimsical and carefree old wind's nose, "This is your signpost: follow your hands and dig."

"Lorca" was conceived in a burst when Livesay walked in Vancouver woods after the news reached her of Federico Garcia Lorca's death. Practically unrevised since its spontaneous creation, it was chosen by Livesay over thirty years later as her "favourite" among her own poems.[17] "Lorca" owes some of that staying power, given the heavy competition of so many of her later poems, to its impassioned transformation of dirge into celebration, its ecstatic movement from night to day, the way the poem quivers with life-force. And another measure of its longevity lies in its dazzling array of perfect images. In death, "voice's door / Is shut forever"; in the constriction of first grief:

> My bed will shrink
> To single size
> Sheets go cold
> The heart hammer
> With life-loud clamour
> While someone covers up the eyes.

Songs of Humanity　　　　　　　　　　　　　　　　　　　　　　　　51

And we hear, coffinlike, "the silence driven in / Nailed down," the word "down" thrice uttered like a tolling bell. A series of "if"s provide a transition, showing nature utterly attuned to Lorca's power and offering the clever symbolism of gulls circling Lorca's head in the socialist equivalent of a halo, a "sickle flight." Livesay finds humble, vivid objective correlatives for his immortality in

> grass flash emerald sight
> Dash of dog for ball
> And skipping rope's bright blink
> Lashing the light!

It is interesting to notice that when a slightly abbreviated "Lorca" appeared in John Robert Colombo's anthology,[18] not one of the four deletions were images; all were abstractions. If excision was necessary, this was only common sense, for who would deliberately scrap striking passages like the following?

> You dance. Explode
> Unchallenged through the door
> As bullets burst
> Long deaths ago, your heart.

Or

> High in cloud
> The sunset fruits are basketed

On the other hand, one addition since the early versions gauges Livesay's honest preparedness to reassess her convictions, to concede a revisionist view. The subtitle to Lorca's name originally read "Spanish poet, shot by Franco's men"; after 1957 Livesay began inserting the qualifying "it was said" after the word "shot." One is reminded of the similar manner in which she candidly remarked about her blind dedication to communism in the 1930s:

I learned a great deal about Communist tactics of penetration and camouflage; but I was too committed to be shocked. It was only years later that the false actions and fractional tactics were revealed to me in their real light. This did not cause me to hate the communists or to red-bait; rather I was disgusted with myself for having been so duped. But I believe I let myself be duped because no one else except the communists seemed to be concerned about the plight of our people, nor to be aware of the threat of Hitler and war. (*Right Hand Left Hand*, 74)

Even the fact that she later reconsidered and regretted the word "duped"[19] suggests her willingness to reevaluate material constantly, her refusal to accept stasis even in her own judgments.

The fact that two-thirds of the poems in *Day and Night* were either originally or eventually dedicated to family and artist friends suggests that Livesay by the early 1940s was shifting away from her previously exclusive focus on social themes. Nearly half of the poems themselves confirm the shift: "Prelude for Spring" (1939) is a paean to nature, "Serenade for Strings   for Peter" (1941) is an almost epic account of birthing her son, the lyrics of the "Five Poems   for Marcia" (1942) are largely dreamlike and cryptically personal, and "Fantasia   for Helena Coleman, Toronto Poet" (1942) is a guidebook to immersion in the freedom of the creative imagination and mythmaking.

When in the years of the Carter administration Americans put aside the ideal of the melting pot to investigate the riches of cultural pluralism, they were embracing an orientation already profoundly familiar to Canadians. The myth of the mosaic is an entrenched part of the Canadian intellectual apparatus, and many Canadian writers have opened windows upon their diverse cultural backgrounds. Select any two Canadian authors for comparison and you will be likely to dip into two cultures—the majority and an unhomogenized minority—operating simultaneously. Moreover, a fair number of Canadian writers, such as Margaret Laurence, Rudy Wiebe, Gabrielle Roy, Mordecai Richler, Yves Thériault, and Farley Mowat, are acquainted with more than one culture, thus embodying within a single canon the ideal of the multiethnic society. Rare, however, is the writer who ventures into more than one "alien" segment of the mosaic, and fewer still are poets. Livesay is unusual in her early, wide-ranging, and enduring poetic interest in the many ethnic and racial components of Canada to which she does not belong except through sympathy and principles of human kinship.

We have already noted the forces for ethnic sensitivity in Livesay's youth—her birth in a city (Winnipeg) and a region (the prairies) that are intensely multicultural; the overworked but cheerful Galician servant girls in the Livesay household; a mother who counted Jews among her best friends and learned Ukrainian in order to do the first Canadian translations of such poets as Taras Shevchenko. At times her "tremulous / protected childhood" (as she refers to it in the poem "Canadiana") and her mother's social innocence left Livesay naively vulnerable and unprepared for encounters with prejudice; years later she would remember

>   the hard darkness
>   of teenage Halloween parties
>   when my mother dressed me
>   in an authentic Ukrainian costume
>   (borrowed from a dancer)
>   to be greeted with:
>   "The girls are all dressed as ghosts—
>   wouldn't you like a sheet?"
>   And shamefully
>   I let them re-dress me
>   in a sheet.
>
>   Late, late
>   cried bitterly
>   on the lone pillow
>   for the gay Ukrainian skirt
>   and my mother's wilful
>   short-sighted love.
>   ("The Halloweens")

Her father, JFBL, was of a sharply questioning turn of mind; a theoretical radical, he encouraged his girls to question received prejudices and espouse high ideals of justice and freedom.

Lest the impression be overdone of an egalitarian family and environment, it must be said that JFBL's essential social conservatism and commitment to notions of Anglo-Saxon cultural and physical superiority would become clearer in confrontation with his rebellious elder daughter. As for her mother, Dorothy was by her late teens beginning to make diary entries about FRL's increasing rigidity and bias: "My mother, most persistent of Christians, says: the white race must survive, because it is infinitely superior to any other race."[20] FRL's gradual narrowing was, apart from the commonplace offshoot of aging, largely a reflection of the WASP elitist attitudes prevalent in Winnipeg well into midcentury. In *Beginnings: A Winnipeg Childhood* stories such as "First Trials" describe the local children's cries of "Yaw, yaw, dirty

Jew," and specific memories of social tension underpin similar chanted slurs in " 'The Times Were Different'?": "EEnie meanie minie mo, catch a nigger by the toe. . . . Rah rah rah. Red white and blue. Your father is an Irishman, your mother is a Jew." Fortunately, however, the model of such intolerance was fully offset both by those crucial early influences and by Livesay's innate sense of social fairness.

Geography and relocation have been major factors in Livesay's expanding consciousness of the "other" in her society. As we have seen, in the early to mid-1930s social work in Quebec and New Jersey sensitized Livesay to the particular plight of immigrants, the lower classes, and blacks, sympathy obviously enhanced by her growing communist commitment. Her 1936 shift to British Columbia introduced her to a new cultural mix, and her combination of the techniques of social work and journalism encouraged the documentary expression of Livesay's growing interest in native peoples and Japanese Canadians. Apart from newspaper articles, verse drama was her preferred medium for exposing the situation of these disadvantaged Canadians.

As in writing about the working classes, Livesay was stepping empathetically beyond her immediate experience, and critics were quick to challenge her right as an outsider to interpret, for example, the Indians. A conscientious scholar, Livesay pointed to her considerable research of the Indians and repeated visits to reservations, retorting, "If the Indians themselves are not heard on the air, at least someone should be speaking for them! . . . The more inter-racial understanding there is, the better."[21] In fact, the status as outsider conferred a desirable objectivity, which, to Livesay, did not reduce but rather increased the artist's social responsibility. Provoked by criticism of "Personal History," her radio drama concerned with anti-Semitism and racism, Livesay declared:

It is up to writers, not personally involved in the clutches of race prejudice, to bring these matters into the open. These are matters which touch not only Negroes in Canada, but Jews and Japanese and Native Indians. And more and more these matters will have to be discussed in the open. I think that anyone who wields a pen is deeply responsible.[22]

There was as well a patriot's concern with the quality of the national culture, the mosaic's need of all its pieces. Writing of her continuing absorption in Canadian minority circumstances, she pinpointed the tragedy implicit in Canada's ignoring

Songs of Humanity

the wonderful creativity of her West Coast Indians. No other race has given this country such an original art; therefore I have been grieved to see, in some Indian Schools, the children being made to do art work that is a copy of European art: or else, asked to model totem poles with no relationship to the legends that the totems tell. I have heard how children are taught to forget the Indian language and to sneer at their own culture: to forget the legends, the wonderful stories, the dances and the art of their people. This is a great loss to Canada as a whole.[23]

Organic in her view of society and indeed the world, Livesay has always regarded the belittlement of any part as the belittlement of the whole. As she would say decades later about the murder of Chile's democratically elected leader in a CIA-orchestrated coup, "What happens to Allende / happens to you and me" ("Unitas," *Ice Age,* 18).

These notions—the dignity and worth of minority cultures; their indispensability to the fulfillment of Canada's potential; the interconnectedness of all destinies; the deep responsibility of the artist to testify to social inequities and promote social harmony—underlie such "poems for voices" as "Prophet of the New World," which appeared for the first time in the *Collected Poems* almost thirty years after its conception. Drafted at a point when Livesay's interest in radio broadcasting was growing, "Prophet" was at least twenty years ahead of its time in lionizing Métis (French half-breed) leader Louis Riel.[24] Canadian history fleshed out, a Canadian hero to foster national pride, timely recognition of native peoples, the quintessential mosaic figure of the mixed-blood Riel: Livesay's verse drama should have been a natural for production by the Canadian Broadcasting Corporation (CBC), given that organization's avowed mission of serving as an instrument of national self-awareness, cultural growth, and unity. But "Prophet of the New World" was never dramatized or broadcast. While the CBC's distaste for some of Livesay's innovative oral techniques played a part, it was primarily a matter of timing. Unlike French Canada, where many regarded Riel as a martyred defender of French culture and Métis rights, in English Canada Riel was until the late 1960s widely regarded as an insane, murderous renegade who had amply deserved hanging. One realizes in retrospect how those very prejudices proved the justice of Livesay's subject and position on that subject.

"Prophet" is structured on a triangulation of voices: a chorus that sets scenes and poses questions; Madame Riel, who chronicles her son's life and, with shifts between the past and a dramatic present, helps the narrative to proceed and Riel to explain; and Louis Riel himself. In a rhythmic combination of free verse and pentameter stanzas, of lyric description, documentary, and declamation, "Prophet" works to several purposes: historical, geographical, sociological, humanist, reformist, patriotic, and poetic.

As historian, Livesay was introducing her fellow Canadians to a segment of their past about which most were mis- or uninformed, and offering a nonestablishment approach to that history. Born on the prairies, she was also interested in making that landscape known to Canadians of other regions, serving in a small way as physical and human geographer. The sociologist and humanist in her wanted to reveal Métis culture, Métis experience, Métis wisdom, Métis dreams, all of which were ignored in academic and popular literature. It does not need elaboration to show how humanitarian, social goals would be met by a poem that told of ruthless government land policies, native malnutrition, and racial hatreds. More subtle were Livesay's hopes of fostering heart and kinship values as opposed to the individualistic, the exploitative, the divisive, the politic. Further, "Prophet of the New World" offered a patriotic vision in which the Métis, "firstfruits of the country," were not dispossessed but given their fair share and proudly willing in turn to share with all the varied nationalities needed to fill the empty arms of Mother Canada. Riel's benevolent prophecy may end for him on the gallows, but Livesay's choral conclusion affirms the "tenacious signal" of the "encircling green," the functional mosaic of a Canada for all Canadians. Finally, a poetic manifesto has been slipped discreetly into "Prophet" when Riel answers charges that he is insane. He begins:

> Mad, did she say mad? Madness is
> the meat of poetry; and every poet's mad
> who has a message burning in his bowels.

While he then launches upon a comparison of his purported madness with the demonstrable insanity of the world, from the viewpoint of poetics the point has already been made. Livesay was defending as vigorously as ever she had in the 1930s the legitimacy and importance of message in poetry. She was speaking out then, as ever since, against obscurantism, against inaccessible, labyrinthine poetry, against the cosmopolitan preferences of poets like A. J. M. Smith, who disliked overt message and gravitated toward verse that was complicated, introspective, mythopoeic, heavily allusive and frequently elusive. She was at the same time appealing to an audience who in the late 1940s and the 1950s became weary of didactic poetry, tired of depression and war, jaded about causes, ethnocentric and isolationist, reminding them that to be truly alive is to care; to cease to care, to forget Riel is to have our heart's "meaning merged into the massing dark."

In the late 1940s Livesay visited two of the British Columbian centers in which Canada's Asians had been confined in wartime, where the uprooted families were still attempting to start life over. She was moved and educated by these inspections, her concern and imagination caught by interviews with social workers and teachers and then reinforced by close friendships with young, second-generation Japanese (called Nisei) who were attending high school and university on the West Coast; in fact a Nisei student, Amy Tabata, lived one winter with her and introduced Livesay to her brother Susumu, who could tell her firsthand of the trauma of evacuation and loss of his fishing livelihood. It was out of this series of experiences that the radio verse drama *Call My People Home* was conceived. The intention, as with her Métis works, was not only to expose injustice and write Canada's underground history, but to acquaint Canadians with the Japanese culture in their midst. The medium was a form of public verse covered with Livesay's stylistic fingerprints: what she called, in a borrowing from the National Film Board's founder John Grierson, a "documentary poem."[25] Its repeated broadcasting by the CBC and enthusiastic reception by the majority of its listeners did much to undercut the *Toronto Telegram* reviewer who sniped at *Call My People Home* as a "cross between Stage 51, an inglorious Milton and News Roundup."[26] Its potentially toughest critics, the Japanese Canadians, saw themselves truly in the poem and were vocally appreciative of Livesay's art on their and other minorities' behalf.[27] Livesay herself, having heard it broadcast, was inclined to consider *Call My People Home*, as both radio and written work, perhaps the best piece she had ever done.

Call My People Home was, as its subtitle in Ryerson's promotional brochure bluntly explained, "An Evacuation Story." The Canadian government had in 1941 violently uprooted Japanese-Canadian fishermen and their families, confiscated their property, and relocated them in the dry interior of British Columbia and on the prairies. No consideration had been shown to keeping families intact or to avoiding shredding the fabric of their lives and plans; no brutalization had seemed unjustifiable under the influence of public and political paranoia about these people's potential as wartime spies for their former homeland. In naming her poem *Call My People Home* Livesay was deliberately echoing the Negro spiritual "Let My People Go," which in turn alluded to the deracination of the Israelites enslaved in Egypt. The cast is extensive: an announcer, a chorus of Issei (Japan-born generation), a fisherman, a young Nisei boy (modeled on Amy's brother Susumu), an evacuated Nisei girl named Mariko, the mayor of the B.C. ghost town that serves as a relocation center, an Issei wife on the prairies, a renegade, and a philosophical Nisei. The speech of each is highly characteristic; for example, the passages about Shig, the defiant young Nisei, are expressed in jazzy, slangy quatrains, his confusion and impatience caught in the abrupt monosyllables and a parenthetical refrain "(Once a Jap, always a Jap)." By contrast, the philosophical young Nisei, Tatsuo, speaks in lengthier lines, polysyllables, with abstractions like grace and the Pythagorean theorem replacing the freight car bunks and robbery charges of Shig's story. In another effective rhetorical strategy more usually the domain of the novel than poetry, the audience enters Mariko's mind through a delicate, poignant letter she writes to her sweetheart describing the conditions she and her mother must endure in the segregated exhibition-ground stables to which they have been confined. With the brilliant objective correlative of a flimsy petticoat hung in a horse stall, Livesay captures in microcosm the horrible invasion of decency and individual rights, the dehumanization, that the Canadian government's policy represents. Mariko writes of her gentle mother,

> she is continually frightened—
> Never having lived so, in a horse stall before.
> My bunk is above hers, and all night I lie rigid
> For fear to disturb her; but she is disturbed.
> She has hung her pink petticoat from my bunk rail
> Down over her head, to be private; but nothing is private.
> Hundreds of strangers lie breathing around us
> Wakeful, or coughing; or in sleep tossing;
> Hundreds of strangers pressing upon us
> Like horses tethered, tied to a manger.

Livesay is also particularly deft at fusing the images of two cultures, in the way "fireflies danced / Like lanterns of Japan on prairie air" or the evacuees sat,

> With idle hands embroidering the past
> Upon a window pane, fed on foreign food
> And crowded together in government huts

In *Call My People Home* she continues to exploit the cumulative and the counterpoint values of successive voices; to mix literary and colloquial idioms; to meld lyrically descriptive, didactic, and philosophical passages; to shift effortlessly between taut narrative and vivid imagery, often merging the two; to weave strong fibers between individual and national destinies. An act of reconciliation, *Call My People Home* concludes without any of the stridency or urgency of her 1930s social utterances, the persecuted, homeless Nisei chorusing with great ecumenical serenity and no trace of rancor:

> Home, we discover, is where life is:
> Not Manitoba's wheat
> Ontario's walled cities
> Nor a B.C. fishing fleet.
>
> Home is something more than harbour—
> Than father, mother, sons;
> Home is the white face leaning over your shoulder
> As well as the darker ones.
>
> Home is labour, with the hand and heart,
> The hard doing, and the rest when done;
> A wider sea than we knew, a deeper earth,
> A more enduring sun.

In between the first draft of "Prophet of the New World" in 1945 and *Call My People Home* in 1948, Livesay managed to sandwich not only a war correspondent stint in Europe, extensive journalism in Canada, her continuing marriage and motherhood of two children, but also the winning of two stellar awards. The Royal Society of Canada in 1947 bestowed upon Livesay their Lorne Pierce Gold Medal for her "work of outstanding distinction," especially commending the aesthetic and ethical sincerity of her art, and praising her ability to fulfill a dedication "to popular causes" in forms that shone with "beauty of pattern and rhythm." More impressive still was Livesay's second Governor-General's Award, in 1947, for her collection of verse named *Poems for People*. Unlike her first coup, almost all of these poems were quite recent, created no more than three years before their publication. And unlike her first award-winner, far fewer of the verses in *Poems for People* have since been chosen to appear in the *Selected Poems* of 1957 and/or the *Collected Poems* of 1972: fourteen of the twenty-four have been passed over on one or both occasions, a fate somewhat surprising for a volume of poetry accorded Canada's highest honor. What is perhaps more pertinent to an inquiry into Livesay as social poet, however—what strongly demonstrates how thoroughly Livesay had mastered a social poetic—is the fact that all but three of the poems so spurned were private, domestic, lyrical, anecdotal, or elegiac, not concerned with concrete social commentary. Of those three socially conscious exceptions, "Improvisations on an Old Theme" and "Lullaby" were reinstated in 1972; the third, "Matins," being both dated and vague, was understandably left in archives. Incidentally, the resurrection of "Improvisations on an Old Theme" in the *Collected Poems* gives the casual reader of Livesay's work a chance to encounter what must surely have been one of the world's first antinuclear poems; crying out against "The dazzling violence of atomic death," it was drafted in September of 1945, mere weeks after the bombing of Hiroshima and Nagasaki.

Literary critics, evaluating the text before it had won the Governor-General's Award, went through their customary range of contradictory judgments.[28] Where A. G. Bailey detected less emotional volume and a narrower awareness of her times than had been evident in *Day and Night,* Mildred Thornton applauded her fourth book as offering a *more* comprehensive view of life, and Earle Birney felt that a reduced focus on causes had been exchanged for a "richer feeling for man in general."[29] Lyon Sharman delightedly quoted at length from the very poem, "FDR," that James Reaney disembowelled at equal length.[30] While "J. T." admired her intensity of feeling and well-controlled metric forms, G. H. Clarke disliked what he called the prosaic quality of the poetry and particularly lambasted Livesay's unrhyming sonnets.[31] If "S. S." called the war poems "the greater Livesay,"[32] Miriam Waddington countered that the best work was on childhood and motherhood.[33] All, however, were prepared to agree that she avoided sentimentality, that she wrote with a spare, striking economy, that her ethical self loomed large among the multiple selves Livesay was so skilled at presenting.

The tripartite structure of *Poems for People* showed Livesay's confidence in the wider social relevance of all parts—personal, social, and environmental—of her immediate world: "Poems of Childhood" and

"Poems as Pictures" formed a triptych around the more obviously socially conscious "Poems for People." Preceding the three sections was "V-J Day," a poetic retrospective on Livesay's struggle to integrate the personal and the public. "It seemed a poor thing to do, to wed," she remembers; "It seemed no time for love" in 1947, when the agonies of China and Spain and the Depression were tearing others' worlds apart. But life is to be lived, and in admitting the personal we do not betray our interconnectedness or sever global ties.

> Now it is eight years after, to the day, to the hour:
> The wrath has devoured itself and the fire eaten the fire.
> And again at sundown over the bird's voice, low
> Over the firs fluted with evening I hear the Yangtse flow
> And the rubble of Barcelona is this moss under my hand.

In "Poems of Childhood" she returns first to her own youth on the prairies, with her ugly duckling self-image and imaginative kinship with wind and the "arrowed alphabet" of migrating geese ("Page One"). Livesay then revisits her father, a raving Lear, a crucified Christ, exploring the mysterious power of that "Inheritance." "Preludium," "Small Fry," "Abracadabra," and "Carnival" are unusual in Canadian literature in their conferring on children's perceptions and baby steps and nursery rhythms a status equal to adult insights, progress, and song: a sort of early children's lib. In a male-dominated literature as well, "The Mother" is remarkable in marvelously capturing both toddler's and mother's world. It is important not only as a beautifully crafted poem and a revelation of the necessary restrictions (and joys) of motherhood but also as a work that, scant years after the passing of legislation declaring Canadian women to be real persons, aids in the expansion of female consciousness and drops a hint to modern society about the burdens of traditional women's roles in this supposedly brave new world.

The title of the second part, "Poems for People," might lead one to expect the kind of proletarian poems Livesay had written in the Depression and early war years. That they are not is a gauge of Livesay's expanded definition of social poetry, her grasp of the interdependence of part and whole, the individual and the masses (a word she had significantly ceased to use in favor of undogmatic diction). These ten poems all bear witness to a world full of dangers, postwar devastation, and emotional isolation, but most do so in the "soft socialist" manner of a Matthew Arnold or an Archibald Lampman. The first of two "Sonnets for a Soldier," "You went wordless; but I had not the will," tells of the private price of war, the permanent estrangement that can come from the separation of a soldier and his beloved; but the second sonnet, "No hands to touch, whom distance separates," affirms the power of love to reunite and declares the importance of the individual's affairs in the larger scheme: "our small doings set a precious pace." "Of Mourners" makes her humanist priorities plain, pressing us to abandon sentimental wailing about human destruction of the landscape and to mourn instead the more crucial pollution and devastation of man's heart and soul, whence environmental ruin springs. And "FDR" uses the interesting ploy of addressing to her early poetic mentor, Walt Whitman, a eulogy about a spirit kindred to them both, President Franklin Delano Roosevelt, whose political and social policies in the Great Depression had so inspired a young Canadian overwhelmed in the slums of New Jersey. Livesay identifies Roosevelt's greatest legacy not as concrete programs or specific social action but as the greater, general ability to conquer fear.

As for that third section, "Poems as Pictures," it is not surprising that all four were omitted from the *Selected Poems*, with only "Autumn in Wales" resurrected for the *Collected Poems*. "Evensong," "Okanagan Pictures," and "Pheasant" did please some of the critics at the time, and they did represent a healthy attention to purely aesthetic interests, but they seem quite weak in hindsight: marred by vagueness, mixed metaphors, dulled imagery. It was as though Livesay had for so long written with a strong sense of purpose and conscious crafting that the pure and directionless lyricism of her earliest writings flowed more sluggishly. She had become a poet as much of mind as of heart.

Chapter Four
More Poems for People

In the 1950s and 1960s Livesay as poet ceased almost entirely to be inflamed social critic, becoming rather an astute but understated observer. Between 1950 and 1968 she drafted no more than nineteen poems that indicted a specific conflict, issued a jeremiad about global conditions, or pleaded for universal harmony, and of those, only eight appeared in print: "Generation," "After Hiroshima," "Of Neighbours," "Hymn to Man," "Wine from Cyprus," "Canadiana," "Centennial People," and "The Metal and the Flower."[1] Nearly half (forty-six percent) of the poems published in those years focused on woman's experience, especially in male-female relationships and in a sexual context. Observations of life and society—character sketches of ferry riders; speculations on human evolution; memories of Canadian Halloween rituals; vignettes in Edmonton, Paris, New York, London, Zambia; history and hippie culture on the West Coast—account for roughly twelve percent of her verse during that time. Another twenty percent or so were personal, introspective, looking at her family, her life, and the prospect of death. Approximately thirteen percent were lyrical, often sensuous description, and the remaining nine percent explored aspects of art, poetry, literary worlds, and such artists as T. S. Eliot, A. M. Klein, and Pablo Picasso.

Of course, it does an injustice to the extent of Livesay's social awareness in Africa to refer only to poetry "vignettes." Much of her social energy in the years as UNESCO teacher went into sharply observant prose: letters, articles, essays, reports, and radio scripts. She had come to Africa via work and study in London and Paris, and that mature reintroduction to places she had known in her college years and in her postwar overseas journalist stint had already thoroughly reinforced her international, nonsectarian perspective. There was a quality of déjà vu in her encounters with the racism of the white Rhodesian elite: accounts of prejudice like "Not on My Verandah" (*Room of One's Own*, 83–91) were familiar updates of the racist-landlady incidents of " 'The Times Were Different'?" and "New Jersey: 1935" (*Right Hand Left*

Hand, 131), with Livesay showing herself as unjaded and freshly indignant as ever she had been in Englewood thirty years before. A vast sympathy with the aspirations of the Africans prompted her to challenge repeatedly even the minor assumptions of white supremacy and to share the African sense of triumph whenever the principles of equality prevailed.

Further, Africa demonstrated for Livesay the viability of a tightly organic society, where "Everyone feels the joy or the sorrow; everyone sings or weeps."[2] The complex interweaving of individual lives, the complicated tribal patterns, the sense of community seemed yet another resolution of the conflict between the unit and the whole, a paradigm for the person within a society, for one culture within a multicultural society, for one society on a planet of many peoples.

The Zambian movement for independence came to a peaceful conclusion while Livesay was there, and she saw firsthand the comparatively orderly dissolution of the British colonial Federation of Rhodesia and Nyasaland with the creation of two new republics, Zambia and Malawi. The elation of the Zambian people, the obvious metaphors of fertility, generation, and birth in new nationhood, the overwhelming rhythmic vitality of the occasion all seemed to call for poetry, a poetry of celebration. As social verse it completed the yearnings of her visionary, millennial poetry of the Depression and the Second World War in that it could document victory over white racism and colonialism after years of struggle, and rejoice at last, after the deep social disappointments of the 1950s and the Korean War, in the achievement of a new social order.

The enthusiasm of bearing witness to Zambian independence did not blind Livesay to the harsher realities of a technologically backward and poverty-stricken society in a frequently parched land. But she paid the Africans the respect of approaching them on their own terms, accepting their values, honoring their ways, replicating their rhythms, speech patterns, and phrases, using their commonplace images of sun and drum, flower and flame, water and millet. There is no noble-savage condescension or sentimental mythologizing of their rural lifestyle and relationship with the land. Of a nameless village she wrote with gripping simplicity:

> They do not love this place, or name it
> they are too much of it
> they smell of grass, of leaves
> of the pitiless dust

> they rise up with the rain
> and die with it.
>
> Between the land and themselves
> they feel no difference
> loving the earth no more
> than a man loves his own hand:
>
> Use it, and live
> or cut it off, and die.
> ("Village," in pt. 2, i, of *The Colour of
> God's Face,* later second poem of
> "Zambia" series in *The Unquiet Bed*
> and *Collected Poems*)

Depicting pragmatic social reality was not her only intention; Livesay also wished to capture impressionist social truths at a heady historical moment. Historical figures like liberation leader and Zambia's first President Kenneth Kaunda or Lumpa sect leader Alice Lenchina are therefore rendered larger than life, cloaked in charisma, redeemers of their people. Detail, albeit fascinating in its own right, is clearly at the service of helping the reader to enter an alien world, see and smell a remote society, make a human connection around the globe. In the end, sound says it all; a black female savior, Alice Lenchina, the African mother-prophet, stands

> rooted as a tree
> a tree singing the new hosannah!
>
> *Lumpa*   (in the highest)
>
> *lumpa*   the drums beat
> *lumpa*   *lumpa*
> *lumpa*   *lumpa*   *lumpa*
> ("The Prophetess," pt. 3 of *The Colour of
> God's Face,* later sixth poem in "Zambia"
> series, *The Unquiet Bed*)

Publication of *The Documentaries* in 1968 signaled a change in Livesay's poetic tone, a newly resharpened edge to her engagement with her society. *The Documentaries* was an assemblage of six narrative poems, four of which are semihistorical: "Day and Night," "The Outrider," and "West Coast" from *Day and Night:* "Call My People Home" from the volume of that name; "Roots" from *The Unquiet Bed,* and "Ontario Story (An Old Woman Remembers)," the only one not previously published. Stimulated by her return to Canada and her renewed involvement with the Canadian literati and Canadian institutions of learning (both high school and universities), Livesay became concerned to provide texts that would introduce to young Canadians their historical, literary, and ethical heritage.[3] The timing was serendipitous, capitalizing upon the unexpectedly widespread nationalist euphoria of Canada's 1967 Centennial.

Prefacing each poem with autobiographical and contextual material, Livesay presented the collection as documents necessary to human as opposed to purely intellectual understanding of the past, and was typically prepared to let the record stand honestly undoctored and unedited for current political or stylistic tastes. In her introductory remarks, Livesay made preliminary notes on her concept of and methodology in the documentary poem.

History deals with the experience of all men during an era; poetry deals with the experience of a few. And so these "documentaries" are not narrative and linear (as history is, as novels usually are) but rather, they draw out of the vortex a whirl of faces. For poetry is a montage, a spiral of experience.[4]

This definition would be elaborated in an important essay presented at the 1969 annual meetings of the Learned Societies of Canada. In "The Documentary Poem: A Canadian Genre" Livesay argued that the Canadian documentary poem, so well illustrated by the long poems of E. J. Pratt, Earle Birney, Anne Marriott, and Livesay herself, was neither simply narrative, national myth-epic, nor objective history. It was "based on topical data but held together by descriptive, lyrical, and didactic elements."[5] Equal weighting is given to "the objective facts and the subjective feelings of the poet"; it is from the dialectic between the researched and the imagined that the documentary poem is born. In the interplay of verifiable, documentable reality with the psychic reality of an invented text, delivered "in a poetic language that is vigorous, direct, and rendered emotionally powerful by the intensity of its imagery," a truth fuller and finer than any of its component parts is created. In her analysis Livesay did not soft-pedal her moral sense, unfashionable though that was in some quarters, or her conviction that moral sensitivity is a national characteristic. The plot is simply "a frame on which to hang a theme" and the human/historical story is told "to illustrate a precept";[6] the "impact is topical-historical, theoretical and moral. For we are a curious breed, we Canadians, who somehow or other imagine we can save man from self-destruction."[7]

Shortly after the appearance of *The Documentaries,* one begins to notice in Livesay's poetry drafts a renewed sense of anxiety and urgency about conditions in the world.

> *I tell you*
> *we live in constant*
> *danger*
> *under the sun   bleeding*
> *I tell you*
>   ("Disasters of the Sun")

This coincides with the decline and aftermath of her grand love affair, the start of a period in which her consciousness of aging, of transience, of decay and mortality began to come to the fore. The sensation of her corporeal frailty paralleled and perhaps intensified her awareness of the earth's fragility and the perilous path humankind is taking. It was also the time when grandchildren started to appear on the scene, the first of son Peter's family of Randal, Jason, and Galen, and daughter Marcia's Martha, David, Benjamin, and Jonathan, a personal investment in the future that prompted her to action. Considering the prospects of children in a nuclear age, being reared in the chemical soup of our modern cities, has in the last decade moved far more passive souls than Livesay's to speak up in protest; the impact, therefore, on a sensibility so innately and historically radicalized as hers comes as no surprise. In the 1970s Livesay rediscovered her penchant for plain, public, politicized poetry and consecrated the innocence and experience of her old age to (in a phrase from *Ice Age*) "tackling the world" and all its parts.

When in 1977 Livesay published a selection of her work under the title *The Woman I Am,* it was in one respect noticeably different from the *Collected Poems* of five years previous. True, as a "selected" rather than a "collected," it could not possibly aspire to the completeness of its predecessor, nor was there space to provide so elaborate a chronological or thematic structure for the volume. But the significant difference lay elsewhere. The *Collected Poems* had taken pains to bring to the surface nearly two dozen "submarine" social poems of a period dear to Livesay's heart: the 1930s. *The Woman I Am,* by contrast, severely ignored all of her social poetry of the 1930s, with the single exception of the sonnet "Comrade," whose focus is as much male-female relations as social struggle. Only one critic seemed to care: in a review entitled "Livesay Distorted," Mary Lee Morton complained, "One extremely important aspect of Livesay's personality—her involvement in social issues and her devotion to justice—is almost completely missing."[8] Given Livesay's annoyance with the frequent dismissal of her political material, how had she come to authorize such an omission? It appears to have been in large part the consequence of a higher priority: wanting above all to be read, to have a chance to "speed" our "arrows," she sought to produce as inexpensive and salable as possible a sampler of her work. First, to be assured that the selection would appeal to young readers, Livesay consulted teachers of Canadian literature and let herself be guided by their choices of the poetry most likely to interest their students; the renewed isolationism of the late 1970s evidently played a part in their recommendations. It is worth remembering as well that 1977 saw the publication of not only *The Woman I Am* but also *Right Hand Left Hand,* a book dedicated entirely to the 1930s and generous in its resurrection of Livesay's social poetry, fiction, expository prose, and drama. With that alternate venue and with her reasonable desire to forego republishing already available poems like "Day and Night," in order to make room for newly topical material, it makes sense that Livesay endorsed the selection she did in *The Woman I Am*. Expense too was a crucial consideration. Atypically for Press Porcépic, the quality of whose layout and printing has often been the envy of the industry, *The Woman I Am* is printed on cheap newsprint, with a flashy cover featuring an unnaturally red-yellow iris (*pace* Vance Packard) and a pair of gothic female faces: one elderly, strong, and almost satanic; the other a chestnut-tressed young woman bearing more than a fleeting resemblance to actress Raquel Welch. Having forfeited many favorite poems to considerations of space, cost, and popular taste, and having acquiesced to such lurid packaging in the interests of marketing appeal, Livesay was understandably vexed to discover that the paperback was selling for $3.95, a price then slightly outside the normal range of the casual buyer and penny-conscious student.[9] She had at least the consolation that the collection did include contemporaneous social verse, for most of the poems of the final section, "1975–1977," show a sharp concern for the times: the health of the Canadian confederation, of the planet, of urban culture, of battered children. *The Woman I Am* is then quite accurate in concluding with the dominant direction of Livesay's poetry in the 1970s and 1980s.

Apart from her musings upon death and art and other ongoing "private" concerns, Livesay has in the last fifteen years been poetically vocal about issues in five large "public" areas. Writing consistently with the postmodernist preference for free verse, in an informal, often prosaic style, she has produced poems serious and light addressing:

(a) war and peace, on a macro- and microcosmic scale, including pleas on behalf of children and of humanistic sanity;

(b) the environment: our relationship with nature and depradations upon Earth;

(c) the faces of modern times: technological, cultural, moral, Canadian national;

(d) conditions of the elderly;

(e) woman's experience, status, rights, and writing.

One poem that touches on three of these four concerns is a blunt manifesto of her position on the relation of art to cause.

Poetry Is Like Bread

Poetry is like bread
Neruda said
It should be shared
by everyone

We women are everyone
beginning to share
Poetry is communication
not a game
played with words:
a poem is a message

. . . .

Our poem—everyone's—
must be a message
for survival
Let it sound out clear
signpost and banner
plain talk:

NO MORE WAR

Self-illustrating in its insistence on "plain talk," the poem has been regarded by Livesay as sufficiently important to be published in the journal *CV/II*, in Livesay's *Feeling the Worlds*, in a handsomely designed broadsheet paired with one of Phyllis Webb's poems, and in a 1985 booklet of Livesay poems entitled *Beyond War: The Poetry*. To some, "Poetry Is Like Bread" seems stunningly unsubtle and unnecessarily prosaic, "talk" instead of "poetry." But one does well to remember that Livesay sees many in the Canadian poetic community—lamentably, many young writers—as effetely and fatally divorced from the real world.

> Pale pale the poets and poetasters
> moving along the midnight mists
> those riverbanks where girls
> white flanked, never refuse
> yield all their mysteries
> ("Grandmother," *Nine Poems of Farewell*,
> rpt. in *Ice Age*)

"It's time to think of the blood / the red searing," she announces in most ungrandmotherly fashion, and the role of writers is in her view more crucial than ever. This is emphatically "not a game / played with words." Write it, say it, read it, do it: NO MORE WAR.

All financial proceeds of the "Poetry Is Like Bread" broadsheet and *Beyond War: The Poetry* have been earmarked for the peace movement, a fundraising device learned by Livesay in the Great Depression and used since on such occasions as the 1964 Children's Fund Drive of the Unitarian Service Committee in Vancouver. Such practicalities are not a footnote but an integral part of Livesay's approach. She believes in becoming involved multidimensionally, and she knows that involvement without cash or equivalent support is sheer sentimentality, idle words without action, song without dance. It cannot be overstressed that all of Livesay's literary-social concerns have been validated by hard work, leg work, research, speeches, enormous expenditures of time, effort, and other personal resources. Poems on Canadian national unity or neglect of children find active parallels in letters to Members of Parliament or the Minister of Health and Welfare; poetic indictments of man's inhumanity to man are reinforced by her membership in Amnesty International; impassioned sentiments about nuclear disarmament are followed up by energetic participation in peace marches and in pacifist organizations in British Columbia; praising verses on women's writing are backed up by countless astute reviews and even laudatory poems, encouraging correspondence with novice women writers, careful (and unpaid!) editing of women's manuscripts.

Livesay's lengthiest piece against war and nuclear doom is *The Raw Edges: Voices from Our Time*. In the Turnstone Press version of 1981, seven voices in eleven sections (both magical numbers, befitting prophecy) speak from the heart. A "sibyl" begins and ends the "conversation," punctuating it at three intervals. The paired recipients of her warning are a male and a female painter, a male and a female "commoner," a poet and a scientist. The language is a spare and honed free verse, rather formal and decidedly poetic in its crafted imagery and oracular diction. As a poem for voices it has a strong declamatory power, and Livesay strikes a balance throughout among visionary abstractions on the order of "sibyl beyond mourning" or "experiments never dreamed," homely references such as "herbs for the steaming cup" or the Saturday "paperboy," and vivid natural images such as "pillowed snow" and "old rain-hammered logs" that "spavined / shoot at fantastic angles."

The first two-thirds of the Scientist's only speech is arguably the most dramatic and compelling passage in this poem for voices. He defines himself to the Poet as "the other side of you / dark side of your moon" and contrasts the fineness of his atomic creation

> so delicate a machination
> it could tear a flower apart
> and put the petals, one on one
> together again

with its grossness, "so violent / it could erupt a mountain," The lines that follow fuse art (western *and* eastern) and life, invoking both Milton's *Paradise Lost* and the sacred Indian text *The Bhagavad Gita*. Further, they implicate the appalled modern scientist, atomic bomb inventor Robert Oppenheimer, who, upon realizing the savage powers he had unleashed, felt inside "the horror and the fascination" of "Milton's satan-saint" and appropriated this Hindu passage for himself: *"I am become Death / the shatterer of worlds."*

Critical and popular audience response to *The Raw Edges* has been minimal, perhaps as much because of the perennial problem of small-press distribution as any lack of interest. One favorably disposed critic, John Bemrose of the Toronto *Globe and Mail,* calls *The Raw Edges* "a lively chat about the gloomy future of the world" (26 September 1981, 17). The liveliness is definitely debatable, however, since almost all of the passages have the stiff quality of set pieces. And "chat" similarly implies far more give-and-take than actually exists. A rare instance of fluidity in someone's position involves the poet deciding that the sibyl is not benign but the bearer of apocalyptic warnings; this change is unfortunately expressed through an etymologically unsound distinction between "sorceress" and "witch," using regrettable lines like "midnight shudders in your eyes." Much of the conversation has the slightly disjointed feeling of people sharing a topic but not quite listening to one another, as in the jerky shifts from sorcery (poet, 5) to cigarettes (male commoner, 6) and spear visions (sibyl, 6) and thence to seashores and a contradictory analysis of man both imposing his names and eradicating his histories (poet, 7). Overall, these semisoliloquies are too abstract to rouse much emotion and too generalized to incite much fear of man's global destructiveness or awake any lotus-eaters to a recognition of the urgency of the situation. *The Raw Edges* does, however, preach a doctrine of time-not-quite-run-out, from the title, which alludes to the fact that the raw edges of a wound are the healing edges, to the upbeat ending. It verifies Livesay's abiding optimism about human potential and her continuing commitment to the responsibility of a poet to afford us glimpses of our best possible selves. As senior sage no less than as fiery thirties radical, Livesay has continued to envision the human spirit, even after a nuclear holocaust, as able

> to sing
> of experiments never dreamed
> of marvels found existing still
> gifts for another universe

"Ice Age," the title poem of the excellent collection published by Press Porcépic in 1975, is a good example of Livesay's preference (optimism notwithstanding) for a frontal assault on mankind's antiprogress, our technological arrogance, "our vain jet-pride" that

> will shriek destruction
> upon the benign
> *yin yang*
> ancient and balanced universe

Eerily anticipating the scientific identification ten years later of the no-win global scenario called "nuclear winter," she accurately prophesies the way

> In this coming cold
> devouring our wheat fields
> and Russia's
> there'll be no shadow
> nor sign of shadow
> all cloud, shroud
> endless rain
> eternal snow

Alliteration ("coming cold"), internal rhyme ("cloud, shroud"), and repeated initials coupled in dimeter lines ("endless rain / eternal snow") are just a few of the devices whereby Livesay achieves a funereal, deliberate pacing. The third and fourth stanzas, by contrast, are passionate, tumultuous, beginning with the overthrow of the man-made Great Chain of Being in the judgmental perspective:

> Worse than an animal
> man tortures his prey
> given sun's energy
> and fire's blaze
> he has ripped away
> leaf
>   bird
>   flower

The nouns spiral down in poignant imitation of those tumbling victims of human violence, the first three of a morgue count of "those who cannot speak" inventoried in another *Ice Age* poem called "Whitepiece." But in "Ice Age" worse damage approaches than even our physical devastation of the planet and all its creatures of earth, sky, and stream: humankind

> is moving to destroy
> the still centre
> heart's power.

It is an extreme, the bitter end already envisaged as early as 1944 in "Of Mourners," where the desecration of "the lovely body of the world" had been a trifle next to the ruination of "Man's building heart, his shaping soul."

Although the heart is her ultimate priority, that does not mean that Livesay regards the environment with any less anxiety or subscribes to her own mini-Great Chain. In "Bellhouse Bay" from *Feeling the Worlds*, she is glad enough of the urban rallies and peace demonstrations that "exhort / SAVE OUR WORLD   SAVE OUR CHILDREN," but she reverses the emphasis of "Ice Age" in reminding us of a nonanthropocentric cause:

> save also   I say
> the towhees under the blackberry bushes
> eagles playing a mad caper
> in the sky above Bellhouse Bay

And admiring the way

> loving survives
> even amongst humans
> always amongst dolphins
> ("On Seeing 'The Day of the Dolphin'")

she pleads with those vibrant finny beings to do her the honor of accepting her as their "next of kin." There is no pecking order; the key is kinship. Both simply and profoundly, as ancient man knew and Dorothy Livesay knows, we all float or we all sink.

In the 1970s and 1980s there has been a return in Livesay's writing to poetic notations on our native peoples—Inuit, Indian, and Métis. Examples, in part or whole, are "Canadiana," "The Artefacts: West Coast," and "The Pied Piper of Edmonton" from the 1971 *Plainsongs;* "Gathering Oysters," "News from Nootka," and "Winter Ascendant" in *Ice Age;* "Who Are the Exiles" and "Reservations" in *The Woman I Am;* and "Bus Trip" in *The Phases of Love.* "Who Are The Exiles" turns the tables on white supremacy, showing the people of the Cree glowingly in tune with and a merely equal, peaceful part of the natural world,

> While above, on the heights we own
> we huddle, white
> enjoying the view
> from our stony houses.

This "Indian Summer" is the Indians' in more than name. They are associated with the golden falling leaves ("a thousand suns") that will "shelter dumb earth / from the next, white numbing invasion," technically of snow but presumably also of the rapacious white man, who sets himself "above" nature, who "owns" nature, who refuses to heed what were in "News from Nootka" called "the ancient messages." Although some liberalized whites do realize their error, it may be a case of too little too late: an unpublished poem called "Editorial Notes" speaks with sardonic directness of the "finer distinctions" Canadians seek, the desire

> to come face to face with
> those we have ousted—the
> rightful owners, the ancient peoples:
> . . . .
> who owned the land, the forest
> the fields, the mountains, the tundra
> We look at them gropingly
> trying to express
> the essence of their experience[10]

Unaware that the very white concept of ownership that has been used in the passage above would block the capacity to understand any wisdom the native could share, the white narrator pleads with those "rightful owners":

> Brothers and sisters, speak to us!
> Without you
> we are explorers   who have
> no home.

We see here an instance of nationalist themes crossing paths with those of native people. "Reservations" reiterates this notion that the ancient people have special knowledge, if only we would be clever enough to listen. Describing Canada as "a necklace of isolates / a belt of bombast," Livesay asks "how can we make out / together" as a nation, and she credits "only the Indians [with] know[ing] / the secret of communications."

Of the forces that threaten to destroy both myth and fact of the Canadian mosaic, Livesay vows fervently in the same poem, "Reservations":

> I would give my little finger
> and my thumb
> if the giving
> could make us
> one

And she asks her Canadian audience:

> What would you give?
> What fire steal
> from what sun?

A committed opponent of Quebec separatism, she laments the barriers between our founding cultures, extols the vitality of modern Québécois literature, deplores the damage that is caused by our lying

> strangers
> locked in our own births
> licking our own wounds
> on the wrong side of knowledge.
> ("Les Anglais: Coming Out of Quebec
> (1974)," *The Woman I Am*)

Canada, supposedly the Peaceable Kingdom, is a crucial microcosmic testing ground for global coexistence. Livesay realizes that she must make us see our interrelatedness on the personal level (as in "Mon Semblable Mon Frère" of *Feeling the Worlds*) and on the national level, if she is ever to win us to her pure and ecumenical vision that

> The world is round
> it is an arm
> a round us

> my fingers touching Africa
> your hand
> tilting Siberian trees
> our thoughts
> still as the tundra stones
> awaiting footprints
> ("Disasters of the Sun")

Livesay often berates modern society for its obscene waste; its malnutrition of mind, body, and spirit; its foolish dependency on machines; its thousands of voluntary disharmonies. In usually brief poems that dive in like strafing jets, she attacks the "improvements" that have complicated, isolated, devaluated life. In the discount store with its inflated wares,

> The shrieking tins
> bottles, prefabricated
> buns
> cry Buy!   Buy!
> demand (like spoiled children)
> immediate attention
> money action
> ("Old Woman in the
> K Mart," *Ice Age*)

On the open highways, the passing cars are "familied boxes" oblivious to the "ditch grasses / bulrush frogsong" ("Thumbing A Ride," *Ice Age*). Night brings only marginally "less polluted air," and we have become so grimly accustomed to technology's "grinding machinations" that we would reject as "fearful noise" the natural sounds of horse, dog, lamb, or cock ("The Takeover," *The Woman I Am*). Our young are prematurely aged, their eyes too jaded, "media-mesmerized / drugged" to appreciate real artists and meaningful human creativity ("Town Topics," *The Woman I Am*). Tyrannized by such "conveniences" as telephones, we accomplish a fraction of what we could ("Conversation Macabre," *The Woman I Am*). These poetic denunciations embrace the momentous and the trivial: at one moment she is sniping at "three hours of Rod and Gun Club / booming racket" disturbing the Sabbath peace on Galiano Island, while the next minute she is exposing the way we heedlessly buy the produce of apartheid regimes without taking responsibility for the atrocities that this perpetuates ("Precautions,"

Feeling the Worlds). Both are aspects of life; Livesay is clearly no thematic snob.

Dorothy Livesay has had a lively interest in woman's experience from the beginning. Daughter to a woman who was almost oblivious to traditional constraints, placing no importance on housework and every emphasis on creativity, Livesay was encouraged from her earliest years not to regard her gender as a barrier to any goal she might desire. But biological, historical, and sociological patterns soon asserted themselves, showing her that what females in the twentieth century faced was not a broad paved way but the tangled path of old. Chapter 5 explores sexuality as, to Livesay, the dominant arena of the female quest, the frame on which all abstractions of identity, freedom, and communication are literally fleshed out.

Livesay has had a tendency to dissociate herself from the feminist movement, speaking of feminists as "them" and characterizing feminists as "stoney" women.[11] In a 1979 *Room of One's Own* interview with Marsha Barber, she made the appallingly misinformed distinctions that she was different from feminists because:

(a) "I like men; I feel that men and women are complementary: they really do need each other";[12]

(b) she thinks men and women "physically and, perhaps, psychologically" dissimilar;

(c) she considers "it is very important for a mother to spend time with her children."

Without descending to an ad hominem (ad feminam?) rebuttal of any of these points, it is sufficient to note that Livesay grossly misunderstood and misrepresented the mainstream tenets of feminism, which do not clash with her beliefs as she evidently thought. What is more germane, surely, is the fact that once again, as in other social spheres, Livesay as theorist is extremely weak tea next to Livesay as intuitive activist. It takes only the merest skimming of her "Faces of Emily" section of the *Collected Poems, The Unquiet Bed, Plainsongs, The Woman I Am, The Phases of Love* (particularly section 3, "Voices of Women"), *Feeling the Worlds* (especially the entire first half), the *Room of One's Own* Livesay double issue, not to mention *Right Hand Left Hand, Beginnings: A Winnipeg Childhood,* and the editing of *40 Women Poets of Canada* and *Woman's Eye: 12 B.C. Poets* to document overwhelmingly the truth that Livesay is a practicing—maybe not a card-carrying, but unquestionably a practicing—feminist.

A sexagenarian when the 1970s began and now honorably into her fourth quarter-century, Dorothy Livesay has done more than any other Canadian poet to investigate the status of the elderly. Her best-known single shot is the often-recited "Salute to Monty Python" (*Ice Age*), in which five feisty old ladies, in hilarious reversal of expectations,

> take on
> the motorcycle gang
> the hold-up guy
> kidnappers and hi-jackers

and send the whole town "scuttling / for cover." Livesay is amused to show the "kiddos" in an agist, youth-obsessed society how they look to their elders, and she enjoys the reversal enough to reprint the poem in *Feeling the Worlds*. She then compounds the point of view by adding "Quartet," a poem that sketches an exhibitionist fourteen-year-old foursome whose antics and crude sexuality fare badly in comparison with the narrator's delicacy and dignity. The point of these two poems is enhanced, of course, by their appearance in a collection (*Feeling the Worlds*) that both argues and illustrates the full emotional, artistic, and intellectual faculties of a septagenarian.

Livesay has also been concerned, however, to investigate what her contemporary, Irving Layton, once aptly called "the inescapable lousiness of growing old." Seven of the *Nine Poems of Farewell* explore aspects of life's final stage: "The Old Bawd," "A Catechism," "Cassandra," "March 26," "Aging," "Grandmother," and "The Prisoner of Time." *Ice Age* is similarly interested in the conditions of old age, what might be thought of as one's personal ice age, although the author shows few signs of banking *her* fires. Apart from five reprints from *Nine Poems of Farewell*, the roster of such poems in *Ice Age* is increased by another dozen poems. A very few, such as "The Cabbage," make wry fun of one's increasing limitations in old age, but most speak with anguish of the "nameless pointless pains" that shatter sleep ("Aging"), the irrepressible sense of shame about a deteriorating body ("Collared"), the plight of the elderly poor ("For Rent" and "Old Woman in the K Mart"), the frustration at still not having good answers to the world's puzzles after a long life ("Walking in the Park"), the return in old age to the nightmares of childhood:

> in my old age
> I am not human

> nor woman
> but terrified hairy beast
> crying for shelter.
> ("Legends")

Livesay's most recent volume, *Feeling the Worlds,* devotes most of the first of four sections, "Family Tree: A Suite," to her interest in generations and the approach of death. She revisits her grandmother in "Photograph"; her parents in "My Mother Myself," "Everywoman Every Man," and "F.R.L."; and various old acquaintances and relatives in "Aunt Helen," "Old Soldier," "To Be Or Not To Be," and "The Inheritors." The portraits that emerge are distinguished by courage—sometimes a determined will to live, sometimes a resolute will to die—but courage in either case. Some, like the nonagenarian in "Old Soldier," mourn the disappearance of conventions like elegiac poetry that gave a grace to dying; he asserts his independence in the deliberate offhandedness of calling himself a weed timely for pulling up, and the metaphor serves also to cast death as a natural, universal process. "Aunt Helen" shows a defiance in dying, stronger than the sweating relations who impatiently wish her gone. Livesay herself expresses a reluctance about "the abrupt leap" in "To Be Or Not To Be" ("But it's not my time yet / . . . or is it?") similar to the assertion back in *Ice Age*'s "The Other Side of the Wall" that

> The wall is death.
> My death. Not to be climbed
> yet.

The concluding line that followed then, "I have no fear," may have been the temporary serenity of one still some distance from the wall, but it testifies to Livesay's enduring conviction that there *is* a fate worse than death. The poem "Euthanasia" ends the "Family Tree" section of *Feeling the Worlds* with the force of a final manifesto, defending the inalienable right to die when one thinks right, before the humilating disintegrations of old age make movement a misery and joy a pretense. Whichever the decision, Livesay calls upon us to respect the decision-maker and to respect as well the "leap into the chasm" as one of the great passages of a life. As artist she reserves the right to perform for herself that last social act, the statement of the epitaph.

In fact, the final poem of what could conceivably be her final volume of entirely new verse is called just that: "Epitaph." Moving from a color chronology/autobiography through to a contrast of textures (touch being perhaps the last sense she will relinquish), with a typical flash of unpretentious humor and a Yeatsian plea for fellow-feeling, the poem begins, as life does for everyone, with "I" and ends, as all things must, with "death."

> I am all mauve now
> and purple
> (not that I'd call myself
> Royal)
> Starting out soft   green   yellow
> flaming mid-life into
> orange   scarlet
> I am all one now
> with lilac and violet
> sleepy colours
> sifted through silver
> I am all worn now
> honed to the bone
> by centuries shifted
> and smoothed into stone
>
> Tread softly on my moss
> step easy on my cushion of grass
> for beneath
> is time's granite
> the warranty of death

Powerful poetry, this, and absolutely authentic, but it is also a bit like Frank Sinatra's multiple retirements and Livesay's own *Nine Poems of Farewell: 1972–1973:* almost certainly premature. Livesay's social involvement continues to flow from deep wellsprings of humanism.

Chapter Five
Songs of Experience: Flesh Made Word

Dorothy Livesay's body has frequently let her down: she suffered from a vaguely identified illness in childhood (possibly chorea), another in early adulthood, and, since then, lung cancer, alcoholism, gout, hypertension, sciatica, and angina. From the beginning she was inclined to view herself as "Misbegotten / born clumsy":

> *Butterfingers*
> father called it
> throwing the ball
> which catch as catch can
> I couldn't.
> ("Ballad of Me," *The Unquiet Bed*)

In time the awkward child became the maladroit adolescent, wanting always to dance, and eventually the frustrated housewife and widow, prematurely stooped. Further, while she has unquestionably led a very active life, Livesay's years are noticeably devoid of athletic activity, of any interest in sports. And yet in spite of all this, she has shown a remarkable focusing on one major aspect of her physical self: the sexual and sensual being. Heir to a body and a national culture that did not encourage such an emphasis, Livesay has nonetheless celebrated the joys of the flesh to a degree that is extraordinary in Canadian literature. And her sexual voice spoke most loudly at a stage of her life when so many have sexually subsided into whispers or even silence.

Livesay has long been willing to declare herself a highly sexual being and to talk about that predisposition in the light of problems of birth control, childbearing, aging, widowhood, traditional roles, and other issues. But she did not learn that candor from her family, a fact that she has in recent years made the material of poems and prose. Livesay's sexual inheritance was one of inhibition and WASP decorum. Consider her mother, FRL, who confided to her diary three years before her repeatedly postponed wedding that she "ought surely to have been a nun; so little does 'sex' appeal to me"[1] and who later "lay in fear / frigid"[2] in her marriage bed, using her daughter Sophie's presence as a shield against sexual overtures from her husband. Consider also FRL's husband, Livesay's father JFBL, who decided arbitrarily that his young wife had not been virginal on their wedding night and thereafter "resented her body and her ways"[3] throughout their life together. The sadness and frustration of her parents' marital dysfunction would replay themselves in her own marriage decades later.

Livesay's early sexual longings and eventual experimentation were, not surprisingly given her attendance at an all-girls school, directed toward women teachers, other girls, and a female cousin. Her adolescent poetry is full of the heightened romanticism, the girlish anxieties, and the images of dominant natural forces that suggest a sexual tension. Staccato pacing and thrust of language reinforce this impression of inexplicit, pubescent desires. Livesay's diaries and memoirs of her late teens and early twenties record a normal progression of curiosity and inquiry about matters of the flesh, but it is not until a very few poems are finally published over forty years later (in the section of the *Collected Poems* retrospectively entitled "The Garden of Love") that one sees her first concrete references to the sexual act. "Again the fever: at last to see you!" (1931) revels in the hotel, the lover, the blankets; "I am merry: 'til I lie alone" (1930) casts her as a "womb where consciousness / can penetrate and throb."

The octave of one blank verse sonnet written in the mid-1930s is particularly eloquent on the ecstasy of Livesay's first consummation with a young suitor named Grant identified in the title simply as "Comrade."

>   Once only did I sleep with you;
>   And sleep and love again more sweet than I
>   Have ever known; without an aftertaste.
>   It was the first time; and a flower could not
>   Have been more softly opened, folded out.
>   Your hands were firm upon me: without fear
>   I lay arrested in a still delight—
>   Till suddenly the fountain in me woke.

It is interesting to note, however, that the sestet thereafter takes the traditional Petrarchan turn and argues from the politicized stance of 1936 that the proletarian struggle has "sealed" them together more completely "Than if our bodies still were sealed in love." It is a continuation of Livesay's lifelong belief in sexual contact as important not only in itself but also as a powerful prologue to human connections and spiritual wholeness.

That flowering and that fountain inaugurated considerable sexual joy in Paris, where Livesay surreptitiously lived with a male fellow student from Toronto, the pseudonymous "Tony" of *Right Hand Left Hand*. Upon her return to Canada, the newly radicalized poet threw herself into not only social work but also a level of sexual activity that seemed appropriate to the shining new world for which she and her free-thinking colleagues were striving. As she has explained in *Right Hand Left Hand* (123), "The final hurdle for the young women in those [activist] groups was that of 'losing your virginity,' " and readings in Havelock Ellis, Emma Goldman, D. H. Lawrence, and others had long since primed Livesay and her companions to expect a full, rich sexual dimension to their lives. Curiously, even her father had contradicted his attitude to his wife's chastity by counselling his daughter in her late teens that "a woman is a fool to be 'virgina intacta'—she misses too much."[4]

Experience, however, had other lessons to teach. In 1933 Livesay published in the leftist journal *Masses* a lengthy blank-verse narrative called "A Girl Sees It!" Subsequently renamed "In Green Solariums," the poem tells an age-old tale: the plight of the single servant girl impregnated by her employers' irresponsible son. Livesay knew whereof she wrote through her field work with unmarried mothers in the Montreal Family Welfare Association, and her intent was in part to show class victimization and brutal social realities in the working class. In addition, however, the poem shows a dark side indeed of sexuality; in juxtaposition to the green sunrooms of the privileged and the blossomings of springtime,

> A girl alone
> Has cause to remember the green roots shooting pain,
> The small sick leaves that sprout, the heavy growth
> Inside the belly, suddenly made plain.

The passage takes on a biographical poignancy in light of the fact that Livesay herself faced an unwanted pregnancy by a fellow leftist, a trauma that produced, both in nine months and in thirty years, not a child but "an outcry of poems."[5] In handling the crisis on her own,

Livesay learned firsthand the unfair limitations that biology and society, even among Marxist comrades, continued to place upon sexual freedom and equality. Nonetheless, despite all those bleak perceptions regarding the wages of sin, "In Green Solariums" does not sacrifice to social and political purposes Livesay's appreciation of the wonders of sex. The servant girl, Annie, is not raped; rather she remembers without bitterness, with evident pleasure:

> O lovely whiteness of you! Lovely body
> Young and burning for me. What a joy
> To seize your mouth and know your hunger there—
> And greater hunger otherwise.

And Annie's life thereafter does not fall into any traditional stereotype of the fallen woman, whether wanton tramp; frigid, embittered single parent; or Scarlet-Lettered isolate. A normal sexual and emotional life is hers: "I have a man now who's not white like snow / But who can take me, and be glad of that—." No visionary celibacy here: even at a time of global depression, when "There's bigger things than love to be worked out," sexual activity has a proper place in the completeness of things.

Marriage in 1937 failed to bring to Livesay the uninhibited lover for whom she longed. Her partner in the "olde daunce" of sex was Duncan Cameron Macnair, a reserved Glaswegian inclined, like her father, to talk a liberated line but tread a conservative one. Diary entries, letters to close friends, and retrospective prose refer to Livesay's sense of her husband's formality, rigidity, impatience with whimsy or romance, and inability to achieve ecstatic abandon.[6] The two were plagued by fears of their children bursting into their bedroom, to the extent for Livesay that such invasions interrupted even her dream fantasies. And an Oedipal confusion of Duncan and JFBL, revealed in later years in dreams and unpublished memoirs,[7] further interfered with the couple's capacity to "dance" together successfully.

In her poetry the deep disappointment of marital sex is suggested indirectly first by the absence of sexual celebration in published *and* unpublished verse of the 1940s and 1950s. This impression is compounded by comparatively frequent images of and allusions to weeping, closed books, constraints, locked doors, clanging gates, incompletion, bleak rather than exciting darkness. Instead of a passionate lover, the poet addresses "The Dark Runner" with "His prying finger";

the remote eagle in his frosty "eyrie" ("Winter Song"); the puritan husband who rejects her "technicolour" Eden for a black and white universe—"Banned from the garden, he forbids / all others entry" ("The Husband"). In "Epithalamium for Susan" pioneer Susan Allison prefers nature as her bridegroom:

> I did not give myself to you.
> For on that wedding night
> I was a girl bound over to the hills,
> my essence pierced with arrows of night air.

In "Letter at Midnight" the young wife and mother of 1942 pleads with her beloved to "Behave to me with love"; in "The Morning After" she fears most the hardened stage *after* tears, "Life on the fringe of feeling." All of this indirection pales before three brief quatrains written in 1951 and published in the 1956 *Selected Poems*: "Wedlock" is the unexpectedly ominous title of a poem that speaks bluntly of the misery of sexual without psychic union. The unhappily yoked ("prisoned") couple are "bereft / And weeping inwardly" at the cruel paradox that, although "so joined in flesh," they with their souls "Achieve no unity."

So explicit an outburst of discontent is rare in the poetry of Livesay's middle years. What is more prevalent is a circumvention of passion from the sexual into the cerebral, of bodily intercourse into aesthetic and intellectual communication. For this she had a truly compatible partner. In her 1972 *Collected Poems* Livesay added the subtitle "for Alan Crawley" to two poems of the 1950s, "Nocturne" and "The Skin of Time." Five years later, in *The Woman I Am,* the poet entitled one section simply "Five Poems for Alan Crawley (1887–1975)." Alan Crawley was the blind publisher of a journal extremely important to the development of modern Canadian poetry, *Contemporary Verse,* on whose founding board Livesay had figured prominently in 1941 and to whose centrality Livesay paid homage in 1975 by naming her own poetry periodical *Contemporary Verse II* or *CV/II*. In Crawley, Livesay found (as did many Canadian writers) a dedicated poetic counsellor and critic, a frequent and enormously helpful correspondent.[8] In addition Crawley was an increasingly intimate confidant to whom she could pour out personal problems and opinions. A fond admirer of Crawley's wife (indeed, sufficiently so as to include Jean in the dedication to her *Day and Night*: "To Alan and Jean Crawley (gardeners)"), Livesay in letters and in person never expressed any inappropriate degree of affection for her mentor; in poetry, however, she felt free to hymn her soulmate, identifiable even then by the references to his blindness,[9] and to rejoice in their "taut / Intensity of thought to thought" ("The Skin of Time"). Those respectful dedications are echoes of Livesay's explanation, in her warmly detailed foreword to Joan McCullagh's *Alan Crawley and "Contemporary Verse,"* that:

Although my friendship with Alan Crawley always remained platonic, in the time of my need I was truly in love with this man (as my poem "Nocturne" testifies). He in his old age (and in his cups!) confided that he had also been in love with me. We sustained each other through some darker years, yet remained loyal to our enjoined commitments.[10]

In verse that final thought became:

> I cannot choose the way
> Of loving you alone:
> The conclave of my memories
> Keeps my allegiance home.
>
> "Accept with grace" was ever the aim—
> Consummation is otherwise:
> To have a habitation and a name
> And time to dust the dark behind the eyes.
> ("The Skin of Time")

In Livesay's 1957 *Selected Poems,* a somewhat pessimistic collection, it is significant that the closing poem should optimistically and brilliantly chart the intersection of art and sexuality, and offer one kind of solution to her psychosexual incompleteness. The title "On Looking into Henry Moore" deliberately invokes the Keats sonnet "On first looking into Chapman's *Homer,"* and its genesis is similarly the poet's epiphanous response to another's work of art, the massive and sleek sculptures of Henry Moore. Her technical achievement is impressive, from the riveting sibilance of the opening command, "Sun, stun me, sustain me / Turn me to stone," through the tight and witty rhyming couplets of the middle section to the verbal turns and internal repetitions of the concluding segment. There is a complex interplay of strong nouns (sun, stone, fire, root, snow, bone, flesh) and abstractions ("green eternity," death, half-self), which supports a series of striking paradoxes and polarities (e.g., "Passivity in fire / And fire in stone").

A tree, teaching that "Aloneness is the only bliss," serves as a paradigm for its own wise lesson, for perfect self-fulfillment. Reassuring the reader humorously that "Self-adoration is not in it / (Narcissus tried, but could not win it)," Livesay reconciles the movement of the tree root "Tombwards" with the branches heavenwards. And like the tree the poet resolves,

> Female and male
> I'll rise alone
> Self-extending and self-known.

In this androgynous vision that anticipates one of Livesay's current interests, the poet sees herself rising phallically and independently (historically male conditions!), purged by fire of her simply female body, "Clad in the armour of the sun" (traditionally male god and male attire for the male pursuit of warring). In this fusion she can achieve an integrated being, "One unit, as a tree or stone / Woman in man, and man in womb."

When Livesay in 1958 received a grant to study in England the creative teaching of English, she leapt at the chance to distance herself from the frustrations not only of high school teaching but of a confining and sexually unsatisfying marriage.[11] At Christmastime[12] in London Livesay wrote her family a special holiday letter, enclosing a poem dedicated to Duncan. In three terse quatrains "The Absences" seems to affirm Dorothy's and Duncan's love and reminisces about the way they once "made mountains move," about the abiding fact that "love we must." But "this diamond, trust" has been cut by "days of disbelief," there are immense "lapses in our love," and—most depressing of all—"For us no future tense, / past tension's set" (*Collected Poems*). When she concedes that "the mould of other times / contains us yet," it is difficult for the reader to be heartened. "The Absences" is a poem whose revisions speak more tellingly than the finished piece. First, it is somewhat atypical for Livesay in the sheer number of changes made in the initial draft—seventeen: at least one in every line, hinting at nervousness, caution, or perhaps irresolution. Then what started as "The Planes of Love" became "The Absences" in rewriting, a far less optimistic approach. The mild declarative "There have been," which originally preceded "days of disbelief" and "lapses in our love," was dropped in favor of the harshly emphatic "What." "Remembrance of other times / Will other hours beget" has become the slightly necrotic, claustrophobic, and tentative "the mould of other times / contains us yet." In the concluding stanza the opening line has been reduced from "Beloved, on these naked plains" to the impersonal geometric pun "But on these planes."

Four months into her fiftieth year, Livesay received word from Canada that Duncan Macnair had died of thrombosis. Since the arrangement of the poetry in the *Collected Poems* presents such a powerful and fascinating autobiographical progression, it is tempting to surrender entirely to Livesay's structural artistry to understand the mesh of art and life in this time of widowhood. Livesay entitles a section "Poems from Exile (1958–59)," which offers: "The Voyage Out," a poem on departure, presumably for England; "Absences," dedicated to Duncan shortly before his death; and then "After Grief," seeking to make peace with death. It soothes one's sense of fitness that the rest of the section tolls with images of dismemberment, burial, black waters, funerals, cold, iron, and bones. Interestingly enough, however, the writing of nine of those fourteen poems preceded Duncan's death, and the centerpiece poem, "Widow," was actually not composed until 1962. So the literary biographer risks vastly oversimplifying the nature of Livesay's "exile" if s/he assumes it, on the basis of the *Collected Poems* groupings, to have been a period of bleak mourning. Widowhood was far from Livesay's only experience and only material for art during that first year abroad. The biographical fact is that Duncan's unexpected death, while certainly an occasion for enormous grief, was eerily on schedule with a provision Livesay had apparently made with her husband at the time of their wedding vows: "I will marry you for the coming years; but I cannot promise you that I will stay married when I am fifty. I might want to start another life."[13] And Livesay's first reactions to widowhood, as she has since admitted with both candor and guilt, were relief and a sense of newfound freedom.

Stimulated by her studies in London, travels to the south of France, and the taking up of a position with UNESCO in Paris, Livesay in one year drafted nearly fifty poems. While a predictable share of this poetry concerns itself with human mortality, loneliness, and impermanence, only five of the forty-six can be considered predominantly pessimistic or negative in spirit. Twenty offer balanced visions, such as an acceptance of death's important place in the natural cycle ("The Immortals," "Vintage," "Persephone," etc.) or a belief in love's power to compensate for life's troubles ("Invocation," "Indian Summer," "Sonnet: the rule I follow," etc.). And fully twenty-one—almost half—of Livesay's poems in her first year of widowhood may be classified as optimistic and even celebratory. The brilliance of Cézanne and Picasso, devotion to her god, high flights of fancy, exquisite provençal landscapes, the joy of poetry and flowers and young lovers are all in evidence, and the sun recurs throughout.

After what Livesay has referred to as her "frozen years," one finds a plainly spoken intention to thaw and reactivate all the senses. Some of this renewed vitality is sensory, as in her delight in the sunflowers whose dancing "Repays all debts, / Delivers me from harm" and makes her "the centre of the world / Immediate and warm."[14] And some is other-directed, such as her savoring her daughter's imminent joining of the dance of life: "tiptoe as a dancer before music's start, / I see you eager to begin."[15] At first Livesay is shy, almost regressing to the virgin days of *Green Pitcher,* fearfully alone in "the blazing sun" and longing

> to lie down
> Under green ferns and fronds
> Lavished with long
> Fingers of wind
> Ravished with rain.[16]

But she does not relegate herself to the passive position of the elderly couple in "Russell Square: Spring,"[17] who may only eavesdrop on the sexual conversation of young lovers. Aware that

> Not he, the naked sun
> Bids me wear widow's weeds
> Nor she, whose silver nudity
> Waxes and wanes[18]

Livesay is by June of that year calling on love, on her guardian angel, on a prospective lover to

> pull the dirge
> Out of my mouth
> Sweeten with taste of summer
> All my north
> ("Articulate Defense")[19]

More than a dozen poems from the year of exile document Livesay's embarking upon a new phase of her sexual life. Particularly striking are her courage and independence. Often, for example, she must reassure a skittish lover that what they have is miraculous, not "disastrous":

> We on love's body
> Are as two hands
> Building delight
> But making no demands
> ("Articulate Defense")

Revelling in her new autonomy, Livesay is at pains to make a distinction between connecting and controlling:

> To be possessed, not owned
> Is to be free for faring; never boned
> Nor bodiced in another's frame.
> ("She Replies to His Pleas")[20]

She detects a fine wisdom in "loving and leaving," a bold act (more usually the male philosophy) that is compared to "snatch[ing] at sun" or "still[ing] the moon's wheeling" ("The Dream").[21] Even if the beloved treats her like a stranger, contact as fleeting as an arm's accidental touch on a bus may cause laughter to hold her "for that second's lift, / Safe from all jostling harm" ("Time tells us we are tall").[22] And she is prepared to take risks: although it may not be promising to "grope together" with another scarred, rejected person, "the dazzling fantasy / Takes fire: our four hands feed the blaze" ("Sonnet: The rule I follow").[23] To those whose sense of decorum is unsettled by such sexual adventuring, and possibly even to the Dorothy who was physically faithful to one incompatible mate all those years, the poet explains that these encounters are not superficial but engage her fully:

> To turn the pages of my loves
> Is no disparity.
> I am each moment; and each song
> Restores my entity.
> ("To turn the pages of my loves")[24]

As is the case with "Poems from Exile (1958–59)," so with the succeeding section of *Collected Poems,* "To Speak With Tongues (1960–64)," one runs the hazard of deducing from the ordering and selection that the early sixties were a great contrast: a sudden burst of energy, curiosity, color, and light. Dating the poems once again shows the creative life to be far more complex: three of the eight actually predate 1960. The sensual "A Conversation" (1958) sees poets as gazelles that "feed on each other's garden" or as submarine, phosphorescent creatures that exchange silvery salutes in the green depths. In "Houdini Eliot" (1959) Livesay quite hilariously denounces T. S. Eliot as a fraudulent "High priest of pomp and poetry" who "sang of sex, but had no bawd," and she vigorously urges the reader to reject Eliot's obscurantism in order to "see man whole." The third, "Picasso Sketching," which is a whirl of audacious images, verbal gymnastics, and artistic admiration, had its original incarnation in April 1959 as (among other tentative titles) "The Clowning Art." The placement of these sunny poems of the "dark period" among the regenerative and vital United Nations and Zambian material of later years tends to compartmentalize the poet's cycles artificially (albeit satisfyingly!) into bad times, good times. The truth is that Livesay has always responded much too thoroughly to all the subtleties, fluctuations, and contradictions of her experience for such simplification to be appropriate.

It is similarly instructive to compare the poetic output of 1959 with that of 1960 through 1963, the years she spent in Northern Rhodesia. The nearly fifty poems drafted in the first year of widowhood far outnumber the sixteen composed in the four years thereafter. Ever eager to express herself in prose, Livesay recorded many of her impressions of Europe and Africa in essays and in personal letters and diaries. It was only after her return to Canada in 1963 that Livesay began to tap the African experiences poetically. "The Second Language (Suite)," which finally surfaced in the "To Speak With Tongues" section of the *Collected Poems,* and the "Zambia" poems, first printed privately by the Unitarian Service Committee as *The Colour of God's Face* (1964) and then made section 4 of 1967's *The Unquiet Bed,* are the two poem sequences most intensely drawn from the years in Northern Rhodesia.

Livesay, in astute self-analysis of her early verse, has noted that "the free verse poems were all solitary, myself talking to the wind; whereas the more structured lyrics envisage a partner."[25] The generalization is reversed in the late 1950s and the 1960s, when a preference in the solitary years for structured poems—particularly blank verse, sonnets, and quatrains—gave way to a preponderance of free verse in the years of renewed quest for that "perfect dancing partner."[26] Partly it was timing: as the twentieth century rolled on, formal regularity in verse became less and less popular. Partly it was the influence of Africa, where European poetic conventions must have seemed less appropriate and where renderings of a fluid and uncorseted society called for parallel qualities in verse. Partly it was an Anglican childhood full of the Psalms, the Song of Songs, Isaiah, and the Anglican liturgy, which made free verse second nature to Livesay and Whitman her avowed "hero."[27] And partly it was personal inclination: the stirrings of unfettered dance in Livesay once again.

There was, of course, a series of subtle preliminary stages. In her fascinating essay "Song and Dance" Livesay has described the encouragement she received from her African students to become reacquainted with her lyric self through singing and dancing. "Best of all, you didn't need a partner," wrote the single, aging woman. "You could dance opposite a girl student as easily as opposite a youth. Not a dance of touch, but one where the rhythm itself created an unseen wire holding two people together in the leap of movement" (46). In this early phase of reawakening, eagerness was counterpointed in inhibition, as she contemplated a deteriorating body and reflected that "No longer any man needs me" ("Widow," *Collected Poems*). An unpublished poem of that period, "The Child on Steps,"[28] emphasizes her wistful sense of standing outside and looking in by comparing her position with that of a prepubescent Rhodesian child watching some teenagers "flashing their new-won sex" and "feeling and knowing / but not belonging." She found herself deeply attracted to a black teacher who became the "you" of many fantasies and poignant passages involving

>   the wanting mouth
>   closed
>   the longing arms
>   clamped.
>   ("The Second Language. For Raphael")

With consummation doubly forbidden them by his marriage and his devout Roman Catholicism, Livesay nonetheless indulged in the sweet torture of wondering:

>   If in the dark
>   I stumbled against your mouth

> would my arms stay pinned
> at my back—
>   or shiver forward
>   white flowering
>   into black?

Since her interest characteristically involved the whole man, and because she respected his beliefs, Livesay chose to view their relationship positively as one of "Moving together, not touching / but moving together" ("Before Independence [Zambia]," *Collected Poems*). In the blazing light of the "dark continent," where the rhythm of the drums "on black curving thighs / thrusts love upwards" ("Wedding," *The Colour of God's Face*), that unseen wire that she had described as holding two people together had become the high tension wire of desire. The rhythm had become specifically sexual; the floor was cleared for a remarkable five-year dance of love with a responsive young Canadian man.

Livesay's poetic drought in the years 1960–63 was followed by a shower of verse in 1964: as in 1959, nearly fifty new poems. She has told of her relief at the enthusiastic feedback from fellow Canadian poets and of her keenness to put her newly sensitized, post-African ear to the test of poetic innovation. Reinforced by subsequent studies in linguistics, a master's thesis on sound and rhythm in contemporary Canadian poetry, and contact with the TISH and Black Mountain schools of the West Coast, Livesay's African experience showed itself in a glittering variety of stylistic experiments.

The drums that had been part of her daily life in Africa informed an incantatory quality that rose in Livesay's verse. Because drumming deals in primary beats, secondary stresses, and the crucial silences in between, the poet became sharply conscious of the power of recurrence, of pause, and of cessation. In the 1930s and 1940s negative associations of repetition had been forged in the poet's mind by the stunning monotony of industrialization with its assembly line; in Africa those connotations were completely neutralized by the transcendent realization, under the influence of a society close to its natural and biological cycles, of the inextricability of rhythm and life. The blood-pumping beat of our hearts, the lunar and solar cycles, the pleasure of patterned movement, the throb and thrust of sex: all were conjured up by the drums. Livesay's rhythms strengthened; her alliteration and consonance multiplied; her fondness for rep-

Songs of Experience: Flesh Made Word 95

etition and internal echoes increased. By 1965 her worksheets showed a conscious deletion of conventional punctuation in favor of white spaces, of lateral and diagonal placement of words. End rhyme almost vanished in her overwhelming preference for the visual and aural options and surprises of free verse. And her mounting interest in the rhythms of human speech prompted her to incorporate conversations almost intact.

Poet Irving Layton had long been given to claiming that Canadian poets were a bloodless lot in comparison with his lusty Hebraic self and that Canada was a Protestant wasteland virtually incapable of producing a sexually inspired woman (hence his choice, for a while anyway, of an Australian mate). When Livesay's *The Unquiet Bed* came out in 1967, it contradicted both of Layton's assertions . . . or perhaps proved them by offering such a striking exception to his rule. Not only did the collection sing of the ecstasies and agonies of sexual passion with a candor unusual among Canada's middle-aged bards and unprecedented among its female poets of a certain age, it also set a model for Canada's younger writers by virtue of its clarity, directness, and honesty about matters many Canadians were still inclined to regard as indelicate. With *The Unquiet Bed* Livesay broke astonishing new ground in Canadian poetry in the sphere of female sexuality, both in an exquisite celebration of a woman's sexual satisfactions and in an unblinking treatment of some of its darker faces: vulnerability, misunderstanding, rejection, withholding, power struggles, agism, and even abortion.

The first section of *The Unquiet Bed* runs the gamut of themes from the dance of sport ("Soccer Game") and British Columbian and prairie snapshots ("Roots") through childhood perspectives ("Spring," "Isolate," "Perceptions") to a series of contemplations about poetry ("Without Benefit of Tape," "The Incendiary"), often in honor of fellow poets ("The Emperor's Circus—for Alden Nowlan," "For Abe Klein: Poet," "Making the Poem—for Jack Spicer, before his death," "Postscript to Phyllis Webb," "For Gwendolyn [MacEwen]," "To a Younger Poet [Al Purdy]"). Section 2 of *The Unquiet Bed* is replete with sensory images: with sun and scents and flowers, with the climax of spurting apple juice in "Eve" and the poet's identification in "Sunfast," under the sway of caressing, probing, and stroking, "with rolling animal life / legs in air." And section 4's "Zambia," a revision of *The Colour of God's Face*, is a vivid documentation of Northern Rhodesia's struggle into nationhood. It is a country's equivalent of the individual song and dance of completion; it is also a reminder for the reader of a major source of Livesay's own renewed capacity to dance and sing.

Sections 1, 2, and 4 of *The Unquiet Bed* form a frame and a context for section 3, which is in many respects the heart of the volume. Its opening poem, "The Unquiet Bed," so important as to lend its title to the entire book,[29] sets the tone, diction, and theme of the dozen poems that follow. Immensely popular, the poem has become a fixture of Livesay's public readings. The small, grandmotherly figure stands with feet demurely together and delivers the lines in her quietest voice. She warns her audience that she "is not what you see," but frequently then disarms them by a self-mocking gesture to her dentures in asserting that "I'm not just bones / and crockery." Livesay stretches out her open hands, to illustrate the abstractions of "longing that love / might set men free," and then brings them together in a fervent handclasp with the hopeful "yet hold them fast / in loyalty." By the time she expresses the affectionate insistence of the closing lines, "move over love / make room for me," the audience is usually won.

Thought of by Livesay as "the little poem of my book," "The Unquiet Bed" does deviate from the free versifying of the volume by being, with "A Letter," one of only two prosodically regular pieces among forty-three. That atypicality tends to highlight it, to emphasize the restrained, almost gnomic quality that might otherwise be missed. The seven original stanzas of the first draft[30] have been pared down, tightly crafted into four quatrains with simple dimeter stresses and *a b c b* rhyme patterning. With sweet reasonableness, the woman declares her identity, her dreams, her past, and her rights. "The Unquiet Bed" is both a manifesto of love and a loving manifesto, acknowledging polarities of love/hate, freedom/constraint, surface/reality, and affirming the space available in one bed for them all.

Livesay was acutely conscious of her society's tendency to mock May-December romances, especially when the December partner was a female, and also to make fun of the notion of older people continuing to be sexually active. Writing at the height of youth cultism in the 1960s, she tackled these prejudices head-on, and in unflinching detail.

In the first of "Four Songs" she explains the rationale for the "bargain" struck between her and her young lover: she will teach him a mature artistic "will"; in turn, he will satiate her profound sexual needs, and perhaps his own too. To reinforce the sense of a balance or fair trade, she creates several parallel structures. "People will say," she begins, "I did it for delight / you—for compassion," and carefully reconstructs it to conclude with the truth of the matter: "You did it from design / I—from compulsion." Since the second stanza is *a b c b* dimeter, it is interesting to note the poet's very deliberate breaking down of such prosodic regularity in the third stanza, first of all by inserting "you said."

> Give me the will, you said
> and in return
> take from my fill
> of passion

As well, she reduces the final line to an amphibrach, which is a single metric foot with one central stressed syllable; its popular name, a rocking foot, reinforces her point about the reciprocal nature of the relationship. At the same time the sheer irregularity of that verse line implies the equal importance of spontaneity and freedom in the mating, the belief that symmetry is not the only consideration.

Since Livesay is hardly the first to discover sex, she naturally draws upon some conventions of love poetry and the courtly tradition. A romantic red rose is given a Keatsian treatment in "A Book of Charms," and eternal is the warning of "Old Song" that, in the face of life's impermanence, one must "catch the bird in season." The horn and "stabbing glance" of the unicorn in "The Dream" are echoes of Renaissance cloaked eroticism and of the romanticism of Livesay's earliest poetry, a reminder of her belief that an older person who falls in love cannot regain her youth but *can* recover her innocence.

Stepping out of maidenly reticence and indirection, however, Livesay is at pains to overthrow the entrenched view that sexual passion is the exclusive territory of the young. She sings boldly of her "hunger," her recurring "thirst," in no way diminished by the possession of crow's feet, wrinkles, or a pendulous bosom. Penises, tongues, nipples, breasts, spread legs—and not all in youthful trim—move out of the mists of euphemism to be named plainly but retain their place in a great mystery.

Radiant joy is everywhere in these love poems: concrete in the way

> the penis completing
> me
> rests in the opening

>   throbs
>   and its steady pulse
>   down there
>   is my second heart
>   beating
>   ("The Touching," 1)

And transcendental in the way his caress puts her in miraculous touch with cosmic regeneration:

>   I'm born again
>   deaf   dumb
>   each time
>   I whirl
>   part of some mystery
>   I did not make or earn
>   that seizes me
>   each time
>   I drown
>   in your identity
>   I am not I
>   but root
>   shell
>   fire
>   each time you come
>   I tear through the womb's room
>   give birth
>   and yet   alone
>   deep in the dark
>   earth
>   I am the one   wrestling
>   the element re-born.
>   ("The Touching," 3)

The swirling disjunctures of line and the possibilities of connection and significance in directions other than the strictly sequential perfectly embody the poet's ecstasy, the movement through love beyond the logical and the conscious and the individual. With love's pride ("A Letter") and love's protection ("The Vigil"), she happily becomes one of a pair of Siamese twins and uses conceits reminiscent of John Donne to show how love can make her whole, "serene— / no longer desperate" ("The Notations of Love," 5).

Drowning and dark earth: vulnerability too is everywhere. The poet is intimidated by her young man's beauty and confidence, next to which:

> My tongue
>   was too long
> my kiss
>   too short
> Inadequate I shrank
>   from perfection
> ("And Give Us Our Trespasses")

Only in the dead of night will he concede her importance; by day he warily withholds, utters "no other word / of praise." "*I was naked / and you clothed me,*" he whispers in the dark, but she feels her own condition is the reverse: "day or night, I / am undressed," for the lover has "undressed me to the bone" ("The Notations of Love," 6). When they must dismantle their home in "Moving Out," she laments the loss of soft sheets and the other familiar "paraphernalia and props" of their love, and must punningly settle for "an upright bed / between your bones." For better or for worse, this love has taught her to "dance / differently" ("Notations of Love").

Sometimes there is a violence or cruelty implicit in Livesay's imagery, as when she writes of her body "needing the knife," compares the lover's tongue to "forked lightning," and masochistically calls his lovemaking a "blow" that "eased me so" ("Four Songs"). He is capable of egotistically silencing her—"Whenever I spoke / out of turn, was it?" ("And Give Us Our Trespasses")—a grievous violation of anyone's rights, but above all of a poet's. And she alludes to betrayal in his tongue being "forked" and in her reference to Dido, "this fire," and "that funeral"; she interweaves the idea of murder with moth, flame, and burning body ("Four Songs"). Dido's destiny was voluntary, however, and so is Livesay's.

"The Taming" specifically explores the peculiar appeal of sexual surrender. As it takes only a few minutes in Livesay's presence for one to detect her strength of will and dominant personality, it is at first surprising that she would be attracted by power greater than her own. On reflection, however, it is quite predictable, for the strong tend to be drawn to the strong. For all that she longs for an equal dance partner, she is honest enough to admit an opposing impulse, the unfashionable desire for a partner who leads and who, in leading her in the dance, releases her from self-consciousness and perhaps responsibility, allows her simply to "Be woman." Indeed, at one point Livesay considered organizing section 3 of *The Unquiet Bed* as a taming-of-the-shrew progression,[31] but such poems as "Sorcery," which would have fit that focus, were held over until the darker sexual explorations of *Plainsongs* in 1969 and 1971.

When *Plainsongs* was republished in 1971, Livesay and Fred Cogswell's Fiddlehead Press had discarded eight of the 1969 edition's twenty-two poems in favor of eighteen more recent pieces. The changes are noteworthy. First, only one of the eight deletions, "The Journey East," had any romantic dimension, and it was also the only one to be reinstated in the *Collected Poems* of the following year. Among the newcomers, almost one-third concerned themselves with matters of heart and flesh. But it should also be remarked that fully half of the eighteen additions are preoccupied with that bane of lovers, time: with history or generations or cycles or aging or love lost. Sometimes in lament, sometimes in the hope of resurrection and

> com[ing] out of the cave
> two
> in one
> ("Easter Saturday")

the revised *Plainsongs* amplifies an already acute consciousness of the Livesay family motto: *Respice ad finem,* or Look to the End.

The subtitle of the 1969 text declares the intended form: *"Plainsongs*—vocal music composed in mediaeval modes and in free rhythm . . . and sung in unison." All of the poems are free verse; all are phases of our common condition ("unison"); all are emphatically meant to be sung, as a chorus of book reviewers had been observing since the arrival of *The Unquiet Bed.* And the epigram of *Plainsongs* confirms that the song will continue to be accompanied by the dance: "In the beginning was the flesh / and the flesh was made word." The biblical derivation of this inverted epigram, Genesis, lends divine sanction to Livesay's convictions about the priority and primacy of the flesh, at the same time implying cosmic application of the individual experience and presenting the flesh as avenue to truth. Further, the indispensability of the poet-lover may be deduced from the participle "made," which gives the agent of transformation (the poet who makes flesh into word) a godlike association and confers on her word a heady status as well.

More than half of the poems of *Plainsongs* reflect some aspect of sexuality, flickering between its glories and its sorrows. The crystal brilliance of sex in "At Dawn" guarantees the anguish of its absence at other times.

> Not to be touched and swept
> by your arm's force
> gives me the ague
> turns me into witch
> ("Sorcery")

But the alchemy can work positively too, can

> magic me
> out of insanity
> from scarecrow into girl again

And the power of sexual love to effect such wonders—to dance her, toss her, catch her in a new springtime—testifies to the legitimacy of the experience; not dependent on props like smooth young bodies, not deterred by breasts like "withered gourds," by shrunken skin, by bristling pubic hair, the lover plunges right to the core, the cunt, the soft and unprotected center of her being.

If the reader is so inclined, it is easy in *Plainsongs* to concentrate entirely on the poet's sense of vulnerability, entrapment, and surrender to a dominating and emotionally stingy lover, who takes her body with elaborate nonchalance "on the unquiet bed" and pretends "no care / save the act done" ("The Cave"). Like her father, Livesay explains in "Heritage," "I am lusty and fearful," and she feels herself "a shell in your hand / to be broken" ("Auguries"). The beloved is cruelly capable of withholding his body ("Con Sequences"), of denying her and so dooming her to a dark garden alone ("Auguries"), of perhaps even pecking out her eyes, blinding her ("Dream"). When he departs, she blames herself in that oh-so-female way for not having managed to become indispensable, for having

> let you find
> a world within
> without me.
> ("The Snow Girl's Ballad")

Bereft, abandoned, she reads a sexual rosary, torments herself with memories of

> how my limbs rose
> and fell   under your loving
> how my breasts pushed upward
> as islands   out of water
> how your hands were the sky itself
> cupping my body
> ("Auguries")

Then, in "The Journey East" across Canada, she acknowledges her lost love's continued power over her: he is "the light I move by" and "I feel you within me / steering." Self-reproach plagues her still:

> I was undressed
> long before I ventured
>   onto the highway
> They were right
>   to give me a ticket
> You were right   also
>   to disown me.

She is left sitting by a window, watching a new generation of dancers in the schoolyard opposite, reflecting

> that I'm only an aging person
> onlooker
> petrified   behind glass
>   ("Where I Usually Sit")

Livesay, however, intends in *Plainsongs* a balance that concludes in affirmation. In "The Woman," for example, sex can both create a "fearful knot of pain" and "untie" it; the pleasure-pain symmetry is reiterated when the lover is frantically urged to "break me again / (until the bliss begins)." And on a larger scale, Livesay organizes *Plainsongs* as a trinity—Loving, Living, and Being—whose conclusions involve (respectively) optimistic images of sky, sea, and resurrection. The "Loving" segment reinforces her positive stance by beginning with the ecstatic "At Dawn" and concluding with her complexly celebratory "The Operation."

A somewhat startling blend of sex and surgery at first glance, "The Operation" deserves a closer look, for it is actually a remarkable intersection of two autobiographical lines involving the flesh: Livesay's five-year love affair and the lung cancer that struck her shortly thereafter, in 1968. The longest poem in *Plainsongs*, "The Operation" in its first of four parts anatomizes the doctor-patient relationship. Taking the poised surgical scalpel and her position as a "victim" into whose arm a needle is "shot," she turns them around. The surgeon becomes a savior to whom she is "grateful," a gifted creator "from bone and flesh" of "a new woman," a sort of lover to whom she is connected by a friendly "warm flame" and to whom she surrenders willingly: "I was his." After the operation, he visits daily and she must each time—whether raging or docile—acknowledge him, her maker, noting "between us still / that intimate   flashing bond." In the final segment of part 1, pronounced healthy, she leaves his godlike powers and territory behind and begins the painful, vital process of breathing deeply on her own.

Part 2 substitutes lover for doctor and shifts to direct address, from "he" to "you." The needle and knife of the beginning section become the penis of this passage, but blood and wounds, gasping for breath and dazed dreams, hurt and healing continue. His power, like the doctor's, moves to the brink of apotheosis: eternally present ("ever there"), dominant and deified ("over me   lord / over me"), like Christ, taking "my pain into your side." The emphasis on gentle comfort, on his "tender rocking ease," is sharply returned to the explicitly sexual and made complete with the colloquial final line: "and a quick come."

In part 3 of "The Operation," Livesay reverses the structure. Where, in the medical relationship, there is a gradual return to health, and the bond between patient and healer is a source of pleasure, in the sexual relationship there is miserable decline, a chilling change of seasons. Their loving becomes "a sickness" or "a kind of disease" in which myriad goodbyes have "swung needles deeper into flesh" than ever the surgeon could and "split the mind's peace." Love becomes a sterile "excuse / for going to bed"; kisses are "transmitted" like viruses; his sperm are love's "antibody" that "I caught between my thighs." The poet uses ambiguous syntax to ironic effect in describing how:

> From my convalescent window
> I see you cured
> jay-walking on robson street
>   a well man
>   free of opposites

Brought low by rain and depression and memories of her recently lost love, she decides "to complete the operation" and the separation, to throw herself into the northern "crystal city of ice," a poetic rendering of her actual move from the West Coast to Edmonton, Alberta. In the presence of her very first lover, the "animal sun," she will heal and grow and inhabit "another kingdom."

The concluding section of "The Operation" restores the equivalency: as at the end of the lung cancer sequence, there is again a vision of autonomy and brilliant prospects. Left to her own devices, "for now the *he* the *you* are one / and gone," she realizes that "I must measure me" and stretch "to reach a dazzled strangeness / sun-pierced sky."

In the 1970s and 1980s Dorothy Livesay has not adopted the role that our society clearly prefers for its grandmothers, that of the sexless sweetie whose romantic memories are veiled in Victorian euphemism. Livesay has felt no genteel serenity about sexual deprivation in old age; instead, as she groans in the second of *Nine Poems of Farewell, 1972–1973*:

> Every bone of me
> is dispossessed
> all merriment
> pretense
>
> for to have known complete
> completion
> then have it wrenched away
> is savage desolation
> ("Down Beat")

Livesay's sense of a double physical betrayal is everywhere: in the "nameless pointless pains" of an elderly body and the jabs of unfulfilled sexual desire. The lover's tongue, of which she made so much in her erotic poetry, multiplies mockingly into "darting tongues" of nighttime pain, which "lick" and "sicken" her ("Aging"). In "Disasters of the Sun" she rejects the sun as benevolent source of sensual pleasure and laments the way her hands, which used to be "tender as green leaves" and skilled at arousing her lover, "pulling you up / into joyous air," have become "knotted bones / whitening in the sun."

While *Ice Age* (1975) is no longer primarily concerned with the poet as sexual being, the volume offers roughly a dozen pertinent poems, none rejoicing, all excruciatingly time-conscious. "Interiors" mourns the departure of the lover with whom it was once possible to "fling / all old age off," and a reappearance of "Aging" from *Nine Poems of Farewell* reiterates the sting of old but unsatiated flesh. "Widow" makes plain the limitations of masturbation, the inability of the hand alone to "recover / the heave and wrestle" or, more importantly, the impossibility of the imagination really being able to duplicate "that bond of flesh / body within body." A similar ranking of the sensory above the intellectual shows itself in "Windows," where, like her plants, she yearns for light, spurns words and thoughts. Elsewhere, in part "1. Waking" of "Morning Rituals" she remembers not her lovers' names but their shapes and recalls with disappointment how her husband "talked more than he made love." She is inclined to turn to nature for solace: in "Morning Rituals" the sun's healing needles upon her labia probe more deeply than could a lover's fingers ("2. Acupuncture"), while "the garden's / wheeling bliss" imprints a blessed pattern upon her eyelids and veins ("3. Blessing").

Men in *Ice Age* seem inadequate, much in need of female sexual and other wisdom. "The Old Bawd" sadly dismisses the men of her current romantic acquaintance as "starved children," a shift from unperceptive to pathetic. In a condemnation of sex without respect, "The Stoned Woman" complains:

> I am become an object
> the man I love
> uses me
> he eats me like breakfast
> and then he shits.

Similarly, "Mathematics" speaks sardonically of the narrator's inability to match her lover's heartless gamesmanship:

> I want to play the great game, darling
> but only you can play it to perfection:
> Much talk . . no bed   Some talk . . some bed
> no talk . . all bed;   and talk tomorrow.

It is not a huge leap from the destructive games of sex to global wargames. Linking sex with male violence, ejaculation with deadly projectiles, Livesay warns that

> The minds of North Americans
> have been so loaded
> with guns   western movies
> hatred of women
> that sex is only a ritual dance
> calling down carnage.
>   ("The Gun")

Livesay is convinced now that, "in love, / women are more committed" ("Last Letter"), and she is prepared to provide a primer for men on women's desires, needs, and potentially world-saving capacity to connect.

> A woman wants above all
> to be touched, caressed,
> massaged and kissed
> and what she carries away
> the next day
> is pride of flesh
> love of link with man
> human to human
>   ("One Way Conversation")

This poem's title suggests skepticism that the message will or can ever get through; nonetheless, she believes that man, "partner to woman," has the choice of the same role—"gently caressing / human to human."

The 1977 selection of Livesay's poetry, under that trademark title *The Woman I Am,* was preoccupied in its new poems with pressing concerns of Quebec separatism, the thermonuclear specter, native rights, and other issues. Four years later, the voice drama entitled *The Raw Edges* (1981) sketched again a world on the brink of apocalypse, but declared Livesay's faith that our salvation can be achieved through the union of hearts and flesh. In a 1982 mimeographed revision of the 1981 Turnstone Press edition, Livesay wrote:

> each man and woman
> common and uncommon
> may learn   in the clutch of loving
> how to rejoice

The "clutch of loving": it seemed a phrase so potent that Livesay used it again at the end of the final poem in *The Phases of Love* (1983).

> teach me to be more human
> and to learn
> in the clutch   of loving
>
> how small miracles
> shatter the facts—
> explode!
>   ("The Sybil")

The Phases of Love is divided in three: 1. Adolescence; 2. Fire and Frost; and 3. Voices of Women. The thirteen poems of "Adolescence," previously unpublished pieces from the middle to late 1920s, are romantic, passionate, confessional, and risktaking. At the other end of the volume and the spectrum and the decades (now the late 1970s), "Voices of Women" offers twenty-five poems of mature and reflective love—love of humanity, love of nature, love of parents and children, love of women, equality in modern love, love remembered and sustaining. Unlike the nervousness of "Adolescence," the sense of a trust in love is here palpable. Then, using the same structural strategy as the one found in *The Unquiet Bed,* Livesay chooses the middle section, the deep center of the book, for thirty-four poems, the fire and frost of the 1960s and early 1970s. Had the reader thought Livesay "beyond" carnal interests? No fear. Her selections bespeak a continuing fascination with the "ancient ceremonies" and sweaty "notations of love." Once again Livesay charts the territory; notes the contradictions; laments and rejoices; approaches and retreats; waxes high-minded, visionary, and inspired; wanes petty, jealous, and inhibited. She anatomizes that now-familiar love affair of the 1960s—its growth, magic, ecstasy, decline, dissolution, and aftermath. And always two insistences:

> I seek more
> than skin, flesh, blood
> I seek the coursing
> heaving heart
> for my soul's food
> ("The hard core of love")

Between her and her former lover, there remain no recriminations:

> only this
> astonishing surprise

> secret and sealed:
> one body and one bliss
> together healed
> ("Now it is done")

In her most recent volume of poetry, sensually entitled *Feeling the Worlds* (1984), Livesay's sexual expression takes a new turn. After the uniform heterosexuality of her previous published love poetry, Livesay evidently felt the times had become sufficiently permissive to let her write explicitly of lesbian attachments. The shift in focus did not come entirely unannounced, however. Five years earlier, in the 1979 Dorothy Livesay double issue of the feminist West-Coast quarterly called *A Room of One's Own,* two poems had obliquely introduced female lovers. "The Secret Doctrine of Women" rhapsodized "one face alight / one woman's hair" as "the solution" that was "always at hand," perhaps overlooked precisely because so "close by," patiently "offering yourself, your love." Identifying pronouns are avoided, no potentially compromising mention of Manitoba survives the rough draft stage, and unisex phrases like "your torso" preserve their privacy, but the intimacy is indisputable.

> I am amazed at me
> so joined
> my blood racing and pounding
> beside yours

In the other poem, "The Enchanted Isle: A Dialogue," Livesay deliberately uses a French word "affairée" to indicate by the final "e" that the "you" that "I choose" is a woman. In the fourth part of the poem she reassures her dear friend that "We are too old to worry what we do / loving is not immoral." Interestingly enough, the excisions made on these two poems for their appearance before the more conservative audience of *The Phases of Love* considerably blunt their sexual allusiveness, encouraging the reader to take them entirely as generalized statements of sisterhood.

One poem from *The Phases of Love* is also relevant to these new directions in the transformation it works upon a major metaphor of Livesay's verse. From the beginning the poet had accepted the mythic conventions of Western civilization, including those of sun and moon. To the Greeks, the sun was the god Apollo (a.k.a. Phoebus), whose hot and phallic rays penetrate the female earth, making her pregnant with all life. In this cosmology the moon is the goddess Artemis (Greek) or Diana (Roman), the pale and inconstant satellite who merely reflects her brother's solar magnificence. As a young virgin, Livesay feared the sun's power and fierceness ("The Shrouding," "In the Street"), but she soon discovered the pleasures of lying naked under the sun, feeling herself "as earth upturned, alive with seed," celebrating his capacity to "magnetize my passion" ("Sun"). Her upbringing on the sun-drenched prairies combined with a year in the sunny Midi of France and three years in the blazing light of Africa to make permanent the linkage of sun with energy, ecstasy, and even specifically sexual possession. Livesay has been intrigued since the 1940s by Sir Thomas Browne's idea of the invisible sun within us all, which makes that power the heritage of both sexes, but she has also had a fondness for the punning potential of sun, son, and Son (of God and of Man), as seen in "Serenade for Strings," "Five Months Young (for Galen)," and "Roots," a pun that undeniably emphasizes the godhead and maleness of that burning sphere.

While the sun god was usually a bringer of comfort and joy to Livesay, in the early 1970s sexual disappointment may have been related to Livesay's turning on her deity, denouncing him as "this most killing / northern sun," warning others in oracular tones:

> *I tell you*
> *we live in constant*
> *danger*
> *under the sun   bleeding*
> *I tell you*
> . . . .
> Sun, you are no good father
> but tyrannical king:
> I have lived sixty years
> under your fiery blades
> all I want now
> is to grope for those blunt
> moon scissors
> 	("Disasters of the Sun")

A few years later, however, the sun has reassumed his status as healing lover, his needles more effective, in fact, than any man's fingers at probing her private parts ("Morning Rituals 2. Acupuncture").

With a title, then, appropriate to her new sexual phase in the 1980s, "Dawnings" in the closing pages of *The Phases of Love* introduces a stunning reversal of these mythic structures.

> When the moon stops by
> with his bag of silver
> I'll not give him
> a look-in
>
> I'll wait for the tender fingers
> of the woman sun
> slipping through the window
> sliding   like love
> into my   skin

When, in the third section of the poem, Livesay calls on an anonymous "you" to "Bliss me with your mouth," we have a clue that it is a woman she addresses, for in an earlier poem called "Breathing" she has already described women of any age as "fresh and sweet-smelling," as she does again here.

Aware of these three harbingers, we can now consider Livesay's explicit expressions of love for women in *Feeling the Worlds*. Livesay's continuing championing of women's rights, more emphatically than ever in recent years, has combined with her "retirement" to a community of women artists to reinforce this sexual development. But there is also a great biographical symmetry operating here. Livesay's earliest sexual inquiries were with her own sex, so her rediscovery in old age of happiness with women has been the completion of a sexual circle. Livesay declares in *Feeling the Worlds* that, unlike her mother, "I grew comfortable with love" ("My Mother Myself"). That claim seems more applicable to her late love affairs with women than the previous ones with men, for with women the elements of kinship, supportiveness, and acceptance surpassed the competitiveness, misunderstanding, and distrust that had plagued her heterosexual relations. In a person so committed to the idea that mind and body are inseparable, it follows that similar bodies prefigure similar minds. And the concept of like loving like, seeing in the lover's face not otherness but sameness, reminds one of the vision of autonomous love explored in "On Looking into Henry Moore" in the 1950s, "Prepar[ing] my half-self for myself." In the security of that recognition, it is then possible to "rejoice in your differences" ("Towards A Love Poem") rather than be puzzled, frustrated, infuriated, or hurt by them.

"Towards A Love Poem" is excellent ground for mapping other changes too. Livesay's heterosexual love poetry was full of images of fire, fever, pain, disease, wounds, war, tempest, and unquiet beds; the woman-loving poetry discards them for images of flying freedom, unshadowed joy, and peaceful gardens. No invader of her privacy, the way a male lover was in "When I got home," "Nothing is Private," and dozens of other poems, this little "sister" inspires Livesay's protective instincts. In contrast with male lovers who "never recognized / my devotion" and "never yielded / to my compassion" ("The Old Bawd"), this young woman, a "surrogate daughter," is a natural and appreciative recipient of Livesay's caring. The benefits are reciprocal: "I too / am learning." And while the sensation of drowning was a frequent phenomenon in her previous love poetry (e.g., "The Step Beyond," "The Operation," "The Touching"), now, through her "undine" or female water spirit, the poet is miraculously learning "to fly / under water."

Where the man buried her beneath his "avalanche of talk" ("This Page my book") or used her as a mirror in which to straighten the "tie" of his thoughts ("I see you trying on an idea"), the woman is her "early morning listener" who has "elected to know me," "elected to love me." Unlike men, who long egotistically to

> create
> the great illusion:
> thundering gods
> at the womb's intrusion
> ("One Way Conversation")

this "lover   explorer" quietly "places the affirming kiss / on my vulva." The lines that follow are a brilliant gauge of Livesay's liberation: "catch as catch can / love in flight   weightless." The last time we encountered "catch as catch can," in "Ballad of Me," Livesay couldn't—couldn't catch, couldn't dance, couldn't please the father whose archetype would undercut her sexual satisfaction for decades. Now she can—can catch . . . and fly . . . and fly in the element that represents her most female, fluid, fertile self—through the love of woman.

One six-line poem in *Feeling the Worlds* succinctly fuses the physical and the idealistic aspects of loving women. Revisiting the redoubtable George Bernard Shaw, whose *Intelligent Woman's Guide to Socialism, Major Barbara, Arms and the Man,* and other works made him a mentor of her early adulthood, Livesay changes one of his titles to "Arms and the Woman."

> My hand within you
> yours in me
> by these crossed swords
> we make a peace
> not of this world
> song without words

The word play on "arms," familiar to participants in the peace movement, turns the military into the pacific and elevates a basic bodily posture of lesbian loving to a covenant, the symbol of a transcendental harmonizing, the model of which could save this precarious planet. There is none of the domination/invasion implicit in the standard heterosexual position; here the hands are symmetrical, perfectly balanced and utterly equal. In the complete communion of the two women, the words that caused so much difficulty between man and woman fall away, and there is simply pure song.

Given that moving, unifying experience, "The Merger" comes as no surprise. Printed directly following "Arms and the Woman," it is a poem one has trouble imagining Livesay writing at any other stage of her life. True, she had many times tried on ideas of androgyny, the perfect union of male and female, and there is no question that in sexuality her orientation is not exclusively heterosexual or lesbian but bisexual, just as her self-image is not simply feminine but androgynous. But again and again in her relations with men, despite the depth and power of the connections, any feeling of peacefulness was fleeting, the anger invariably built, and often she was left puzzling wryly,

> If we are two halves
> of the same fruit
> why must we fight
> over the stone?
> ("The Search for Wholes")

Now, in achievement at last of the dream of the Henry Moore poem, rising "Self-extending and self-known," Livesay explains:

> When I was *two* people
> . . . .
> always there was
> an intermittent war
>
> Now I am *one*
> I go hand in hand
> with myself
> linking our laughters
> ("The Merger")

The last poem of *Feeling the Worlds* is called "Epitaph," and its final word is "death." But before that inevitable sloughing off of the physical—surely the ultimate surrender of the flesh—there is still time for the regenerative sun to touch her again and work new magic in an old body. In an unexpectedly fierce autumn sun, Livesay shows herself Sun Libran to the end:

> My cranky ankles   knees
> melt in the blaze
> and I am again
> young naked girl
> lulled on a bed of leaves
> ("September Equinox")

Chapter Six
A Poet's Prose

In June 1983 Dorothy Livesay told me, "I'm moving toward a more open form . . . prose poems. It's not my choosing. I'm just writing what's told to me. It's a coincidence that it's all the mode right now." The phrasing makes her inclination toward prose seem a totally new direction, but in fact Livesay's love affair with prose had started back in childhood. And it is in that childhood that one finds the sources of the powers—both external and subconscious—that Livesay Platonically alludes to in declaring prose "not my choosing."

Livesay's mother, a poet, was also an experienced writer of several forms of prose, being a journalist, translator of many Ukrainian prose legends, and author of *Savour of Salt,* stories about a little girl's experiences in an Irish settlement in early twentieth-century Ontario. Playing no generic favorites, FRL encouraged her elder daughter from late infancy to write little tales as well as rhymes. Even when Livesay became widely known as a poet with two Governor-General's Awards for Poetry to her credit, FRL did not forget or slight Dorothy's prose efforts, reading her manuscripts carefully and offering thoughtful if not always appreciated advice. At least once, in the late 1940s, she even went so far as to try (unsuccessfully) to place for publication a thoroughly unimpressive story called "Apple-Dear" that had been written by Dorothy at age 5.[1] As a reticent Randal, FRL energetically fought in Dorothy the Livesay impulse to confessional prose, repeatedly deploring in private correspondence those occasions when Dorothy in her writings had aired the family linen in public about animosities, alcoholism, debt, and other problems. But in this as in so many respects Dorothy was her father's daughter, prepared to let the portrait stand, warts and all.

From her father, JFBL, Livesay inherited not only that unblinking candor but an unequivocal preference for prose. In fact, in defiance of an age-old ranking of poetry as the supreme literary form, JFBL considered fiction the indisputably superior genre. A reader and teller of stories from his boyhood in Ireland, he had written children's stories in his early days and was still working on fiction after his retirement, a collection published posthumously under the title of *Peggy's Cove*. His *The Making of a Canadian,* edited by his wife and published by Ryerson three years after his death, overflows with sketches, anecdotes, impressionistic family history, war narratives, and a startlingly autobiographical short story called "The High White Bed." The literary models he enthusiastically brought to his daughter's attention were all novelists, and female at that; as Livesay wrote to her own daughter in 1970, JFBL's "passionate admiration for Jane Austen and the Brontës and Virginia Woolf certainly brushed off on me . . . and he wanted it so."[2] Ironically, therefore, the poet from whose pen verses have flowed like water has instead craved from the start a gift for prose and has considered prose far more difficult than poetry. As she confided to her diary at the age of eighteen:

> How little poetry matters to me! I must confess it.
> Terrible achings after the elusive power-depriving [*sic*] story-telling possess me.[3]

Those "terrible achings" underlie Livesay's opinion that any real poem is the nucleus of a story and that "in some ways my poems are just shorthand for stories I'd like to write."[4] To this day Livesay has reiterated her fascination with and determination to master prose of all sorts—fictive, expository, argumentative, descriptive, and narrative—and retained her identity with her father as frustrated novelist.

Since Livesay is now known almost exclusively as an extremely skilled poet, it comes as a surprise to many to discover the dimensions of her accomplishments in prose. As fiction writer, literary critic, journalist, and autobiographer/biographer of a decade, Livesay has been richly productive for over fifty years.

Poet as Fiction Writer

While "No More Hankies,"[5] written by Livesay at the age of nine, cannot be said to have showed more than the mildest promise, it interestingly exhibited many of the characteristics of her best fiction since. First, it had a strong development, the stage-by-stage, tearful, drenched-handkerchief loss of three bells that had been attached to three rattles that had adorned three dolls owned by three children whose three mothers were married to the only survivors of the story. It fulfilled Livesay's enduring conviction, slightly overstated in her diary of 1929, that "the chief function of a story should be to express movement. There must be progress—backward, forward, or in a circle. But from the direction of that progress the reader must be able to see what the rest of the movement will be, to the end of life."[6] Second, children were at the heart of it, as the child's perspective would inform the stories of *Beginnings: A Winnipeg Childhood*. Third, it eschewed the easy or the happy ending, as has most of Livesay's fiction over the years. Fourth, the parallelisms and refrains anticipated the poetic cadences of her adult prose style. And the sheer repetition of internal plot in that brief tale foreshadowed Livesay's tendency to resurrect drafts, both fragments and entire stories, at intervals throughout her career. Some material resurfaced in all three of her greatest phases of prose visibility: in the late 1920s, in the early 1950s, and in the 1970s.

Of the twenty short stories that Livesay has published between 1929 and 1977, more than half have appeared first in a periodical and then taken their place as units in larger Livesay volumes. "Six Years," "Case Supervisor," and "A Cup of Coffee" joined the previously unpublished "Herbie," "Out West," "Two Women," and "Zynchuk's Funeral" in *Right Hand Left Hand;* "See the World Clearly" (which eventually regained its original name, "The Other Side of the Street"), "First Crocus" (later part of "A Prairie Sampler," which was in turn part of the final "Preludes"), "Matt," "The Sparrows," "The Two Willies," and "An Immigrant" were interwoven with eight other stories, five of which dated from at least the 1950s, in the collection of short stories ultimately entitled *Beginnings: A Winnipeg Childhood*. Two more have moved from journals to anthologies: "The Mother-in-Law," renamed "The Wedding" for a selection of Albertan fiction,[7] and "The Glass House," which, in being chosen for *The Best American Short Stories of 1951*,[8] put Livesay in such heady company as John Cheever, Bernard Malamud, and Tennessee Williams.

Having from the start thought that "the only thing to do was be a novelist," Livesay has at least five times drafted full-scale novellas and novels. Several of these had their first incarnations in short stories, sketches, letters, diaries, and fragments penned in the late 1920s or the 1930s. In the late 1940s she began to reconsider and regroup early materials, seeking ways to convert short stories to the purposes of novels. *The Intruder* (or, *The Glass House*), for example, began in 1929 as "Autumn Day," evolved into the 1949 short story "The Glass House," which became in turn the first chapter of a four-part novel of intense psychological interaction.[9] Diary entries, essays, and short stories from her youthful stay in the south of France were the source of *Pavane,* a twenty-chapter novel, that was first assembled and expanded in the 1950s and then recirculated for consideration by publishers in the late 1970s, and was even submitted to the McClelland & Stewart First Novel Competition in 1977 under the pseudonym "Daphne Wilson." The most phoenixlike of all the proposals was *Her Father's House,* whose part one alone was a thirteen-chapter, twenty-nine subsection intertwining of the stories of a man and his daughter: with origins in early memoirs, letters, diaries, and fragments, it became in the 1950s a fullblown novel. Failing to find a publisher, Livesay eventually returned *Her Father's House* to its component short stories, four[10] of which were published in periodicals and nine of which provided part or all of chapters[11] for *Beginnings: A Winnipeg Childhood* in 1973.

"The Cage," a short story written after the Second World War, became the opening chapter of *Give My Love to London,* a four-part novella of forty-eight pages, whose action alternated among London, Montreal, and the British zone of Germany. While entirely a tale of "a postwar world where moral and social values have vanished,"[12] *Give My Love to London* in part 4 draws on Livesay's experience of Montreal and of social agencies in the 1930s; one characterization in particular, Jake, appears to be drawn from a specific friendship in New Jersey of 1934–35. Another exception to the five-decade pattern, in fact a one-shot phenomenon, *The Husband* was also really more novella than novel at eighty-nine pages. Epistolary in form, it appears to have been composed in the mid 1960s, entirely after Livesay's return to Canada, and to have been based particularly on her New Brunswick and African experiences (although one part has a debt to the Knister relationship and drowning of the early 1930s). Unlike *Her Father's House, The Glass House,* or *Pavane,* once rejected for publication *Give My Love to London* and *The Husband* seem to have been consigned to the void.

That Livesay has abandoned projects like *The Husband* but persisted with versions of such works as *Her Father's House* almost certainly has to do not just with their intrinsic quality but with their closeness to her heart and personal history. Most of Livesay's forays into fiction, right back to the 1920s, have had an autobiographical element, and none more than *Her Father's House,* which traced JFBL's life and work and her own relationship with him in highly verifiable detail. So thin, indeed, was the veil between the novel and Livesay's family history that her mother vehemently opposed its publication as an invasion of their privacy. That veil had been gossamer from the start; for example, in the numerous stories of 1928 that she wrote from a female child's viewpoint, Livesay (whose nickname, one remembers, is "Dee") named her protagonist "Elizabeth," nicknamed "Zee," even (in "The Lie") "Zee L——."[13] In such stories the child's sister is sometimes an unmasked "Sophie," and the baby brother whose arrival unsettles her is explicitly "Arthur." For Livesay, then, in fiction as in poetry the distance between art and life has been minimal.

The themes of Livesay's fiction, published and unpublished, have tended to parallel her preoccupations in poetry. Social realism has played an important part from the 1930s onward: stories like "Six Years" (*Right Hand Left Hand*) are typical in showing Depression conditions among the working classes via idiomatic, conversational accounts, written variously in the first and third person but consistently from a single point of view, individualized and chatty rather than omniscient and formal. An even more dominant focus has been interpersonal relations: man and woman, parent and child, siblings, co-workers, friends. In the short story "The Glass House" the Chekhovian action rests almost entirely upon the subtle interplay of personalities: the delicate Celia, her sturdy daughter Charlotte, her sensitive son John, her effete nephew Lawrence, the earthy servant girl Anna. The early fiction, like Livesay's early poetry, shows strong interest in faltering or failed romances, in frustrating marriages, and in family triangles of father, mother, and child. And many of the youthful tales explore maiden fears of intimacy. In one particularly symbolic 1927 piece called "Flight," a pale, large-eyed, mustachioed(!) girl goes through the cycle of the seasons in a half-finished house called "The Wing"; she comes to know nature and to love it, then fear it, be pursued by it, be caught and held by it, and surrender to it in an almost sexual embrace.[14]

"Flight" raises the point that nature looms as large in Livesay's fiction as in her poetry, lyrical descriptions of landscape, wind, and sky often having the presence or force of a persona in the plot. Sometimes, in fact, Livesay's mood pieces overshadow and overwhelm her characters, fragmenting the reader's sense of direction and forfeiting that precious effect of inevitability in the unfolding of both internal and external action. It often seems the case that her ear for nature's voice is more acute than her ear for human speech, resulting in passages of stilted dialogue but powerful description.

For the public as opposed to the literary scholar, the one work on which Livesay's reputation as a writer of fiction rests is *Beginnings: A Winnipeg Childhood*. As has been noted, by the time it arrived in assembled form in 1973, most of its chapters had appeared in journals or anthologies or been broadcast on the CBC. The promotional blurb on the back cover of the New Press edition (1975) was explicit about the autobiographical origins and the poetic equivalents of the material:

Canadian poet Dorothy Livesay has sifted her childhood experiences through her poetic imagination to create a collection of prose reminiscences containing all the magic of her verse.

This volume presents fifteen "reminiscences"—fifteen pictures of the adult world as seen through the eyes of a child and written in fictional form. All those who wish to savour the excitement of Winnipeg during the unforgettable second decade of this century will find new insights into the era, the city, and the misunderstandings that have always existed between generations.

The publication of the book, first by Pequis Press in Winnipeg as *A Winnipeg Childhood* and then by New Press in Toronto as *Beginnings: A Winnipeg Childhood,* marked the end of a long struggle with publishers, who had since the 1950s resisted the manuscript in its varied forms. As late as 1971 Livesay was defending to an editor of McGraw-Hill Ryerson the appropriateness of its structure as a series of sketches in the tradition of Gabrielle Roy's *The Road Past Altamont,* Margaret Laurence's *A Bird in the House,* or Ethel Wilson's *The Innocent Traveller.* As she further argued, "The point of view, I feel bound to insist, is perfectly legitimately third person over the shoulder; and the child is consistently a little girl moving from six to nine years old, her horizon and understanding of adults gradually expanding."[15]

Livesay was correct. The world of Winnipeg during and shortly after the Second World War and the eternal prairie landscape serve as social and physical backdrops to the real organizing principle of the book: the child Elizabeth's consciousness. And there are other effective structural devices: the frame of V-wedge geese headed north in the first and final chapters; the house that shrinks as the little girl grows; the everpresent wind, sun, snow and flowers that similarly unify Livesay's entire poetic canon. There is also the fledgling social sensibility of Elizabeth, who intuitively knows the cruelty of baiting a retarded boy ("Matt") or a Jewish playmate ("First Trials"), hates condescension to native peoples ("Anna"), and is genuinely disturbed by the new idea that in war both sides are human and suffer ("The Guardian Angel").

Beginnings: A Winnipeg Childhood is a book distinguished by honesty. Young Elizabeth, so obviously Dorothy as a child, is not always astute, not brilliantly precocious. It is a narrow, Protestant, middle-class realm that this girl child occupies and Livesay is at pains to show not only her flights of imagination but also her inherited limitations. Elizabeth sometimes comes only very slowly to a glimpse of the truth: that it was really her adored Big Willie who stole her money ("The Two Willies"); that spinster Aunt Maudie really has been a mother after all . . . to Elizabeth herself ("The Uprooting"); that her confident mother is not always positive of her actions ("The Other Side of the Street"). And she can be blind, missing the point that the adult reader catches: oblivious to World War I in any real way ("The End of the War"); insensitive to Jenny's new ambitions ("A Week in the Country"); untouched by her infant brother's death ("Father's Boy"); indifferent to the emotional wars of her parents ("The Party"). Livesay deliberately, authentically makes her so, for Elizabeth is a child awed, confused, and often repelled by the "grown-up world. A tangled mass of evidence which the child could not sift; a clash of emotion, of love and hate, with which the child could not sympathize." Livesay steps briefly into omniscience to explain that, like Pearl in Hawthorne's *The Scarlet Letter*, Elizabeth's "own soul had not opened; love had not reached her. And so she recoiled, drew closer to Peggy, to the street, trying to avoid, at every turn, the strange atmosphere where tall people moved" (68).

A multifaceted prose poem, *Beginnings: A Winnipeg Childhood* is unified by its lyricism. The language is liltingly simple and straightforward, apparently deceptively so to the rare one or two critics who were fooled into thinking the book slight or superficial. In actuality, the directness is resonant, and the sensate details of daily life viewed from a height of three feet are rendered in a way that implies their inherent mystery. The following paragraphs illustrate such qualities:

Nuts, tangerine oranges, cluster raisins—all the treats of Christmas—and a sachet, a hankie, a tiny celluloid doll, just right for the doll's house. She dreamed an hour away, tingling with the newness, the differentness. Having new things, however small, made oneself feel new again. The old Elizabeth had fallen asleep on Christmas Eve and a new one arose clothed in golden garments, bursting with song. ("Christmas," 39f)

What did she care anyhow if Rita Green was going to get heck? Rita had never cared for her—nor for Peggy, either. It was as if the big girl had cobwebs on her face, and kept stroking them aside, trying to see the world. Elizabeth was much smaller, but she could see the world clearly, the flawless sky, the sunshine a great golden roof vaulting the street. Nothing on the pavement but hot white light, ribboning the dull boulevard. Nothing moving. Only in the hollow concrete ditch near the sewer, some sparrows were having a dusty bath. ("The Other Side of the Street," 81)

The images are sharply realized; the language is immediate, sensual, and precise; the content reaches down into the deepest phases of our perception of the world.

In this collection, Livesay late in life looks back to her beginnings, both her early life and her early writings about that life. Far from a departure from her poetic self, these stories are lyrically in keeping. By prefacing the stories with her poem "Isolate," Livesay cements the connection between two genres and confirms *Beginnings: A Winnipeg Childhood* as poet's prose.

Poet as Critic

When Livesay was a young woman studying overseas, her father wrote to her affectionately that he missed her sharp chin poking fiercely at him. The image captures an element of Livesay's makeup familiar to all who know her personally: a sharp and inquiring approach, a disinclination to suffer fools gladly, an assertive rather than a retiring presence, the self-assurance born of having done the spadework and expecting as much of others, and the pride of conviction. Those characteristics have clearly marked her in her capacity as literary critic.

From her first diary musings, Livesay has showed an interest not just in practicing her art but also in understanding it, especially as practiced by others. She has throughout her career pondered the essence of literature and has particularly tried to define the relationships among poet, poem, nature, and society. Part of this inquiry led her as early as 1928 into publishing literary criticism, both essays and reviews. That she felt from the start inspired, entitled, and able to comment on the literary scene is indisputable. In *St. Hilda's Chronicle,* a periodical of the University of Toronto's Trinity College, she tackled with equal confidence the contemporary fiction of New Zealander Katherine Mansfield and the poetry of Canadian E. J. Pratt.[16] In the years since, while she has ranged widely in her reading and appreciation of other literatures, the bulk of her critical efforts have been directed toward Canadian writing.

From a reading of Livesay's critical prose over the last half century, certain principles or recurring tendencies emerge. There is, first of all, an initial nonjudgmental receptivity, an attempt to approach the artist on his own terms. Indeed, considering her strong opinions, it is impressive to see Livesay's openminded interest in and curiosity about what other writers are doing. If the writer manages well what he seems intent upon doing, Livesay will commend the accomplishment. True, she may venture an aside on problems with that intent in the first place, but she will nonetheless give credit where it is due. Connected with that forbearance is a second characteristic, Livesay's clear respect for historical context. She believes in viewing a writer in his own times with an informed sensitivity to the assumptions and limitations of those times.

Third, as befits her personality, Livesay is most willing to be evaluative. Once she has made what she regards as suitable allowance for time, intent, and even inexperience, she exercises fully her option to assess, to call something excellent or partly marred or downright unsatisfactory. She praises what she can and then roundly and even angrily condemns any sloppiness, misinformation, stupidity, affectation, or (in Livesay's view) wrongheadedness. This content frequently provokes a like style, flying with strong declarations, rises and descents in rhetoric, passionate tones, and a quiverful of exclamation points. Nor would she have it otherwise. Livesay has long denounced those two other breeds of critic: those who mealymouth about, terrified of saying anything concrete and vulnerable to counterattack; and those who distort the truth because, apart from the fact that they "have not studied the past, have not done their homework," they are crippled by their "fear of sentimentality."[17]

When the subject of one of her analyses—from a poet's words to a policy decision of the League of Canadian Poets—verges even slightly on the issue of world peace, Livesay instantly puts aside all scholarly decorum or worry about being perceived as too emotional. She writes earnestly and urgently, aware of but indifferent to the likelihood that she will strike many people as overwrought and naive.

Livesay's early contemplations of art stressed intensity of experience, the power of personal revelation. Communication, while extremely desirable, might not come at once, and the artist had to reconcile himself to the possibility that his fit audience would perhaps not arrive for awhile. From 1932 on these priorities were reversed, and the relations between art and society was, for Livesay, paramount. As a critic commenting on the work of others, Livesay has since clearly preferred to detect wider horizons than just the personal and has tended to applaud poets who "speak . . . less for themselves and more for us."[18] She has also favored writers who express positive, humanist values over those with an ambiguous, ironic perspective. And Livesay has had a marked inclination toward those who, like her, believe in poetry as plain talk, meant to be accessible, clean, and spare of construction.

This social conscience and the sense of writers and critics as organic parts of their country and culture have manifested themselves in important ways that would earn Livesay a place in Canadian literary history even if she had never penned a verse. The first is the attention that she has paid to and fostered in the national literature. From that fledgling article on Pratt to her numerous reviews of young women poets fifty-seven years later, Livesay has published on the order of ninety articles and reviews discussing the health and achievement of Canlit and its practitioners. A. M. Klein, Louis Dudek, Anne Marriott, P. K. Page, Pat Lowther, Mazo de la Roche, Milton Acorn, Alan Crawley, Emily Carr, Pat Lane, Miriam Waddington, and dozens of others have all had their profiles heightened by her astute commentaries. As one who has been an avid participant in and alert observer of most of its developments in this century, Livesay is justified in priding herself on her knowledge of Canadian literature, aptly dubbing herself a literary-historical "resource." She has also had an active hand in introducing a new generation to its national writers, having taught undergraduate- and graduate-level Canadian literature courses at universities from the West Coast to the Maritimes and lectured widely around the country from the 1930s to the present.

Particularly dear to Livesay have been two major efforts of literary resurrection. Working tirelessly as a sort of unofficial literary executor, Livesay has helped to assure the reputations of Raymond Knister (1899–1932) and Isabella Valancy Crawford (1850–87). In the case of Knister, it was through her energetic offices that Ryerson Press published his *Collected Poems* in 1949, with an intimate, speculative memoir by Livesay as its introduction. She has since then rarely missed an opportunity to bring his name and work back to memory, and she was the logical choice of *Canadian Literature* to review his *Selected Stories* when they were edited by Michael Gnarowski in 1972.[19] After exhaustive and groundbreaking work on Crawford (as evidenced in the huge files of her research material in the University of Manitoba Special Collections,[20] Livesay presented her findings to the academic community in 1969,[21] following that up in 1973 with two lengthy and crucial articles on Crawford, "The Hunters Twain"[22] and "Tennyson's Daughter or Wilderness Child? The Factual and Literary Background of Isabella Valancy Crawford."[23] Subsequent academic inquiries into Crawford and Knister could be argued to be founded almost entirely on Livesay's pioneer scholarship.

Writing many valuable critical articles and reviews on Canadian authors and texts and teaching Canadian poetry and prose in public and university settings over fifty years are not the entire measure of Livesay's critical contribution to her country's literature. She has also, in a five-pronged approach, nurtured the writings of those outside the dominant tradition: the writers who lacked the preferred combination of gender, location, ethnic affiliation, political philosophy, and status. These have included women, native peoples, westerners and maritimers, non-Anglosaxon immigrants, Marxists, and young unknowns.

The little magazine or periodical has been one of her main tools to usher these disadvantaged writers into print in Canada: in the 1930s, as part of the editorial board of the leftist journal *New Frontier;* in the 1940s, as a founding member of the West Coast journal *Contemporary Verse;* in the 1970s, when she founded and financed a new prairie poetry magazine, *CV/II.*

A second device for encouraging such writers has been producing two anthologies, both devoted to female writing. *40 Women Poets of Canada* (1971), edited by Livesay with the assistance of poet-teacher Seymour Mayne, attempted to redress the gender imbalance of most of Canada's poetry anthologies and textbooks, and also to represent, however imperfectly, all ages and regions. In an innovative strategy, Livesay explained these ambitions not in a formal introduction, which might have dominated the selection, but in a review that she wrote of her own anthology, published under the title "Livesay's Choice."[24] Critics (all female, as it happens), while not altogether comfortable with women writers being "segregated"[25] and also somewhat fixated on the superficial impression that "the topics dealt with in the poems [were] not unlike those dealt with in men's poetry,"[26] generally applauded the acquaintance the book afforded with forty women poets less often anthologized than their poetic brothers.

Three years later, in direct response to the sad fact that neither *40 Women Poets of Canada* nor its publisher, Ingluvin of Montreal, were still on the market, Livesay brought out a second women's anthology, concentrating on poets from Canada's westernmost province. Once again she strove for a range of ages, of experience, of style and theme. And she made a point of selecting recent verse, largely unpublished, so that her anthology would not simply survey old territory. This time she did provide a foreword, arguing bluntly that the poems were not indistinguishable from male verse, that there was a recurrent *"way of looking* that is distinctly from *woman's eye;* and *a way of feeling* that is centred in *woman's 'I.'* "[27]

Livesay's other three methods of encouraging new writers have been more personal. One has been the thankless composition of dozens of grant recommendations on their behalf. Despite her self-help instincts, her own fierce independence, and her ambivalence about grants as a potentially dangerous force for flabby "self-indulgence," especially in young writers,[28] Livesay has given her energetic backing to a large number of grant applications.[29] In a similar vein she has long pressed the League of Canadian Poets, the Canadian Authors Association, and other literary organizations to pay special attention to the attraction and nurture of new, young writers, by way of lecture-/reading-tour subsidies, publishing and moral support, and a more inclusive membership policy. And, finally, Livesay has put exceptional effort into her writer-in-residenceships from New Brunswick to British Columbia.[30] When it would be so easy to regard such a position as a year off, a free time to pursue one's own work entirely and be largely invisible, Livesay has consistently done quite the reverse. She has set up and observed generous office hours; made herself extremely accessible outside of that formal schedule; spoken to any groups who showed interest; responded in detail to any submitted student writing; given frequent poetry readings; immersed herself in campus literary, cultural, and political issues; supportively offered her own work to relatively obscure local periodicals; and issued comprehensive and thoughtful reports (whether required or not) at the end of her residenceships. During her stay at the University of Alberta, for example, Livesay's anxiety about the absence of Canadian authors in university and secondary school English courses moved her to submit a brief to the Moir Committee, urging that a conference take place to begin to address that problem. And at the University of Manitoba she saw the need for a western literary outlet, particularly for the encouragement of young poets: *CV/II* was the result. Always she has viewed an academic appointment as involving the explicit responsibility—in her affirmative wording, "opportunity"— for the writer "to share his or her experience with younger people,"[31] to embody for and introduce to a new generation a living literary tradition. In that ambition the functions of writer, teacher, nationalist, humanist, and critic merge.

Poet as Journalist

Northrop Frye was not the first but is certainly the most famous observer of the fact that Canadians have a deep fondness for narrative. Many of Canada's finest poets have occupied themselves as energetically with narrative as with lyrics, and frequently with a fascinating combination of the two. The Canadian impulse toward narrative frequently has a historical bent, and major poets from Lampman and D. C. Scott through Crawford and Pratt to Livesay, Birney, Purdy, Atwood, Marlatt, and Kroetsch have set themselves to document imaginatively the Canadian past and present. Livesay's inquiry into "The Documentary Poem: A Canadian Genre" identifies as distinctive to Canada the long poetic narrative "which is valid as lyrical expression but whose impact is topical-historical, theoretical and moral." The corpus of Livesay's poetry, as examined in chapters 3 and 4, amply demonstrates her unceasing interest in "topical data" and her determination to comment upon it. Less familiar is her role as a journalist, as articulate chronicler of current events, as pragmatic sister to her own poetic self. Like her experience as teacher, social worker, critic, anthologist, editor, and activist, Livesay's journalistic career is not a dilution of or aberration from her primary path of poetry; rather the functions are interlocking and mutually supportive, the one a "popular," productive parallel of the other.

The bloodlines for Livesay in journalism were impeccable. Her paternal grandfather, John Gillett Livesay, had been the *Times* correspondent on the Isle of Wight, so that her English-born father, JFBL, was (in his own words) "brought up in it [the world of journalism]."[32] Livesay's parents, both journalists, met on the editorial staff of the Winnipeg *Telegram* in 1904. JFBL established himself firmly in Canadian journalism through his skills in what the family called "the newspaper game" and his conspicuous ability as an administrator. Before meeting his future wife, JFBL, thanks to his understanding of British soccer, had been sports editor for the Regina *Leader Post;* on the *Telegram* he rapidly became telegraph editor and maintained an interesting sideline as reporter of British horseracing. During World War I he served as battlefield correspondent in France, and the image he cast as the absentee adventurer at the far-off center of what was happening would resurface decades later in his daughter's *Beginnings: A Winnipeg Childhood*. After the war, JFBL settled down in Toronto as the general manager and prime mover of the newly created Canadian Press, a news agency cooperative that quickly became the core of the newspaper trade in Canada. His documentary account of the war, entitled *Canada's Hundred Days,* would be praised by such distinguished reviewers as Charles Bruce for its excellent reportage and fine prose.

Compounding the journalistic influence was Livesay's mother, who had been contributing literary pieces to *Massey's Magazine* and, around the turn of the century, took a post as social reporter on Parliament Hill for the Ottawa *Journal*. During an assignment as English teacher to Boer children in South Africa, FRL sent home articles, about her pupils and postwar conditions, to the *Journal* and the Winnipeg *Telegram*. Upon her return to Canada, she realized that what she most wanted to do was write and that she had a talent for reportage. This led not only to her employment on the *Telegram* and marriage with JFBL but also to an active life for many years in Manitoba journalism; she wrote several columns in the Winnipeg *Free Press,* became a member of the Canadian Women's Press Club, and met stimulating writers like Nellie McClung. After she moved to Ontario, FRL kept up her journalistic work as a freelancer.

Livesay was introduced early to the print world, her infant lispings and precocious toddler remarks appearing often in FRL's column under the heading "Dorothy's Sayings." Both parents strongly encouraged her to publish as soon and as often as possible; even in her teens they heartily promoted all phases of her writing through their personal and professional connections. They were in touch with the major literary/ cultural movements of Canada, and young Dorothy's autograph book featured such names as Sir Charles G. D. Roberts, E. J. Pratt, and Mazo de la Roche. From such a background, Livesay acquired a sense of the important link between journalism and the development of a country. Since her family was—far more than most—involved with Canadian events from 1905 to 1925, Livesay has long been tempted, despite fairly consistent lack of publisher interest, to write a book focusing on her parents' role as pioneer journalists in Canada's cultural-historical evolution.

At the same time as her youthful dynamism in poetry, Livesay began to make a mark of her own in journalism. In a Danish interview,[33] Livesay has mentioned having worked one summer at university as a cub reporter for the Winnipeg *Tribune,* and *Saturday Night* accepted a piece from her on Cape Breton in 1927. In 1929–30 she took advantage of her university year abroad to send back tourist articles on architecture ("Modern and Medieval Seen in Arromanches-Les-Bains" for the *Star Weekly*) and fashion ("French Women Consider Convenience Not Fashion" for the Toronto *Daily Star*).[34] Both articles demonstrate sharp observation, concrete social information, lyrical description, and pains taken to draw connections with the Canadian/North American experience. The assured, competent tone strongly suggests the work of a journalist much older than twenty; thus she was by no means over her head at the 1930 Imperial Press Conference in London, which she attended with her father.

In the 1930s, Livesay did not produce many articles, although she has mentioned her father's encouragement "to use my languages and get into the diplomatic service or into journalism." She felt, given the Great Depression, that social work offered a more solid future and a better chance "to see how the other half lives."[35] Nevertheless, in her connection with the leftist periodical *New Frontier,* Livesay did travel to the West Coast, thence as a reporter for *New Frontier* and the *Nation* to coal-mining towns in Alberta and company towns in the interior of British Columbia. As she recounts in *Right Hand Left Hand,* she had scarcely completed interviews and a handful of exposés—on Corbin, on Blairmore, on agricultural and mining monopolies, on union struggles and government repression—than she was ejected from the Bridge River Hotel for radicalism and (circumstantially) from journalism as well for more than a decade. Livesay's trenchant comment on society was therefore expressed through the medium of poetry until the end of World War II.

Now, it would be a distortion of the facts not to concede that for all the Livesays a hierarchy of kinds of writing did exist. Journalism was viewed by them as an activity of less moment, of less substance and art, of a less enduring nature than what they and most of us would distinguish as "creative writing." Dorothy's father more than once lamented his thwarted novelist hopes, blaming the fact that he had "got too deeply into journalism to re-emerge."[36] Yet he concluded with some modest satisfaction, "now I know I will die in the harness, a not unworthy employ." JFBL was inclined to minimize his wife's journalistic success in the same way that his son-in-law, Duncan Macnair, would years later dismiss Dorothy's moneymaking prose as trifles. Ultimately, she shared that perspective from the larger, creative context, but Livesay has always had a clear notion of practical intent and a burning desire to reach her audience. Lyricism might have to be sacrificed to journalism, but the 1930s had developed her pragmatic priorities, and as her poetry moved toward the rhythms of common speech, the distance between poetry and journalism began for her to decrease. And, as she wrote to her husband from a journalistic assignment in Paris with such plain mission: "Your remarks, I gather, suggest that in spite of your criticisms you are satisfied w[ith] what I am doing [writing for the Toronto *Daily Star*]. . . . I seem to be reaching the common man, which is all I am concerned about. Letters to the *Star* indicate that I am waking people up. Which is what I came for."[37]

There is another consideration: Livesay has mentioned in letters how journalism seemed to her an avenue to freedom from a domestic trap. She was impressed by a reading of Storm Jameson's *Three Kingdoms*, which argued the virtual impossibility of maintaining at one time more than two of these three: a job, a husband, and children. As well, Livesay had written in her diary in the 1920s: "One cannot have both flesh children and book children. It will have to be one or the other."[38] But there she was in the 1940s with both book children and flesh children. A way of lessening the pressure, of resolving the conflict, seemed to be journalism. At the basest level it offered money—and the Macnairs were as plagued by financial troubles as had been Dorothy's parents and her grandparents. The money permitted a housekeeper and help with child care, double freedom for the woman already longing for the mountain snows of the Three Emilys. Journalism also afforded a way of getting out to what was happening in the world—and Livesay has always wanted to see for herself, to have that direct contact that then emerges in so many different forms in her poetry, fiction, drama, and articles. Finally, journalism helped her to reach the common man in a way poetry unfortunately was unlikely to do. With strong thematic concerns a major element in her writing, Livesay could not dismiss that advantage.

It is clear, to return to the documentation of a documentor, that in comparison with the trickle of newspaper articles produced by Livesay in the 1930s and 1950s through 1980s, the immediate post–World War II years were her heyday as a journalist. Shortly after the war, she proposed to the Toronto *Daily Star* a series of articles on postwar Britain and the idea was accepted. The resulting articles, although more politicized, were to be mildly reminiscent of her own mother's dispatches from post–Boer War South Africa.

Livesay flew to London in early September 1946, even her journey spinning off an article on air travel. In less than three months' time she filed thirty-nine timely and authoritative reports on an impressive variety of topics, such as food shortages, housing, leisure activities, the persisting class system, industry, women in the Labor Party, the reconstruction of Coventry, Winston Churchill, Wales, Birmingham's day nurseries, and British morale. Around the beginning of November, the *Star* wired permission for her to travel on to France and Germany to compare conditions there. In France she had an opportunity to report on a UNESCO conference in which Canada was participating; in Germany she was allowed to visit the Ruhr, Cologne, Hamburg, Berlin, the French and British zones.

Certain characteristics recur throughout this series. The articles generally demonstrate research, imagination, and balanced treatment of subjects. Facts and figures are always skillfully presented in human terms and are, where appropriate, corroborated by quotations from "average" civilians. British conditions are translated into Canadian equivalents, and, whenever possible, the Canadian connection is raised, whether as a reference to Canadian-made goods, a comparison with a Canadian city, or a compliment to Canadian aid and services to the United Kingdom. Livesay's evident social vision is interwoven with her attention to small, enlivening details. And there is an intriguing pattern to the sequence of article topics: tending first to the practical/ the flesh, then to the spirit; first to housing and food, then to recreational activities; first to meat and then to morale in England, France, and Germany.

The momentum of this journalistic surge continued after Livesay's return to Canada in December 1946. The *Star* wanted her at once to cover farmers' conferences in Regina and Edmonton. Articles on a new set of Canadian topics began flowing into the pages of the *Star,* the *Star Weekly,* and *Saturday Night*: immigrants; minorities (especially the Indians and Japanese Canadians); regional interests (particularly western and northern); women's themes; problems of the disabled, the elderly, the alcoholic; labor and political issues. Livesay's prolific outpouring went on throughout 1947 and into 1948.

It is as interesting to note the rejections as the acceptances in these busy months. The *Star* found Livesay's suggestion of an article on arms to China, for example, "a little too controversial," and it twice rejected proposals on women's status in Canada as "too negative and generalized."[39] In fairness it should be mentioned—and this is as well a tribute to Livesay's versatility—that the *Star* also turned down uncontroversial and specific pieces about B.C. salmon fishing, arthritis, and the Grouse Mountain Ski Village.

While Livesay's European sojourn had only mild poetic impact ("London Revisited: 1946," "Autumn in Wales," "Matins"), the return to Canada and Canadian issues was mirrored sharply in her poetry: much of *Poems for People,* the subsequent *Call My People Home,* and additional periodical poems. It takes no critical supersleuth to notice the concurrence of a poem like "Indian Graveyard" with an article like "A Better Break for the Indian." In fact Livesay, in a letter to B. K. Sandwell, confided a deliberate socio-political strategy for the timing of *Call My People Home* complementary to such of her articles as "Canada's Japanese Problem," "B.C.'s Imaginary Headache—the Japanese," "More Population—Less Penury: Japanese Pioneers Prove It," "Greenwood," and "Will B.C. Let Bygones Be Bygones for the Japanese Canadian?" *Call My People Home* was written in the fall of 1948 and winter of 1949 "with a view to helping the Japanese case when the Federal ban [legislation against Japanese Canadians] is lifted March 31."[40]

Apart from its literary merit, *Call My People Home* is an illustration of how genres and media can intersect with a specific historical, topical intent. Its subtitle, "A Documentary Poem for Radio," indicates Livesay's increasing interest in broadcasting. As early as 1936 Livesay had given a talk on CBC about the social irrelevance of much modern poetry;[41] by 1946 she had collaborated with Mary Alexander on a Canadian historical program called "Flags for Canada" and had successfully proposed to the CBC six broadcasts on postwar Europe. Although a Louis Riel docudrama (also 1946) was not accepted—the penalty of being twenty years ahead of her time—a 1950 documentary on the Canadian Indian did find favor. Thereafter, as her correspondence with the CBC shows, Livesay was an active contributor and counsellor on specific proposals and on programming generally.

Livesay's movement from print journalism in the 1940s into broadcast journalism in the 1950s was reinforced by her growing faith in the power of the voice, the immediacy of first person "testimony," whether in poetry or prose. This did not mean, as it might first appear, a retreat from rhythm and lyricism, for those elements were inherent in speech and even in individual words: "I am always hearing this other *beat* behind the ordinary spoken language and I'm always hearing the melody," Livesay explained. With the gradual simplification of her style towards normal speech rhythms and that related belief in the musicality of human utterance, as well as her new interest in the found poem, the line between Livesay's poetry and her journalism became less precise. Her fondness for "topical data" informed her approach to both.

Livesay's main journalistic endeavors in the 1960s involved her work in Africa, again lightly paralleling her mother's dispatches from South Africa over half a century before. To the CBC, to newspapers and periodicals, she offered pieces on Northern Rhodesia, race relations, Kenneth Kaunda, Zambian independence, third-world conditions, and so forth. Although she was discouraged by Canadian apathy toward other societies, she was heartened by the rise of interest in the Canadian "locus" and Canadian history. In an intelligent foreword to *The Documentaries* in 1968 she explained her journalistic sense of the sanctity of those "social histories":

Generally it has seemed better to leave the work untouched, as a record of the times; for, though some of the lines and patterns are not all that might be desired, I believe that the veracity of the material and mood is more important than the occasional sentimentality of expression or the lack of polish in style. I am "ornery," and I like authenticity in reportage.

A new type of social journalism, as innovative in its way as that of a Michael Herr or Tom Wolfe, was brought into being in 1977 with Livesay's remarkable retrospective of a decade, *Right Hand Left Hand*. A collage of photos, letters, poems, stories, articles, plays, documents, and paintings is held together by unapologetic commentary, the cohesive power of Livesay's assertive personality, and the overriding force of the Dirty Thirties themselves. She is not often arrogant in her perspective, not inclined to exercise smugly the prerogative of age and insist that only she as a veteran can pronounce what really happened. Indeed a distrust of memory probably underlies to some degree her insistence on photo and document, on unedited letters, on letting much of the material speak for itself in the best documentary tradition. It is not that art doesn't ultimately enter into it—how can it fail to with an artist at the controls?—but that objective impulse bespeaks an aspect of Livesay that has received less notice than the passionate, intimate, subjective self.

Offering a format since widely imitated, *Right Hand Left Hand* is part of Livesay's abiding interest in the historical—the once topical if you like—the eternally topical if you subscribe to a notion of history's repetitiveness, as Livesay has said she does. As an articulate writer and thinker looking back on nearly sixty years of vital comment, Livesay feels entitled to proclaim patterns and to write, almost simultaneously, of conditions in Depression Canada and modern Bulgaria—to write passionately in poetry and analytically in prose, and sometimes the reverse. The closeness of the two modes is illustrated in the way Livesay's journalistic efforts can be so easily included in the remark she once made about being a poet: "I believe completely . . . in the thing being given to you, and you are the vessel and you must record it."

Chapter Seven
A Woman's I:
Right Hand Left Hand

If *Right Hand Left Hand* was innovative as social history, it was also a groundbreaker in the realm of female autobiography. As historians of that genre are quick to remind us, autobiography has not been around as a developed and widely practised form for more than a few centuries. The Renaissance increase in historical sense and self-consciousness is credited with fostering the rise of autobiography, a trend compounded in the late seventeenth century by the new popularity among Protestants of religious autobiography. The literary historians who study this are themselves very much a recent, twentieth-century development. And those few who focus specifically on female autobiography are almost entirely the phenomena of this last decade. Small wonder—small field. Until very recently, women writers have shown a remarkable aversion to overt autobiography. One constantly sees autobiography veiled by fiction and by poetry, but rarely finds a woman writing in proud and unobscured prose of the circumstances and texture of her life and times. Women's literature (to flog the irresistible punning metaphor of eye and I) has traditionally covered with demurely lowered lids and fringing lashes the personal woman's "I."

In Canada this generalization on the paucity of women's autobiography is easily documented. When Cynthia Pomerleau, in her article on women's autobiography in England, lamented that English women of the seventeenth century, although more than half of the population, produced only ten percent of the autobiographies written in that century,[1] she might as well have been speaking of Canada from the precolonial period through the mid-twentieth century. William Matthews's compilation of Canadian diaries and autobiographies to 1950 draws upon unpublished as well as published manuscripts; it even lists magazine excerpts of autobiographical material and such obscure items as an eleven-page, unpublished diary of a fourteen-year-old in the mid-nineteenth century.[2] This exhaustive approach to the literature of two centuries yields only 1276 autobiographical pieces, however, and of that modest return exactly ten percent—only 128—were by women. To beat the eye symbolism to death, in Canada one is unfortunately reminded, regarding autobiography, of Atwood's grisly metaphor, wherein the open female eye gets impaled on a fishhook.[3]

Such was the case until the end of World War II, but the impression has arisen that the blossoming of women's consciousness in and since the 1960s has promoted overt female autobiography. Examination of Canadian literature in the last twenty years, however, shows a continued preference for autobiography-via-fiction in Laurence, Munro, Atwood, Thomas, Gallant, Engel, and many others. Indeed, Laurence has steadfastly denied specific autobiographical dimensions in any but *A Bird in the House,* and Atwood has repeatedly grumbled that North Americans (unlike Europeans, she says) have a fallacious and foolish obsession with finding the autobiographical in her work, an element she dismisses outright. One is hard-pressed, then, to cite (sight!) many overtly open eyes (I's) in contemporary Canadian women's literature. In the (twi)light of dashed expectations about the liberation of female autobiography, a new appreciation develops for Livesay's 1977 *Right Hand Left Hand, A True Life of the Thirties: Paris, Toronto, Montreal, The West and Vancouver. Love, Politics, the Depression and Feminism.* When she brought it out at the age of sixty-eight, Livesay had already published considerable verse and some short fiction in the mode of veiled autobiography. Adolescent anxieties, first loves, sexual reawakening, politicization, marriage, childbirth, parenting, marital conflict, travel, widowhood, sexual rediscovery, teaching, aging, grandparenting—all figured in her poetry and prose. Identifiable people and events were named and explored—but, like Emily Dickinson whom she has quoted on the matter, Livesay preferred to "tell it slant." With *Right Hand Left Hand* that obliqueness was put aside, and so were a lot of the conventions of both male and female autobiography.

Right Hand Left Hand is divided into nine unnumbered segments of varying length, roughly chronological, actually beginning in 1928 with Livesay's late girlhood in Toronto. Each heading is a location and a date, such as "Montreal 1933–1934" or "Spain 1936–1939," except for the seventh section, named for the leftist periodical "New Frontier 1936–1937." Within each part, introduced by an epigram of Livesay's own wording drawn from text within that chapter, there are combinations of a baker's dozen of types of material.

First, marked off by Livesay's large, scrawled initials—boldly devoid of daintiness, elegance, or "feminine" reticence—are passages of retrospection, in which Livesy explains contexts, serves as archivist, provides transitions. Then there are artifacts: the handcrafted menu from a summer of 1931 coffee shop enterprise; Livesay's union membership card; a full program, including back-cover advertisements, of the Workers' Theatre play *Eight Men Speak;* the covers of several issues of *New Frontier;* comic doodlings entitled "D. L. in Love," showing a stick figure Dorothy in postures ranging from "resolution" and "fortitude" through "weakness" and "despair" to "collapse" and "oblivion." Among other memorabilia are the even more intimate photocopied pages of young Dorothy's diary, full of confession . . . and pretension . . . and acute longings. A fourth sort of autobiographical document is letters, both reproduced in their original handwriting and reset in modern type. Some are short notes among close friends and family; others are lengthy self-analytic letters about life, art, and politics; there is considerable business correspondence related to *New Frontier,* including an hilariously acid exchange between *New Frontier* editor Lon Lawson and Livesay's husband, Duncan Macnair. Not all of the letters are from Livesay herself; in telling her story she often lets the letters of others speak for (and about) her.

Woven among these retrospective passages, artifacts, diary excerpts, and letters are five varieties of Livesay's own creative writing. Naturally, there is poetry. Twenty-two poems provide a lyrical counterpoint to the prosaic material; all mirror, directly or indirectly, the humanist and political preoccupations of their author. As well, there is short fiction. Seven short stories demonstrate Livesay's sharp concern for the working class and her first-hand experience as a social worker in Canada and the United States. Further, there is drama. Livesay includes two representations of an entire other sphere of her accomplishment: a radio play that has also seen stage production, and an agitprop mass chant. A fourth extension of her public voice is found in examples of a very vibrant brand of journalism that she practised some thirty years in advance of the so-called "new journalism" of the 1960s: investigative, personal, humane, tough; articles like "Blairmore," "Indians at Caughnawaugha," and "Corbin: A Company Town Fights For Its Life" offer a superior blend of fact, argument, and the human factor, in clean, incisive prose liberally laced with interview responses and vivid descriptions of shocking conditions among Canadians stricken at every level by the Depression. On the more academic side, and to acknowledge the substantial contribution Livesay has made to Canadian literary criticism, *Right Hand Left Hand* reprints five of her articles, all to a greater or lesser degree reflective of her intense politicization in the thirties: from a memoir of Raymond Knister to a review of Morley Callaghan's *They Shall Inherit the Earth*. One piece, a denunciation of the decadence of modern bourgeois poetry, was broadcast on CBC radio in 1936; another, a study of manifestations of the Spanish Civil War in Canadian poetry, is actually retrospective scholarship of the 1970s, some forty years later, an interesting discarding of manmade time restrictions when the material is so obviously germane. And scholarship makes Livesay herself the subject in an interview, with one of Livesay's oldest friends replying frankly to questions about Livesay's family, personality, and career.

In a stratagem that seems both pertinent and generous, *Right Hand Left Hand* also includes milestone articles by others: Sean Griffin's and Steve Brodie's compelling accounts of Vancouver's Bloody Sunday, Ted Allan's interview with Ernest Hemingway, Leo Kennedy's "Direction for Canadian Poets," for example. They are invaluable to a biography of the decade of the thirties and subtly effective documents in Livesay's autobiographical intention of giving the reader a feel for her life and times. In the same vein, Livesay offers the reader a selection of newspaper clippings. Some are accounts of her various distinctions and public addresses in the 1930s while others are tributes to the accomplishments of respected friends, such as the glowing review of Jim Watts's Vancouver direction of *Waiting for Lefty,* or simply pertinent historical analysis such as the excerpts from Sandra Souchotte's excellent feature on workers' theater in Canada. It is apparent that for a person strongly integrated with her times, a document need not be produced by her mind alone to earn a place in her autobiography; it was sufficient that it reflected her world and her thought.

The use of photographs in *Right Hand Left Hand* hardly seems an innovative stroke on the surface of things, but a closer look reveals a very creative combination of the personal and the public. The photos are not all of one kind: there are formal newspaper portraits of the young, braid-crowned poetess; pictures of the parental home at Clarkson, Ontario; snaps of close friends and family, including an unexpected but tasteful picture of Dorothy and two chums daringly topless; informal photos of workers' theater groups; and the striking final image of a female friend marching confidently off to war. Such is perhaps to be expected of personal autobiography, particularly (stereotypically) a woman's. But the notion that these images mattered—and of course that Livesay's personal story mattered—was the first courageous assumption. Intermingled, then, with these private photographs are more "official" images of the times—a wide selection from the Public Archives, especially of Canadians on relief, in distress, scrabbling for a living in the Depression. Livesay's unselfconscious adoption of these establishment pictures, albeit ones not much flaunted by the Canadian government then or now, is an extremely rare tactic in female autobiography, far more the province not even of male autobiography but of male documentation of (capital H) History. The brilliance is less in the pictures themselves, for all their intrinsic interest, than in the perceptive decision to include them. Ditto the addition of still photographs from *Los Canadienses,* the National Film Board production on the participation of Canada's volunteer battalions in the Spanish Civil War.

The thirteenth and final vehicle for revelation of self and times is also visual. It is art: reproductions of oil paintings, of lithographs, of charcoal sketches, of what have the appearance of woodcuts, of acrylics, of pen and ink—on subjects ranging from rummage sales to the despair of the jobless. It is a graceful and fitting recognition by a verbal artist of her ties with and indebtedness to artists in other media.

From the perspective of autobiography it is necessary to consider the characteristics and achievement of *Right Hand Left Hand* less in isolation than in comparison with both traditional/male autobiography and the now differentiated concerns of female autobiography.

Estelle Jelinek, in an essay called "Female Autobiography and the Male Tradition," has made a persuasive case for the idea that, contrary to our impression of autobiography as the "genre of disclosure," it has actually traditionally hedged its bets, kept (in Hawthorne's phrase) "the inmost Me behind its veil." "The admission," of Jelinek, "of intense feelings of hate, love and fear, the disclosure of explicit sexual encounters, or the detailing of painful psychological experiences are matters on which autobiographers [male *and* female] are generally silent."[4] Not so Livesay, who is atypical not only in her preparedness to talk about extremely private topics but also in her willingness to look silly, vain, pigheaded, manipulative, misguided, or insensitive. She does not excuse: she does not excise. The candor is astonishing.

Right Hand Left Hand: among other significances, the title declares itself of two worlds: the right hand, female, tied to the kitchen sink; the left side, involved in male activism/socialist politics. But the polarity of the physiology is not that simple, for that male-associated left hand takes its orders from the right side of the brain, which governs such female terrain as body language, nonverbal communications, color perception, the unconscious, patterns of urges and sudden insights, holistic and intuitive thought. And the right hand is directed by the left brain, controlling muscular activities, speech and logic, linear thought.[5] How then does the left brain, the male autobiographical tradition, show itself in *Right Hand Left Hand?* First, in Livesay's clearly being both an active participant in the movements of her time and a bold demonstrator of her links. In declaring the connection of her self and her private worlds to the larger worlds of Canadian industry and the Spanish Civil War and the Soviet-German Pact. In assuming, moreover, that her personal story is important—no more important, no less important—both of itself and in the context of the larger story of the tumultuous 1930s. It is, among other things, a useful reminder of the relation between large events and little people: not dominance but interdependence.

How else is *Right Hand Left Hand* atypical of female autobiography? It is different in its confident vision of women like Jean ("Jim") Watts marching off and sharing fully in the great struggle. Nor does Livesay place her work humbly in the background, camouflaged or minimized. Atypical of female biographers generally,[6] she discusses her various careers and specific aspects of her work; when marriage interferes with her job, she does not sigh stoically but laments plainly. And she does not emphasize people and domestic detail at the expense of social developments or philosophical and aesthetic inquiry. She is atypical as well in her commitment not exclusively to the power of the imagination (almost the only power accessible to women for centuries) but also (some think antithetically) to the power of society (which has traditionally ignored women) and the power of action (traditionally, too, the male domain).

Livesay's personal style in *Right Hand Left Hand* is not in the feminine tradition of humility and self-effacement. A strong-jawed, strong-minded persona comes through at once: a partial but utterly accurate perception, as anyone who knows Livesay can testify. Neither is the literary style stereotypically "feminine"—by which is conventionally meant such adjectives as "genteel," "sentimental," "refined," "sedate," "discreet," or "tender" (with occasional interlinear implications of "silly," "incompetent," "shallow," "vacuous," or "inconsequential").[7] The ideas in *Right Hand Left Hand* are often forceful, didactic, and challenging. And the language in which those ideas are expressed is hard, bright, impassioned, sometimes intemperate, often the antithesis of "ladylike." Technically, Livesay favors the longer sentence length and exclamation point that Mary Hiatt in *The Way Women Write* has demonstrated statistically to be male prose characteristics.[8]

Right Hand Left Hand: on the other hand, Livesay shows herself in the female autobiographical mainstream in dozens of other ways. There is her frank discussion of confusion and uncertainty, eschewing the male autobiographical "success story" conclusion in her preference for the female tentative hopefulness. Livesay's female hand writes plainly of the sense of conflicting obligations: leftist dreams and practical duties. Livesay demonstrates a very female consciousness of the price to be paid for any triumphs and a female disinclination to build a myth of the self or proclaim great and permanent achievement. She ends the book and the struggle in 1939, we must remember, with these words: "We were all in high hopes again that this time it truly would be a war that would change the world. Instead, we received Hiroshima."

Further, Livesay is typical of women autobiographers in revealing intense personal relationships, although it is interesting that many reviewers did not notice this or thought it nullified(!) by the expression of equal devotion to writing and to social concerns. That misjudgment may have derived from the fact that Livesay is apparently typical of women autobiographers as well in often understating her emotional commitments while intermittently being markedly passionate about her writing. It is instructive, of course, to compare the critics' treatment, so positive and approving, of male writers who are devoted to *their* work.

Livesay is typical, again, in speaking, in that chameleon way women learn early, in multiple voices—representing multiple, often contradictory roles. She is atypical and clever, however, in celebrating those voices with the mechanical variation of holographs and sundry typesets (Garamond Italic, Times Roman, Andover Roman).

Right Hand Left Hand embodies as well the typically female collective sense of *our* struggle—our female but also our human/social struggle—rather than the individualistic sensibility that more often operates in male autobiography. Livesay speaks frankly and consciously of her female spiritual forerunners and of the necessity to her development of their example.

In a variety of other details, Livesay conforms to the female autobiographical model, as detailed by Jelinek. There is her identification with the stronger parent, in her case her father; there is also that more-female-than-male inclination to be introspective and to blame the self. There is an (according to Hiatt) characteristically female preference for parenthetical asides and for use of the dash for added comment rather than emphasis or conclusion. Typical too of her sex (Hiatt again), Livesay uses more than men the verbs of intuition (seem, sense, feel, believe, love, fear, guess, think, imagine) but uses as often as men the verbs of reason (prove, solve, decide).

These matters are, however, minor considerations next to the pronounced typicality of a most important aspect: the structure of *Right Hand Left Hand*. As is generally the case with female autobiography, the book does not pursue the male autobiographical goal of an "interpreted past," emphasizing objectivity, distance, and conclusions. Rather it is a very female goal, involving the renunciation of a simple center and any progressive, continuous design. Given the female autobiographical aim of knowing/revealing the woman *as she is,* and the assumption that external imposition of a definition is to be avoided because she is already fine just *as she is,* a logical structure (tightly chronological, progressive, linear, rational, synthetic) is not a female priority. Instead the emphasis is on the cyclic, diurnal, the cumulative; it is a matter of *process.* "Dailiness matters to most women," Suzanne Juhasz has written, "and dailiness is by definition never a conclusion, always a process."[9] And to quote, for balance, a man of the same persuasion, psychologist David MacClelland has argued that "Women are concerned with the context" while "men are forever trying to ignore it for the sake of something they can abstract from it."[10] MacClelland writes of a male belief in getting to "the point," as compared with a female distrust of "the point" and belief instead in circumstantial, complex, and contextual answers to "simple" questions such as "What happened?" Immersion and texture instead of breadth and analysis are regarded as more urgent considerations in female autobiography.

Little wonder, then, that *Right Hand Left Hand* has a structure that may seem random to some but is willing to sacrifice "less logical" to "more truthful." Livesay's subtitle is no accident: "A True Life," neither conventional autobiography nor memoir. *True life:* both words are significant. It is a *life* in its multiplicity, Livesay and her world reflected in so many mirrors as to be truly rounded and rounded truly; *true* in the sense that the details exist in their own right, without having to function as cogs in a highly oiled wheel. What some critics have dismissed as a cluttered grab bag of items actually conforms to the conviction of one West-Coast commentator that "As ordinarily experienced, life doesn't have the feel of a well-ordered novel."[11] Well-ordered, perhaps the book is not; but much method lies in this female lunacy, for the blend of the personal, the social, the aesthetic, and the historical is a powerful one, and *Right Hand Left Hand,* in accord with a higher autobiographical vision than just recounting or interpreting the past, captures a life as it was being lived.

Chapter Eight
Conclusion: Measure of a Writer

When Dorothy Livesay brought out her first fine book of verse in 1928, modern Canadian poetry was decidedly in its infancy. Three of the four "Confederation Poets" who had fathered a national verse in the 1890s were still literarily active and honored.[1] The First World War, the new influence of poet E. J. Pratt, and the rise of the innovative young Montreal poets—A. J. M. Smith, F. R. Scott, A. M. Klein, and Leo Kennedy—had not yet prodded the bulk of Canadian writers out of a certain nineteenth-century and Georgian twilight, either thematically or stylistically. Into this poetic time warp stepped a thoroughly modern young woman who knew Roberts and Carman personally and accepted their senior encouragement but not their literary models. Abhorring romantic excesses of sentiment, image, or idea, loving the imagist clarity and precision of such American women poets as H. D. and Elinor Wylie, Livesay was from the start in the vanguard of poetic modernism in Canada. Since that auspicious beginning, Dorothy Livesay has—by action or reaction—been a vital part of the development of the national literature through more than half of this twentieth century.

How is one to take full measure of sixty years of literary accomplishment—dozens of books and hundreds of articles, songs sung and lives touched? Livesay herself leans to the historical approach, telling audiences at home and abroad the tale that is both her life and Canada's.

The poetry of *Green Pitcher* and *Signpost* pointed the way with a new sort of nature poetry, often expressed in the as-yet unaccepted *vers libre* and in stark, spare imagery that celebrated the power of nature in itself rather than simply as metaphor for human conditions. Also departures were the particular directness and spontaneity of *Signpost* and other early poetry in speaking of intimate relationships—their fears, frustrations, and failures. In the 1930s Dorothy Livesay was among the first to respond to hard times and turn her talent to social purpose. Livesay's acute consciousness of a poet's social responsibility, stimulated by Canada's sufferings in the Great Depression, did not abate in the 1940s, even after the trauma of World War II had ended and many poets were retreating into introspection and psychological, metaphysical, or mythical allusion. With twenty years' prescience Livesay concerned herself unfashionably, in poetry and in prose, with native peoples, minority groups, multiculturalism, and women's experience, and she continued, equally unmodishly, to argue the importance of direct and accessible communication in poetry.

After a hiatus in Europe and Africa, Livesay again burst on the Canadian literary scene with *The Unquiet Bed,* unquestionably some of the most electrically open sexual poetry Canada had ever read and certainly the most candid any female Canadian had ever published. It was written with that attention to sound and speech rhythms that Livesay had always practiced but that had only recently come into vogue. Her interest in Africa foreshadowed the current interest of Canadian poets in other countries and other cultures; her sensitivity to aspects of old age in *The Unquiet Bed* and the subsequent *Plainsongs, Ice Age, The Phases of Love,* and *Feeling the Worlds* anticipates the changing priorities of an aging (but still ageist) North American population. Further, Livesay's "documentary" poems on the Canadian past, one dating from as early as 1936, joined her other shorter pieces on Canadian culture on the cutting edge of her nation's self-absorption in the late 1960s through the 1970s, as witnessed in part by the surge of quasi-historical narrative poetry in Canada in recent years. As well, Livesay's remarkable multigenre volume on the 1930s met the needs of both a rediscovery of that passionate decade and a growing emphasis on women's studies, providing a new model for female autobiography. Today, at seventy-seven years of age, she shows no signs of slackening in her pace, dulling of her perceptions, or stiffening of her receptivity to the challenges of life and art.

With so dazzling a track record, the question inevitably arises: why has Livesay been comparatively neglected by literary critics in her homeland? Why have less accomplished and significant authors been studied in monographs and full-length books, sometimes repeatedly, while Livesay has gone without any equivalent of such critical attention until now, until this present study? One of myriad illustrations of the peculiar lack of extended, serious scrutiny of Livesay's work is Tom Marshall's *Harsh and Lovely Land: The Major Canadian Poets and the Making of a Canadian Tradition.*[2] In that survey, apart from glancing reference, only pages 51 through 53 are devoted to Livesay, and almost an entire page of the three is spent not in review or analysis but in quotation from two of her poems. As Stephen Scobie remarks, "Much as I admire the best work of Klein, Birney and Layton, I do not see why they are worthy of a chapter apiece, while Dorothy Livesay, whom I would hold to be a finer poet than any of them, must make do with three pages."[3] Scobie might be argued to overstate, and literary pecking orders are rarely useful anyway, but Livesay is indisputably the equal of these three peers, and Scobie is painfully accurate in exposing the preferential treatment that continues to be accorded others even into the 1980s. Why, then, has this particular prophet been, relatively, so studiously ignored by the critical elite?[4]

There seem to be several pieces to this puzzle, and even assembled they do not quite form a complete, intelligible picture. One factor is certainly timing: the ill luck, first, of being in the wrong place at the right time, the happenstance of relocating in 1936 from Ontario to British Columbia and thus operating thereafter outside the orbit of the Eastern cultural establishment. Equally a matter of timing have been Livesay's thinking and seeing too far (usually thirty years) ahead of her time: proposing Louis Riel topics from the late 1930s; defending native and minority perspectives in the 1940s; writing, with a handful like F. R. Scott and A. M. Klein, poems of social protest years before they became even mildly acceptable to the majority of readers; exploring motherhood and other aspects of female experience decades before they became intellectually respected themes; revealing all about late-life sexuality (a topic whose time has yet to arrive) to a generation obsessed with exclusively youthful sexuality. And literary fashion completes the triad of timing. Livesay was E. J. Pratt's poetic heir in her delight in narrative and in her commitment to verse accessible and interesting to Everyman. To the poets (and critics) of the mythopoeic, cosmopolitan, more obscurely allusive mainstream in the 1940s and 1950s, her poetry often seemed too simple and inartistically straightforward; to the traditionalists who longed for the poetic diction, elevated imagery, and reliable verse forms of yesteryear, her vernacular language, urban images, and experimental prosody offended the sense of poetry as sublime utterance.

The lack of literary allegiances has been another barrier to critical attention, especially from literary historians who tend to think in movements and trends. Livesay has refused throughout her career to identify herself with any single school or confining category. She has acknowledged the influence of American imagists like H. D. and Amy Lowell, but argued that her debt is primarily to their example of freedom, both in experimental verse forms and in a throwing off of exhausted Georgian images in favor of ones that were spare, precise, resonant with meaning. In the 1930s and 1940s her connection with the social poets of the Montreal Group, later the *Preview* Group, was strained not only by her shift to the West Coast but by her distaste for what she regarded as their "obscurantist" other face, the sophisticated poetry of overt erudition, metaphysical imagery, and cryptic introspection. The sense of isolation from Canadian poetry that she acquired during the late 1950s and early 1960s in Europe and Africa quickly evaporated upon her return to Vancouver in 1963, and at first she delighted in her colleagues' new poetic attention to colloquial idiom and oral rhythm, the sound and song so innate to her. But she soon came to view the TISH movement as a derivative and ultimately limited colonist of the American Black Mountain school of poetry. She emphatically rejected the theory of the garrison mentality, wherein the Canadian attitude to nature is one of awe and terror and a sense of siege, even though that notion had been given the weight of gospel by the identity of its creator, Northrop Frye, and its main prophet, Margaret Atwood. And she refused to enter the orbit of the Canadian Broadcasting Corporation (CBC) and surrender meekly to the authority of Robert Weaver, despite the fact that alienating such powers almost certainly reduced the amount of attention and air time given her work.[5] In the 1970s Livesay persisted with direct social protest when the hippie generation had aged into the "me" generation and become isolationist, cerebral, convoluted, and self-absorbed. And the 1980s have seen all too many critics eager to confine Livesay in the gilded cage of Ancient Sage, trying to impose on a person to whom involvement is life a serene, oracular detachment. Livesay has shrewdly resisted the pressure to enter even that comfy category, to surrender to the restrictions of even so complimentary and well-intentioned a pigeonholing as "the original earth-mother of Canadian poetry."[6]

Much of this rugged independence has to do with Livesay's lifelong passion for freedom. Less voluntarily, it is also connected with that acute sense Livesay has always had of being an "isolate," of "not belonging," of standing outside the established groups, schools, and cliques[7]—perhaps a lonely but frequently a productive position. And the nonalignment with literary schools is related as well to the individualism of women artists. Back in 1948 Henry H. Wells had refereed

Conclusion: Measure of a Writer

Livesay's grant proposal to the Guggenheim Foundation on women's poetry; in the course of his strong support of her application he had observed that in poetry "The women don't goose-step like the men. They don't fall into schools. Their personalism keeps them from this peculiar practice of the men."[8] What Wells expressed as an advantage and virtue has its darker side: the chronic isolation of women writers, the shortage of artistic camaraderie. And timing returns to compound this female isolation. As Livesay remarks in the important opening paragraph of *Right Hand Left Hand:*

The other Canadian artists of my era were those men born soon after the turn of the century: Raymond Knister, Earle Birney, Robert Finch, A. J. M. Smith, A. M. Klein (1909), Leo Kennedy and Irving Layton (1913). No companion women poets were born until the end of the First World War: P. K. Page, Miriam Waddington, Ann Wilkinson, Anne Marriott, Margaret Avison, and Phyllis Webb. So until they began to make their mark in the forties, I always had the feeling I was struggling alone to make a woman's voice heard. I admired the men—particularly those who encouraged me—Knister, Klein and (for a time) Smith, but I felt curiously detached from them in a literary and life-style sense.

This puts a finger on a more controversial charge, that Livesay has suffered some degree of neglect because she is female. Unquestionably she received considerable support—from parents, from coactivists, from prestigious older writers such as Sir Charles G. D. Roberts and E. J. Pratt, from critics like W. E. Collin and Alan Crawley, from her husband and many friends. But a sexism sleuth might begin with her bizarre exclusion from *New Provinces: Poems of Several Authors* (1936), a "landmark" collaboration of six male poets from Montreal and Toronto claiming to illustrate the new directions Canadian modernists were taking. That sleuth might pause in thought over Ralph Gustafson's 1958 *Penguin Book of Canadian Verse,* which offered five poems by Birney, six by Smith, six by Scott, and only three by the woman who had won two Governor-General's Awards for Poetry. It would be hard not to be nonplussed by Gary Geddes's overlooking of Livesay in his 1970 *15 Canadian Poets*; as a clumsy afterthought he added her to the roster in the 1978 edition, retitled crudely *15 Canadian Poets* + *5*.[9] And at a 1983 York University conference on the long poem, Livesay, one of its senior and most accomplished practitioners, was noticeably unfêted and even slighted while a tight circle of male poets and critics gave congratulatory papers upon one another's work. Even the younger women Livesay cites as the bright lights succeeding her—Page, Waddington, Wilkinson, Marriott, Avison, and Webb—might well share the opinion that gender had some part to play in their lesser visibility, the smaller critical attention paid them. One may at least claim with some assurance that, until the late 1960s and the rise of feminism, Livesay's being a woman was not an asset.

One other piece in this incomplete puzzle is the personality of the poet herself. Livesay is a person who has annoyed and offended many, some beyond recall. Her character is strong, passionate, contradictory—beautiful and ugly, generous and jealous, accommodating and manipulative, helpful and obnoxious, joyously in harmony and seething with a thousand angers, sharply ambitious and simultaneously self-deprecatory. "The woman I am / is not what you see." Delicate grandmother one moment and raging activist the next; anti-American with McDonald's burger wrappers on her table; a figure of gracious elegance in batiked silk, hours after having hitchhiked to the campus; strident evangelist and adaptable pacifist; irritated haranguer of young women to cut off their long hair and inspiring mentor of those same young women as poets: Livesay is fully each of these. Her family and friends, who know more than one facet, can all testify to these contradictions—with annoyance and with admiration, with exasperation and with love. Ultimately, however, these vexing polarities have been the crucible from which an extraordinary sensibility and powerful art have emerged. The time is overdue for the anglophone world to take notice of Dorothy Livesay.

Notes and References

Sources frequently cited will be identified by the following abbreviations:

ALTA The Dorothy Livesay Collection
 The Bruce Peel Special Collections Library
 Rutherford South
 The University of Alberta
 Edmonton, Alberta, Canada T6G 2J8

MAN The Dorothy Livesay Collection
 Department of Archives and Special Collections
 Elizabeth Dafoe Library
 The University of Manitoba
 Winnipeg, Manitoba, Canada R3T 2N2

 (This entire collection has recently been reorganized; a lengthy finding aid was published in the spring of 1986.)

QUEEN The Dorothy Livesay Collection
 The Archives
 Douglas Library
 Queen's University
 Kingston, Ontario, Canada K7L 3N6

Chapter One

1. "Poetry," *Times Literary Supplement,* 20 December 1928, 1014.
2. Charles Bruce, "Green Pitcher," unidentified newspaper review, n.p., n.d., n.pag., Box 18, folder 1, MAN.
3. Raymond Knister, "Modes Conservative and Chic," *Saturday Night,* 3 November 1928, 12.
4. W. E. Collin, "The Power of Imagery," *Canadian Forum* (February 1933):192.
5. Pratt to Livesay, 5 December 1935, Box 14, folder 7, MAN; quoted in *Right Hand Left Hand,* ed. David Arnason and Kim Todd (Erin, Ont.: Porcépic, 1977), 154.

6. W. O. Raymond, citation of the Royal Society of Canada, Livesay-Ryerson correspondence, November 1947, folder 1, ALTA.
7. "Song and Dance," *Canadian Literature* 41 (Summer 1969):40–48.
8. Hans Jewinski, "Poetry," *Quill & Quire* (January 1976):25.
9. Since the preparation of this study, Livesay has published a new "selected," *The Self-Completing Tree* (Victoria: Press Porcépic, 1986).
10. Richard Wilbur, interviewed on Canadian Broadcasting Corporation radio, circa 1983, according to Livesay in a conversation with Lee Thompson, Galiano Island, June 1983.
11. "The Enchanted Isle: A Dialogue," *Room of One's Own* 5 (1979):122.

Chapter Two

1. Preface to *Down Singing Centuries: Folk Literature of the Ukraine*, trans. Florence Randal Livesay (Winnipeg: Hyperion, 1981), 11.
2. "Song and Dance," *Canadian Literature* 41 (Summer 1969):40.
3. Diary entry, "Music and Prose," 5 December 1924, Box 31, folder 2, MAN.
4. Bruce, "Green Pitcher," Box 18, folder 1, MAN.
5. Knister, "Modes Conservative and Chic," 12.
6. Pierce to Livesay, 14 September 1928, folder 20, Livesay-Ryerson Correspondence, QUEEN.
7. "B. L.," interview with Dorothy Livesay, 29 April 1975, Box 20, folder 4(b), p. 5, MAN.
8. "Girl Wins Coverted [sic] Prize," *Evening Telegram* (Toronto), 12 January 1929, n.pag.
9. Diary entry, 20 April 1928, Box 31, folder 2, MAN; rpt. in *Right Hand Left Hand*, 23.
10. Ibid.
11. Dorothy Livesay to Florence R. Livesay, 31 December 1929, Box 30, folder 25, MAN.
12. Dorothy Livesay to F. R. Livesay, 30 March 1930, Box 30, folder 25, MAN.
13. Francis Cecil Whitehouse, "Literature," *Daily News* (Nelson, B.C.), 7 January 1933, n.pag., Box 10, folder 3, MAN.
14. Peter Grant, "*Sign-Post.* A Review on a Late Book of Poems by Dorothy Livesay," *St. Catharines Standard*, 6 December 1932, 7.
15. "A Distinct Contribution to Canadian Letters," *Free Press* (London), 3 December 1932, 6; D. W. B., "*Signpost,*" *Herald* (Lethbridge), 8 December 1932, 9; "Dorothy Livesay Writes Terse and Homely Poetry," *Daily Star* (Toronto), 10 December 1932, 4; E. J. R., "A Young Poet," *Spectator* (Hamilton), 10 December 1932, 20; J. P. C., "New Books," *Gazette* (Montreal), 10 December 1932, 10; Charles Bruce, "A Canadian Poet," *Star* (Halifax), 10 December 1932, 10, 15; "Winnipeg Girl Brings Out Second Successful Book

of Verses in East," *Free Press* (Winnipeg), 14 December 1932, 11; E. J. P[ratt?], "Promising New Book by Young Canadian Poet," *Advertiser* (London), 14 December 1932, n.pag., Box 10, folder 3, MAN; Francis Cecil Whitehouse, "Literature," *Daily News* (Nelson, B.C.), 7 January 1933, n.pag., Box 10, folder 3, MAN; W. E. Collin, "The Power of Imagery," *Canadian Forum* (February 1933):191–92; Theodore Goodridge Roberts, typed copy of a review of *Signpost*, n.p., n.d., n.pag., Box 10, folder 3, MAN; Burnett, typed copy of a review of *Signpost, Charlottetown Guardian*, n.d., n.pag., Box 10, folder 3, MAN.

    16. "A Distinct Contribution to Canadian Letters," *Free Press* (London), 3 December 1932, 6.

    17. E. J. P[ratt?], "Promising New Book."

    18. W. E. Collin, "The Power of Imagery," 192.

    19. Livesay, "Time," manuscript versions, pt. 1, 14 July 1929; pt. 2, 20 September 1929, ALTA.

Chapter Three

    1. Diary entry, 22 April 1930, Box 32, folder 15, MAN.

    2. Ibid.

    3. "Proletarianitis in Canada," in *Right Hand Left Hand*, 230.

    4. *Right Hand Left Hand*, 91–96. Livesay does not explain why she chose to use a pseudonym, Katherine Bligh, for this article.

    5. Ibid., 112, 114.

    6. "At English Bay," *Saturday Night*, 5 March 1938, 2; "Lullaby," *Province* (Vancouver), 1938, n.pag.; "We Are Alone," *Saturday Night*, 18 November 1939, 3.

    7. "Joe Derry," *Masses* 2, no. 10 (September 1933):15.

    8. *Eight Men Speak and Other Plays*, ed. Robin Endres (Toronto: Hogtown Press, 1976), xix.

    9. *Right Hand Left Hand*, 97.

    10. "Dominion Day at Regina," poetry worksheets, July 1936, ALTA.

    11. 1942: Earle Birney's *David and Other Poems*; 1943: A. J. M. Smith's *News of the Phoenix*.

    12. L. M. S., review of *Day and Night, Star* (Halifax), 20 May 1944, n.pag., Box 18, folder 2, MAN. The other seventeen reviews still accessible either in libraries or in Box 18, folder 2, MAN, are as follows: L[ouis] A. M[ackay], "Day and Night," *Contemporary Verse* 10 (April 1944):15–16; J. E. Middleton, "The Current Manner of Poetry and Dorothy Livesay's Art," *Saturday Night*, 13 May 1944, 28; Anita Freeman, "New Book of Poems Published," *Kingston Whig-Standard*, 18 May 1944, n. pag.; see same newspaper review entitled "Every Friday: Books . . . Dorothy Livesay's Poems," *Victoria Times*, 19 May 1944, n. pag.; and "Dorothy Livesay's Poetry Expresses Social Philosophy," *Ottawa Journal*, 20 May 1944, n. pag.; and "New Book

of Poems by Dorothy Livesay," n.p., n.d., n.pag.; M. V. Thornton, "Woman Writes With Moving Power: Virile Work of Canadian Poet," *Vancouver Sun,* 27 May 1944, n.pag.; Sally Townsend, "Poetry of Dignity and Depth," [Toronto newspaper], 2 June 1944, n.pag.; Margaret Avison, "Books of the Month," *Canadian Forum* (June 1944):67; Helen Lorraine Honey, "*Day and Night* By Dorothy Livesay," *Narrator,* June 1944, n.pag.; Amabel King, "Reviews," *Canadian Poetry Magazine* 7, no. 4 (June 1944):41–42; G[eorge] H[erbert] C[larke], "New Canadian Verse," *Queen's Quarterly* 51 (Summer 1944):227; "Portrait of a Poet: Introducing Dorothy Livesay," *Quill & Quire* (July 1944):29–30; Doris Ferne, "Book Review," *Western Recorder,* October 1944, 1–2; F. R. Scott, "Day and Night," *First Statement* 2, no. 10 (December–January 1944–45):23, 24; Ruth Stephan, "A Canadian Poet," *Poetry* (Chicago) 65 (January 1945):220–22; [Watson Kirkconnell], "*Day and Night,*" *Canadian Poetry Magazine* 8, no. 3 (March 1945):39; Henry H. Wells, "The Awakening of Canadian Poetry," *New England Quarterly* 18 (March 1945):11–12; E. K. Brown, "Letters in Canada: 1944. Poetry," *University of Toronto Quarterly* 14 (April 1944):262–63; "Poems Worth Studying," *Canadian Author & Bookman* (March 1946):20.

13. See Avison, Brown, C[larke], [Kirkconnell], and Stephan, above.
14. Stephan, "A Canadian Poet," 221.
15. Brown, "Letters in Canada: 1944," 262.
16. Avison, "Books of the Month," 67.
17. "Lorca," in *How Do I Love Thee: Sixty Poets of Canada (and Quebec) Select and Introduce Their Favorite Poems from Their Work,* ed. John Robert Colombo (Edmonton: Hurtig, 1970), 10–12.
18. Ibid., 12.
19. "Dorothy Livesay, Unabashed Romantic," in *In Their Words: Interviews with Fourteen Canadian Writers,* ed. Bruce Meyer and Brian O'Riordan (Toronto: Anansi, 1984), 77.
20. Private papers, Galiano Island, B.C., Canada, 1979.
21. Ibid., 21.
22. Dorothy Livesay to Gordon Sinclair, 8 August 1950, folder 1, QUEEN.
23. Dorothy Livesay to W. A. Martin, 7 May 1953, folder 1, QUEEN.
24. Indeed, six years before "Prophet" was started in 1945, Livesay had already written a sonnet about Riel that used visionary imagery to dub him "Bare headed prophet of this brimming world!" "Louis Riel," unpublished poem, ca. 1938 or 1939, poetry worksheets, ALTA.
25. "The Documentary Poem: A Canadian Genre," in *Contexts of Canadian Criticism: A Collection of Critical Essays,* ed. Eli Mandel, rev. ed. (Chicago: University of Chicago, 1977), 267–81.
26. "Four Chapbooks," *Toronto Telegram,* 3 February 1951, n.pag.
27. See correspondence of 29 March 1949 and 5 March 1953, for ex-

ample, from Japanese-Canadian groups to Livesay, thanking her profusely for her effective poetic plea, in Business Correspondence, folder 1, QUEEN.

28. J. T., "Strong Social Sense Shown by New Poems," Canadian Press Release, Toronto bureau, 24 June 1947, in Box 18, folder 14, MAN; Mildred V. Thornton, "Poems of Distinction," *Vancouver Sun,* 26 July 1947, 5; S. S., "Poems for People," *Province* (Vancouver), 2 August 1947, n. pag.; Earle Birney, "Reviews," *Canadian Poetry Magazine* 11, no. 1 (September 1947):37–38; Alfred G. Bailey, "New Books," *Dalhousie Review* 27 (October 1947):383–84; George Herbert Clarke, "Recent Canadian Verse," *Queen's Quarterly* 54 (October 1947):394; James Reaney, "Quiet Poetess," *Varsity* (Univ. of Toronto), 20 October 1947, 5; Miriam Waddington, "Books Received," *Canadian Forum* (October 1947):165; Lyon Sharman, "Review and Tribute," *Carmel* [California] *Pine Cone-Cymbal,* 30 January 1948, n.pag.

29. Bailey, "New Books," 384; Thornton, "Poems of Distinction," 5; Birney, "Reviews," 37.

30. Sharman, "Review and Tribute," n.pag.; Reaney, "Quiet Poetess," 5.

31. J. T., "Social Sense," n.pag.; Clarke, "Recent Verse," 394.

32. S. S., "Poems for People," n.pag.

33. Waddington, "Books Received," 165.

Chapter Four

1. "Generation" and "After Hiroshima," in *New Poems,* ed. Jay Macpherson (Toronto: Emblem, 1955); rpt. in *Collected Poems* (Toronto: McGraw-Hill Ryerson, 1972); "Of Neighbours" and "Hymn to Man," in *Selected Poems* (Toronto: Ryerson, 1957); rpt. in *Collected Poems,* 1972; "Wine from Cyprus," in *Collected Poems;* "Canadiana," in *Plainsongs* (Fredericton: Fiddlehead, 1971 ed. only); rpt. in *Collected Poems;* "Centennial People," *Saturday Night* (July 1967):26; rpt. in *Other Voices* 3, no. 3 (November 1967):5; rpt. in *Plainsongs,* 1969 ed. only; "The Metal and the Flower," *Scan* 4 (April–May 1968):14; rpt. in *Plainsongs,* 1969 ed. only.

2. Notes, "Africa," Livesay private papers, Galiano Island, 1979.

3. Livesay promoted this point on many occasions, including an article for the *English Quarterly* 1, no. 1 (June 1968):31–38, entitled "A Creative Climate for English Teaching." All three of her conclusions (p. 38) are pertinent to her own practices as a poet.

First we need a teacher for whom literature is a revelation of life, and who sees the necessity of relating it to the students' level of experience. Next we need an attitude which uses the students' everyday speech patterns to reveal the structural backbone of English: less formal grammar and more enjoyment of words, idioms, slang—a study of language, in short, so related to life that the learning motivation of "tests" is no longer necessary. Lastly, especially in Canada, we need the widest possible search for texts drawn from our own literature and history; and a wise use of current weeklies and journals, public affairs programs and films.

    4. Livesay to Robin Farr, 24 June 1968, Livesay-Ryerson Correspondence, QUEEN.
    5. In *Contexts of Canadian Criticism: A Collection of Essays,* ed. Eli Mandel, rev. ed., 269.
    6. Ibid., 269.
    7. Ibid., 281.
    8. Mary Lee Morton, "Livesay Distorted," *Branching Out* 5, no. 3 (1978):41.
    9. This was the amount I paid in St. Catharines, Ontario, in 1978. I note with interest that the current Press Porcépic catalog lists *The Woman I Am* at one dollar less . . . eight years later and in defiance of inflation. That reduction suggests that Livesay's wishes have prevailed.
    10. "Editorial Notes," unpublished poem, 1971, *White Pelican* file, Box 24, folder 23, MAN.
    11. "The Feminist," unpublished poem, December 1968, ALTA.
    12. See also "Self-Portrait: The Androgyne," in *The Phases of Love* (Toronto: Coach House, 1983), wherein she describes men as easily made fearful of her, unlike the "women-children" who detect her warmth and softness. "Rare," she says, was the young man who realized otherwise: " 'Why, you love men!' he cried / and hugged her." The point is obviously a reaction to feminist extremists in combination with defensiveness about the hostility she has so chronically stirred in men.

Chapter Five

    1. Florence Randal Livesay, diary entry for 11 April 1905, in the possession of Dorothy Livesay.
    2. "My Mother Myself," in *Feeling the Worlds* (Fredericton: Fiddlehead, 1984), 17.
    3. "The Origin of the Family," in *The Phases of Love,* n.pag.
    4. J. F. B. Livesay to Dorothy Livesay, 26 January 1930, Box 32, folder 12, MAN. That Dorothy challenged JFBL's inconsistency—requiring virginity in his bride but thinking it wasteful generally—is evidenced in an unpublished poem in Dorothy Livesay's possession, " 'On my wedding night.' "
    5. "Ballad of Me," in *Collected Poems,* 266.
    6. See, for example, Livesay, "At the Back of My Mind, (1958–9)," *Room of One's Own* 5, no. 1/2 (1979):38. Bluntly she reports, "Our sexual life was not a success."

7. E.g., Livesay, autobiographical notes, one dated 20 March 1953, Box 31, folders 25 ("Autobiography") and 28 ("Autobiography. Dreams 1946–1974"), MAN.

8. See ample Crawley-Livesay correspondence, QUEEN.

9. Crawley, having lost his sight in the middle of a fine legal career in Winnipeg, had retired to the West Coast on that account.

10. Foreword to *Alan Crawley and "Contemporary Verse"* (Vancouver: University of British Columbia, 1976), xvii.

11. "At the Back of My Mind (1958–9)," *Room of One's Own* 5:41.

12. Incorrectly dated January 1959 in *Collected Poems* and in the ALTA manuscript. See the original draft in Box 16, file "R," MAN.

13. *Room of One's Own* 5:37.

14. "Vase," unpublished poem, 1959, ALTA.

15. "Letter to My Daughter," unpublished poem, 1959, ALTA.

16. "Girl Child," unpublished poem, 1959, ALTA.

17. "Spring in Russell Square," *Canadian Forum* (December 1959):201–2; rpt. as "May in Russell Square," *Delta* (January–March 1960):20–21.

18. "Persephone," *Atlantic Advocate* (September 1966):86.

19. "Articulate Defense," unpublished poem, 4 June 1959, ALTA.

20. "She Replies to His Pleas," unpublished poem, 1959, ALTA.

21. "The Dream," unpublished poem, 1959, ALTA.

22. "Time tells us we are tall," unpublished poem, 1959, ALTA.

23. "Sonnet: The rule I follow," unpublished poem, 1959, ALTA.

24. "To turn the pages of my loves," unpublished poem, 1959, ALTA.

25. "Song and Dance," *Canadian Literature* 41 (Summer 1969):43.

26. Ibid.

27. Livesay to C. Boylan ("Charlot"), 2 May 1967, Box 3, folder 26, QUEEN.

28. "The Child on Steps," unpublished poem, 1963, ALTA.

29. Livesay also proposed *The Notations of Love, The Skin of Time,* and *Sunfast* as titles for *The Unquiet Bed.* Livesay to editor Earle Toppings, 12 July 1966, Livesay-Ryerson correspondence, QUEEN.

30. "The Woman I Am," poetry worksheets, 1966, ALTA.

31. Livesay to Earle Toppings, 17 December 1966, Livesay-Ryerson correspondence, QUEEN.

Chapter Six

1. "Apple-Dear," unpublished short story, Box 31, folder 23, MAN.

2. Dorothy Livesay to Marcia Macnair, 25 August 1970, Box 28, folder 23, MAN.

3. Diary entry, 20 April 1928, *Right Hand Left Hand,* 23.

4. In Marsha Barber, "An Interview with Dorothy Livesay," *Room of One's Own* 5, no. 1/2 (1979):29.

5. "No More Hankies," unpublished short story, Box 29, folder 7, and Box 3, folder 18, MAN.

6. Diary, December 1929, Box 31, folder 2, MAN.

7. In *Wild Rose Country: Stories from Alberta*, ed. David Carpenter (Ottawa: Oberon, 1977), 129–38. Livesay was loosely eligible for this category by virtue of her years of teaching at the University of Alberta. Previous publication of this story under the name "The Mother-in-Law" was in *Branching Out* 1 (December 1973):16–19. The story was first drafted in 1929 (Box 20, folder 28, MAN).

8. In *The Best American Short Stories of 1951*, ed. Martha Foley (Boston: Houghton Mifflin, 1951), 218–27. The story originally appeared in *Northern Review* 3, no. 5 (June–July 1950):1–10.

9. See Box 20, folders 11 and 20, MAN, and folders 1 and 29, QUEEN.

10. "First Crocus," *Canadian Forum* (March 1952):276; see also "A Prairie Sampler," *Mosaic* 3, no. 3 (Spring 1970):85–92; "Matt," *Canadian Forum* (January 1953): 227, 229–30; "The Two Willies," *Journal of Canadian Fiction* 1, no. 1 (Winter 1972):27–30; "The Other Side of the Street," *Literary Half-Yearly* 13, no. 2 (July 1972):96–103.

11. "Preludes," "Matt," "The Two Willies," "Christmas," "First Trials," "Father's Boy," "The Other Side of the Street," "The End of the War," "A Week in the Country," Box 22, folder 46, MAN.

12. "Give My Love to London," synopsis, Box 20, folder 29, MAN. See also Box 20, folder 11, MAN, for the original short story.

13. "The Lie," unpublished story, 20 January 1928, Box 10, folder 4, MAN.

14. "Flight. A Fragment," unpublished short story, 8 September 1927, Box 1, folder 25 (3), MAN.

15. Livesay to Toivo Kiil, 1971, Box 24, folder 18, MAN.

16. "Katherine Mansfield," *St. Hilda's Chronicle* 17, no. 43 (Easter 1928):21; "The Poetry of E. J. Pratt," ibid.:22.

17. "Getting It Straight," *Impulse* 2, nos. 3 & 4 (1973):29.

18. "Review," *CV/II* 1, no. 2 (Fall 1975):37.

19. "Knister's Stories," *Canadian Literature* 62 (Autumn 1974):79–82.

20. I. V. Crawford material: Boxes 5 (folders 30, 32), 11 (25 folders), 12 (11 folders), MAN.

21. She did so first via the perhaps inappropriate avenue of a presentation to the Association of Canadian University Teachers of English (York University, 12 June 1969), ostensibly talking generally (and quite brilliantly) about "The Documentary Poem: A Canadian Genre" but actually seizing the opportunity to devote nearly half of her paper to Crawford and her long poem "Malcolm's Katie." This was later published in *Contexts of Canadian Criticism*, ed. Eli Mandel, rev. ed., 267–81.

22. "The Hunters Twain," *Canadian Literature* 55 (Winter 1973):75–98.

23. "Tennyson's Daughter or Wilderness Child? The Factual and Literary Background of Isabella Valancy Crawford," *Journal of Canadian Fiction* 2, no. 3 (Summer 1973):161–67.

24. "Livesay's Choice," *Canadian Dimension* 10, no. 8 (June 1975):15.

25. Anne McDougall, "The Trouble With Hen Parties . . . ," *Victoria Times*, 11 March 1972, 14.

26. Lorraine Vernon, "Forty Women Poets Redress Balance," *Vancouver Sun*, 13 October 1972, 37A.

27. Foreword to *Woman's Eye: 12 B.C. Poets* (Vancouver: Air, 1974), v.

28. See Florida Town, "SFU Writer-in-Residence Suggests Life Too Soft for Today's Artists," *SFU Week* 15, no. 6 (11 October 1979):2.

29. See, for example, Box I, folder 8, "Canada Council (1974–1975)," folder 9, "Canada Council (1973–76)," and folder 22, "Dorothy Livesay Support Requests from Others for Grants '77."

30. The titles have changed from one appointment to the next; the Livesay style—total involvement—has not: 1965–66 Lecturer in poetry, Department of Creative Writing, University of British Columbia; 1966–68 Writer-in-residence, University of New Brunswick, teaching a graduate course in Canadian literature during the second year; 1968–71 Associate Professor of English, University of Alberta; 1972–74 Visiting lecturer, University of Victoria; 1974–76 Writer-in-residence, St. John's College, University of Manitoba, teaching graduate seminars in Canadian literature at the University of Manitoba during the second year; 1977–78 Writer-in-residence, University of Ottawa; 1980–81 Writer-in-residence, Simon Fraser University; 1981–82 Creative writing seminar, Simon Fraser University; 1983–84 Writer-in-residence, New College, University of Toronto.

31. Livesay, quoted by Florida Town, *SFU Week*, 2.

32. J. F. B. Livesay to Charles Bruce, 1 March 1944, Box 31, folder 7, MAN.

33. Jørn Carlsen, untitled interview with Livesay, *Kunapipi* 1, no. 1 (1979):130–34.

34. "Modern and Medieval Seen in Arromanches-Les-Bains," *Star Weekly*, 9 November 1929, 9; "French Women Consider Convenience Not Fashion," *Star Weekly*, 16 November 1929, 24.

35. David Arnason, unedited transcript of interview with Livesay, 30 May 1976, Box 3, folder 15, p. 9, MAN.

36. J. F. B. Livesay to Dorothy Livesay, 26 January 1930, Box 32, folder 12, MAN.

37. Dorothy Livesay to Duncan Macnair, Box 28, folder 18, MAN.

38. Undated diary entry, Box 31, folder 2, MAN.

39. *Star* (Toronto) editors to Livesay, 20 January 1948, 22 October 1948, and 30 May 1949, Box 1, folder 21, QUEEN.

40. Livesay to B. K. Sandwell, 28 February 1949, Box 1, folder 25, QUEEN.

41. "Decadence in Modern Bourgeois Poetry," Box 3, folder 15, MAN; published in *Right Hand Left Hand,* 61–67.

Chapter Seven

1. Cynthia Pomerleau, "The Emergence of Women's Autobiography in England," in *Women's Autobiography,* ed. Estelle C. Jelinek (Bloomington: Indiana University, 1980), 21.
2. William Matthews, *Canadian Diaries and Autobiographies* (Berkeley: University of California, 1950).
3. Margaret Atwood, "you fit into me," in *Power Politics* (Toronto: Anansi, 1972), 1.
4. Estelle C. Jelinek, "Introduction: Women's Autobiography and the Male Tradition," in *Women's Autobiography,* ed. Jelinek, 13.
5. Livesay is aware of this. See her undated notation, Box 3, folder 29, MAN.
6. Jelinek, "Introduction," 7–9. Patricia K. Addis, in her *Through a Woman's I: An Annotated Bibliography of American Women's Autobiographical Writings, 1946–76* (Metuchen, N.J.: Scarecrow, 1983), is particularly conscious of this practice of self-erasure. In her introduction Addis defends the apparently controversial inclusion under "Autobiography" of letters, diaries, journals, memoirs, reminiscences, and travel accounts as legitimate phases and faces of female autobiography. It is a proviso necessary to permit inclusion of the 2217 entries she then locates in the postwar period. She apologizes for indexing some of the authors as "wife of" but defends such subordination on the grounds that those women consider/ed those relationships "the single most important factor in their lives." Thus one finds 17 doctors versus 25 doctors' wives or daughters; 7 members of the armed forces versus 25 wives of such; 8 ministers versus 45 ministers' wives or daughters. And that "reflected glory" phenomenon—woman earning the right to tell her story as the admiring appendage of an important person—shows up most starkly when one compares the category of "Relative [husband, daughter, mother, sister] of a Famous Woman" with "Female Relative of a Famous Man": 7 to 104. Women in our emancipated era, it appears, have been no more inclined to document their sisters' lives and accomplishments than they have their own.
7. Mary Hiatt, *The Way Women Write* (N.Y.: Teachers College, 1977), 5.
8. Hiatt, chapter 3, "Longwindedness Versus Shortwindedness," and chapter 4, "Who is Scatterbrained?"
9. Suzanne Juhasz, "Toward a Theory of Form in Feminist Autobiography," in *Women's Autobiography,* ed. Jelinek, 224.
10. David MacClelland, "Wanted: A New Self-Image for Women," in *The Woman in America,* ed. Robert Jay Lifton (Boston: Beacon, 1967), 181.

11. Ronald Hatch, "Livesay Has Her Say," *Vancouver Sun*, 2 December 1977.

Chapter Eight

1. Bliss Carman, with only a year to live, was in 1928 awarded the Royal Society of Canada's Lorne Pierce Gold Medal that young Livesay would win in her turn nineteen years later. Charles G. D. Roberts, seven years away from a knighthood, had won the first Medal in 1926 and remained a prominent figure in Canadian letters despite the rise of new literary movements, until his death in 1943. Duncan Campbell Scott, nearing retirement from the Civil Service and nursing a dying wife, was nonetheless working tirelessly to promote the reputation of the fourth "Confederation Poet," Archibald Lampman, who had died young in 1899. Scott would also, in the course of his later years, publish four more books of his own poetry and prose.
2. Tom Marshall, *Harsh and Lovely Land* (Vancouver: University of British Columbia, 1979).
3. Stephen Scobie, "Tunnelling Toward a National Dream," *Books in Canada* (August–September 1979):14.
4. While my focus here is on the gap in literary criticism, the phenomenon of neglect or willful omission is widespread in anthologizing as well. Eli Mandel, for example, who put together *Five Modern Canadian Poets* (1970) and *Eight More Canadian Poets* (1972), never did find space for Livesay, although such lesser lights as James Reaney and Jay Macpherson were admitted. John Newlove, under more pressure to be representative in his *Canadian Poetry: The Modern Era* (1977), nonetheless allowed only four Livesay poems in comparison with thirteen by Leonard Cohen, fifteen by Alden Nowlan, nine by Reaney, eight by Macpherson, seven by George Johnston, and so forth.
5. For at least four years, the argument raged between Livesay and Weaver over whether she would be allowed to read her poetry on radio. Livesay argued the absolute necessity of having the actual poets read their own work, as opposed to a paid reader. Earle Toppings, her Ryerson Press editor, several times warned her that offending "czar Weaver" on this issue could be damaging to her career, causing her to be "ostracized." Livesay-Ryerson Correspondence, Box IV, QUEEN. See especially the Livesay-Weaver letters of 20 June 1964, 24 February 1965, 13 April 1967, and 27 November 1968, and the Livesay-Toppings letters of 13, 15, and 17 April 1967.
6. Tom Marshall, "Major Canadian Poets III. The Modernists," *Canadian Forum* (January–February 1979):16. Ditto Bob Harvey, "Poetry: A Cry To Stave Off Evil," *Edmonton Journal*, 14 November 1969, whose praising pigeonhole was " 'grande dame' of Canadian poetry."
7. E.g., *Right Hand Left Hand*, 20.
8. Livesay, "Personal Correspondence," folder 24, QUEEN.

9. *15 Canadian Poets,* ed. Gary Geddes and Phyllis Bruce (Toronto: Oxford University, 1970); *15 Canadian Poets* + *5* (Toronto: Oxford University, 1978). Indeed, four of the five belated additions are women: Livesay, P. K. Page, Phyllis Webb, and Pat Lowther; except for Lowther, all are in Geddes's own category of "established poets," obviously consciously passed over in the first edition.

Selected Bibliography

PRIMARY SOURCES

1. Poetry
Beyond War: The Poetry. Vancouver: Private printing, 1985.
Call My People Home. Toronto: Ryerson (Ryerson Poetry Chapbook #143), 1950.
Collected Poems: The Two Seasons. Foreword by Dorothy Livesay. Toronto: McGraw-Hill Ryerson, 1972.
The Colour of God's Face. Vancouver: Unitarian Service Committee, 1964.
Day and Night. Boston: Bruce Humphries, 1944; Toronto: Ryerson, 1944.
Disasters of the Sun. Burnaby, B.C.: Blackfish (Broadsides Folio #3), 1971.
The Documentaries. Foreword by Dorothy Livesay. Toronto: Ryerson, 1968.
Feeling the Worlds. Fredericton: Fiddlehead, 1984.
Green Pitcher. Toronto: Macmillan, 1928.
Ice Age. Erin, Ont. Porcépic, 1975.
Nine Poems of Farewell 1972-1973. Windsor: Black Moss, 1973.
New Poems. Edited by Jay Macpherson. Toronto: Emblem, 1955.
The Phases of Love. Toronto: Coach House, 1983.
Plainsongs. Fredericton: Fiddlehead (Poetry Books), 1969. Rev. and exp. Fredericton: Fiddlehead (Poetry Books), 1971.
Poems for People. Toronto: Ryerson, 1947.
The Raw Edges: Voices from Our Time. Winnipeg: Turnstone, 1981.
Selected Poems of Dorothy Livesay [1926–1956]. Introduced by Desmond Pacey. Toronto: Ryerson, 1957.
Signpost. Toronto: Macmillan, 1932.
The Unquiet Bed. Toronto: Ryerson, 1967.
The Woman I Am: Best Loved Poems from One of Canada's Best Loved Poets. Erin, Ont.: Porcépic, 1977.

2. Short Stories
A Winnipeg Childhood. Winnipeg: Peguis, 1973, rpt. as *Beginnings: A Winnipeg Childhood.* Toronto: new press, 1975.

3. Multigenre Collection
Right Hand Left Hand. Edited by David Arnason and Kim Todd. Erin, Ont.: Porcépic, 1977.

4. Books Edited

Collected Poems of Raymond Knister. Foreword by Raymond Knister. With memoir by Dorothy Livesay. Toronto: Ryerson, 1949.

40 Women Poets of Canada. Edited by Dorothy Livesay and Seymour Mayne. Montreal: Ingluvin, 1971.

Woman's Eye: 12 B.C. Poets. Foreword by Dorothy Livesay. Vancouver: Air, 1974.

5. Selected Articles

"Aspects of Symbolism," *Modern Quarterly* 17 (January 1967):114–26.

"Canadian Poetry and the Spanish Civil War." *CV/II* 2, no. 2 (May 1976):12–16. Reprinted in *Right Hand Left Hand,* 250–55.

"Carr and Livesay." *Canadian Literature* 84 (Spring 1980):144–47.

"Commentary." *West Coast Review* 12, no. 2 (1977):69–70.

"A Creative Climate for English Teaching." *English Quarterly* 1 (June 1968):31–38.

"The Documentary Poem: A Canadian Genre." In *Contexts of Canadian Criticism: A Collection of Critical Essays.* Rev. ed., edited by Eli Mandel, 267–81. Patterns of Literary Criticism, no 9. Toronto: University of Toronto, 1977.

Foreword to *Alan Crawley and "Contemporary Verse,"* by Joan McCullagh, vii–xvii. Vancouver: University of British Columbia, 1976.

"Fred and the *Fiddlehead.*" *Atlantic Advocate* (May 1967):26–28.

"The Hunters Twain." *Canadian Literature* 55 (Winter 1973):75–98.

Introduction to *In Due Season,* by Christine Van der Mark. Vancouver: New Star, 1979.

"Livesay's Choice." *Canadian Dimension* 10, no. 8 (June 1975):15–16.

"Mazo de la Roche: 1879–1961." In *The Clear Spirit: Twenty Canadian Women and Their Times,* edited by Mary Quayle Innis, 242–59. Toronto: Canadian Federation of University Women/University of Toronto, 1966.

"The Native People in Our Canadian Literature." *English Quarterly* 4, no. 1 (Spring 1971):21–32.

"On the Way Out." Editorial. *CV/II* 3, no. 2 (Summer 1977):2.

"Poet's Progress." *New Frontier* 2, no. 3 (July–August 1937):23–24.

"Poets Yap, Writers are Suppressed—Why Can't Canada Be Just Like Bulgaria?" *Globe & Mail,* 16 July 1977, 6.

"The Polished Lens: Poetic Techniques of Pratt and Klein." *Canadian Literature* 25 (Summer 1965):33–42.

"Remembering Mazo." In *Selected Stories of Mazo de la Roche,* edited and introduced by Douglas Daymond, 11–13. Ottawa: University of Ottawa, 1979.

Review of *The Collected Poems of Red Lane. Far Point* 2 (Spring–Summer 1969):51–57.

Room of One's Own 5, nos. 1-2 (1979): "Ambivalences," 95–96; "At the Back of My Mind 1958–9," 37–41; "At the World's End; Where I Am Now," 113–14; "Diary Notes (May/June 1979)," 77–82; "Doctors," 92–94; "Leftovers," 98–99; "No Rape," 97; "Not on My Verandah," 83–91.

"The Sculpture of Poetry: On Louis Dudek." *Canadian Literature* 30 (Summer 1966):26–35.

"Search for a Style: The Poetry of Milton Acorn." *Canadian Literature* 40 (Spring 1969):33–42.

"Song and Dance." *Canadian Literature* 41 (Summer 1969):40–48.

"Tennyson's Daughter or Wilderness Child? The Factual and Literary Background of Isabella Valancy Crawford." *Journal of Canadian Fiction* 2, no. 3 (Summer 1973):161–67.

"This Canadian Poetry." *Canadian Forum* (April 1944):20–21.

"Tip of an Iceberg." Review of *New Provinces: Poems of Several Authors*, edited by F. R. Scott, A. J. M. Smith, et al., rev. ed., introduced by Michael Gnarowski. *Essays on Canadian Writing* 7–8 (Fall 1977):145–50.

"Two Women Novelists of Canada's West." *Review of National Literatures* 7 (1976):127–32.

"A Writer in the Depression." In *Essays in B.C. Political Economy*, edited by Paul Knox and Philip Reznick, 65–73. Vancouver: New Star, 1974.

6. Journals Founded and/or Edited

Contemporary Verse. Founding committee, 1941.

CV/II. Founder/editor, Summer 1975–Autumn 1977.

New Frontier. Regional editor, April 1936–October 1937.

Northern Review. Regional editor, December 1945–Summer 1947.

White Pelican. Guest editor, with Rudy Wiebe, Special Issue on the Canadian North, 1, no. 2. Fall 1971. Also listed as member of editorial board for 1, nos. 1, 3, and 4; 2, nos. 1 and 3.

7. Manuscripts and Audiovisual Materials

Department of Archives and Special Collections, Elizabeth Dafoe Library, University of Manitoba, Winnipeg, Manitoba. 39 boxes: poetry worksheets, articles, fiction, radio plays, correspondence, photographs, memorabilia, tapes, etc. This collection has recently been entirely reorganized; a lengthy finding aid is available.

Bruce Peel Special Collections Library, University of Alberta, Edmonton, Alberta. Livesay-Ryerson correspondence; poetry worksheets to 1974; photocopies of literary correspondence (originals at Queen's).

Douglas Library Archives, Queen's University, Kingston, Ontario. 4 series/104 folders: literary correspondence 1933–70; photocopies of poetry worksheets and of Livesay-Ryerson correspondence (originals at Edmonton).

Special Collections, Simon Fraser University, Burnaby, British Columbia. 15 tape recordings: interviews, poetry readings, music, lectures.

David Tucker, dir. *The Woman I Am*. Toronto: Film Arts/D.L.T. in association with the Canadian Broadcasting Corporation, 1981. Broadcast on *Spectrum*, CBC television, Toronto, 17 March 1982. Since rebroadcast on CBC several times.

SECONDARY SOURCES

1. Bibliography

The Papers of Dorothy Livesay: A Research Tool. Manitoba: University of Manitoba, 1986.

Ricketts, Alan. "Dorothy Livesay: An Annotated Bibliography." In *The Annotated Bibliography of Canada's Major Authors*, edited by Jack David and Robert Lecker, vol. 4, 129–203. Downsview, Ont.: ECW, 1983.

2. Journal Issue Devoted to Livesay

Dunn, Margo, Janice Pentland-Smith, Gayla Reid, Helene Rosenthal, Gail van Varseveld, Eleanor Wachtel, and **Jean Wilson,** eds. *Dorothy Livesay Issue* [*Room of One's Own*] 5, nos. 1-2 (1979). Collection of essays and a poem about Livesay and her writing as well as poems, diary notes, sketches, an open letter, and essays by Livesay, an interview with her, and six photographs.

3. Sections of Books, Articles, and Reviews

Arnason, David. Introduction to *Right Hand Left Hand*, edited by David Arnason and Kim Todd. Erin, Ont.: Porcépic, 1977. Presents literary-historical context of Canada in the 1930s and influences on Livesay during the Depression.

Aspinall, Dawn, Anne Marriott, Pat Lowther, and **Charles Lillard.** "Book Reviews." *Prism International* 13, no. 1 (Summer 1973):137–41. Condensed transcript of a four-way discussion by a Canadian literature specialist (Aspinall) and three poets about Livesay's *Collected Poems*. The male participant is noticeably less impressed than the females.

Baugh, Edward. "Dorothy Livesay, *Collected Poems*." *Quarry* 22, no. 4 (Autumn 1973):2–4. West Indian critic sees her humanity "enlarged" by her years of social poetry, but her "strongest bent is towards the intimate and lyrical." Calls her "one of the most prolific and consistently delightful poets of this century."

Boylan, Charles. "A Dancing, Vivid Palette." *Edmonton Journal*, 8 December 1972. A very approving review of the *Collected Poems* by the Marxist author of an unpublished M.A. thesis on "The Social and Lyrical Voices of Dorothy Livesay" (U.B.C., 1969).

Brown, E. K. *On Canadian Poetry.* Rev. ed. 1944. Reprint. Ottawa: Tecumseh, 1973. Major critic admires equally Livesay's intellectual, social and nature poetry.

———. "Letters in Canada: 1944. Poetry." *University of Toronto Quarterly* 14 (April 1945):262–63. Here a marked preference for her lyric over her political voice, focused on *Day and Night.*

Cogswell, Fred. "Reviews." *Fiddlehead* 79 (March–April 1969):112. Sees in *The Documentaries* evidence of the "artistic unity" and movement toward freedom of Livesay's poetic development.

Collin, W. E. "My New Found Land." In his *The White Savannahs.* 1936. Reprint Literature of Canada: Poetry and Prose in Reprint, no 5, 147–73. Toronto: University of Toronto, 1975. The first extended introduction to Livesay's work, complimentary about *Green Pitcher* and *Signpost,* but approving and encouraging her subsequent turn to Depression themes.

Crawley, Alan. "Dorothy Livesay—An Intimate Biography." 1945. Reprinted in *Leading Canadian Poets,* edited by W. P. Percival, 117–24. Toronto: Ryerson, 1948. Reminiscence of his friendship with Livesay since 1938, her life on the West Coast, and analysis of her poetry.

Davey, Frank. "Dorothy Livesay." In his *From There to Here: A Guide to English-Canadian Literature Since 1960.* Vol. 2 of *Our Nature–Our Voices,* 168–72. Erin, Ont.: Porcépic, 1974. Overview, seeing Livesay as one of the most important Canadian poets of the last half-century, the "finest lyricist of her generation," and a forerunner of the natural voice poetry of the 1960s.

———. "Dorothy Livesay (b. 1909)." In *The Oxford Companion to Canadian History and Literature,* edited by William Toye. Toronto: Oxford University, 1983. Bio-critical survey, generally approving but somewhat dismissive of her publications in the 1940s (two of which won Governor-General's Awards).

Dykk, Lloyd. "A Gallant Poet Speaks Her Mind." *Vancouver Sun,* 11 September 1981, L40–L41. Enthusiastic overview of Livesay's themes, beliefs, and style, well disposed to her social poetry past and current.

Fetherling, Doug. "Canada, Country You Loved With Hate. . . ." *Saturday Night,* March 1973, 37. Review of the *Collected Poems,* regarding her poems as becoming "meatier" over the years and calling the book "not only an important document on the evolution of Canadian poetry but also . . . a good book."

Foulks, Debbie. "Livesay's Two Seasons of Love." *Canadian Literature* 74 (Autumn 1977):63–73. Feminist analysis of Livesay's work, detecting opposing and unreconciled visions of love.

Frye, Northrop. *The Bush Garden: Essays on the Canadian Imagination.* Toronto: Anansi, 1971. Livesay is only fleetingly mentioned in Frye's *University of Toronto Quarterly* poetry entry for 1955, but is discussed at some length in the 1957 article, identified as an imagist throughout her private and public phases.

Geddes, Gary, and Phyllis Bruce. "Dorothy Livesay." In their *15 Canadian Poets + 5.* Toronto: Oxford University, 1978. Brief, bio-critical summary, identifying Livesay primarily as a "Realist" and terming her recent work "stridently" feminist.

Gibbs, Jean. "Dorothy Livesay and the Transcendentalist Tradition." *Humanities Association Bulletin* 21, no. 2 (Spring 1970):24–39. Argues a "Thoreauvian" transcendentalism in Livesay's poetry, a quest to achieve "sphericity," a oneness with "the larger order of things."

Harrison, R. T. Review article on *A Winnipeg Childhood. World Literature Written in English* 13, 2 (April 1974):266, 272–74. Emphasizes the sense of prairie isolation that informs the structure and content of the book.

Kiverago, Ron A. "Thirties Revisited." *Essays on Canadian Writing* 10 (Spring 1978):101–3. Warmly approving review article on *Right Hand Left Hand.*

Knister, Raymond. "Modes Conservative and Chic." *Saturday Night,* 3 November 1928, 12. Very early review of *Green Pitcher,* admiring her modernist originality of language, by the writer whose poetry Livesay edited after his death.

Kreisel, Henry. "The Poet as Radical—Dorothy Livesay in the Thirties." *CV/II* 3, no. 1 (Winter 1979):19–21. Lengthy, approving review article, by the prairie novelist, on *Right Hand Left Hand,* combined with a tracing of Livesay's social consciousness over the years.

Lane, Patrick. "The *Collected Poems* of Dorothy Livesay." *Blackfish* 4–5 (Winter–Spring 1972–1973):n. pag. Detailed, lengthy, chronological review, tracing Livesay's "passionate struggle to understand herself and her [mind-body] schism," and the way that has committed her to the "great social themes" of this century.

Leland, Doris. "Dorothy Livesay: Poet of Nature." *Dalhousie Review* 51 (Autumn 1971):404–12. Thematic study of Livesay as a poet offering a vision of "man's acceptance of himself as a part of nature."

M[acKay], L[ouis A.]. *"Day and Night."* *Contemporary Verse* 10 (April 1944):15–16. Review of *Day and Night,* applauding its "remarkable" unity, seen as the "organic" consequence of a central theme of "human liberty and social justice."

Marshall, Tom. *Harsh and Lovely Land: The Major Canadian Poets and the Making of a Canadian Tradition.* Vancouver: University of British Columbia, 1979. Brief overview, identifying her true voice as terse and laconic, paradoxically dubbing her "the original earth-mother of modern Canadian poetry" but, like so many other critics and anthologists, according her work very little space or attention.

Mathews, Robin. "Right Hand Left Hand." *Ontario Report* (April 1978):34–35. A probing, opinionated, radical-nationalist review article that praises the book in many respects but argues that it is misleading, incomplete, ultimately colonial and sloppy-liberal in its thinking.

Mitchell, B. " 'How Silence Sings' in the Poetry of Dorothy Livesay." *Dalhousie Review* 54 (Autumn 1974):510–28. Based on the *Collected Poems*, a lengthy study of Livesay's thematic and stylistic poetic development and of specific poems.

Morley, Patricia. "Learning and Loving During the Lost Years." *Atlantis* 3, no. 2, pt. 1 (Spring 1978):145–50. Balanced review article on *Right Hand Left Hand* for a feminist journal, considering form as well as content.

Morton, Mary Lee. "Livesay Distorted." *Branching Out* 5, no. 3 (1978):41. Challenges the omission from *The Woman I Am* of nearly all socially conscious poems of the 1930s and 1940s.

New, W. H. "Canadian Literature and Commonwealth Responses." *Canadian Literature* 66 (Autumn 1975):14–30. A comparatively rare approach to Livesay's poetry—specifically her African poems—from the perspective of the artistic impact of British Commonwealth consciousness.

Nowlan, Michael O. "With Freshness Is a Leaf." *Fiddlehead* 119 (Fall 1978):5–6. On the occasion of the fiftieth anniversary of Livesay's first book, *Green Pitcher*, a tribute to Livesay's poetry, literary nationalism, and spirit.

Pacey, Desmond. Introduction to *Selected Poems of Dorothy Livesay* [1926–56], xi–xix. Toronto: Ryerson, 1957. Bio-critical overview to the mid-1950s.

———. "Books Reviewed." *Canadian Forum* (April 1968):21–22. Review of *The Unquiet Bed*, praising the "mature humanity," "intense vitality and honest self-revelation."

Pratt, E. J. "Dorothy Livesay." *Gants du ciel* 11 (Spring 1946):61–65. Study by a major Canadian poet of Livesay's poetic development over the years, with an assessment of *Day and Night* as the best social poetry Canada has produced.

Purdy, Al. "Reviews." *Tamarack Review* 47 (Spring 1968):88–89. Review of *The Unquiet Bed* by a prominent Ontarian poet, expressing a strong preference for her "wise, witty, and warm" current poems over her earlier ones.

Rapoport, Janis. "Winnipeg Childhood." *Tamarack Review* 61 (November 1973):76. Review of that book, sensitive to the child's consciousness as an organizing principle.

Rashley, R. E. *Poetry in Canada: The First Three Steps.* Toronto: Ryerson, 1958. Identifies love as Livesay's answer to mankind's problems; sees her poetry as "a somewhat cold and intellectual realization" of "an emotional attitude toward the contemporary world."

Resnick, Philip. "Ontario Story." *Canadian Dimension* 6 (July 1969):38. Review of *The Documentaries* in a leftist journal, predictably applauding its social consciousness and its "good poetry, clearly and cleanly expressed."

Rogers, Linda. "A Woman for All Seasons." *Books in Canada* (January–February 1973):50. Review of the *Collected Poems*, admiring most her poems of "the private event" in a book Rogers approaches as both "the portrait of a woman made whole through joy and suffering" and "a history of 20th-century Canada."

Skelton, Robin. "Everything Lives." *Canadian Literature* 35 (Winter 1967):91–92. Review, by West-Coast poet, of *The Unquiet Bed*, praising the "superb sense of music" and the successful fusion of "romantic, archetypal imagery with a simple and spare diction."

———. "Livesay's Two Seasons." *Canadian Literature* 58 (Autumn 1973):77–82. A long, generally favorable review of the *Collected Poems*, noting defects of language, rhythm, and image, but arguing that one is inclined to indulge them in the face of "such passionate honesty of feeling and such consistent moral courage."

Steinberg, M. W. "Dorothy Livesay: Poet of Affirmation." *British Columbia Library Quarterly* 24, no. 2 (October 1960):9–13. Brief thematic overview to late 1950s.

Stephan, Ruth. "A Canadian Poet." *Poetry* (Chicago) 65 (January 1945):220–22. Review, in the prestigious American journal, of *Day and Night*, vastly preferring the social poems over the romantic lyrics.

Stephens, Donald. "Words and Music." *Canadian Literature* 60 (Spring 1974):93–95. Praising article on *A Winnipeg Childhood*, judging it to have the same qualities as the best of her poetry.

Stephens, Peter. "Ideas and Icons." *Canadian Literature* 40 (Spring 1969):76–78. Review of *The Documentaries*, emphasizing Livesay's honesty as offsetting her polemicism and calling the book "essential reading."

———. "Out of the Silence and Across the Distance." *Queen's Quarterly* 78 (Winter 1971):579–91. Stylistic and thematic study, stressing darkness, silence, and isolation, as embodied in form and content.

———. "Dorothy Livesay: The Love Poetry." *Canadian Literature* 47 (Winter 1971):26–43. Reprinted in *Poets and Critics: Essays from "Canadian Literature" 1966–1974*, edited by George Woodcock, 33–52. Toronto: Oxford University, 1974. Lengthy thematic discussion of Livesay's love poetry early and late, seeing throughout a consistent and successful emphasis on "honesty and candour."

Thompson, Kent. "Reviews." *Fiddlehead* 73 (Summer 1967):79–83. Review of *The Unquiet Bed* from the viewpoint that East- and West-Coast poets have quite different poetic strategies, but that Livesay successfully draws from them both.

Thompson, Lee Briscoe. "A Coat of Many Cultures: The Poetry of Dorothy Livesay." *Journal of Popular Culture* 15, no. 3 (Winter 1981):53–61. Discusses the development of Livesay's consciousness of multiculturalism and her three artistic and creative responses.

Varma, Prem. "The Love Poetry of Dorothy Livesay." *Journal of Canadian Poetry* 3, no. 1 (Winter 1980):17–31. Discusses love as a major and evolving theme.

Vernon, Lorraine. "Livesay's Coming of Age." *Lakehead University Review* 6 (1973):246–50. A praising, substantial review of the *Collected Poems*, arguing that the collection should dispel "a mistaken image of a public/private Livesay" and reveal a woman of social convictions who strives always in her poetry to "bring the world together, in one large, human need."

Wallace, Bronwen. "Profile: Dorothy Livesay." *Canadian Writing Newsbulletin* 2, no. 1 (Spring/Summer 1983):1–2. Livesay at age 73, writer-in-residence at the University of Toronto.

Weaver, Robert. Editorial. *Tamarack Review* 75 (Fall 1978):5–7. Another tribute to Livesay on the fiftieth anniversary of her *Green Pitcher*, admiring its "youthful freshness," as well as the passion of her latest work, *Right Hand Left Hand*.

Woodcock, George. "Playing with Freezing Fire." *Canadian Literature* 70 (Autumn 1976):89–91. Review article on *Ice Age*, the theme of aging, and Livesay's development over the previous decade.

Zimmerman, Susan. "Livesay's Houses." *Canadian Literature* 61 (Summer 1974):32–45. Discusses the image of the house as it illuminates complex social, sexual, and personal choices implicit for a woman torn between hearth and freedom.

4. Interviews

Beardsley, Doug, and Rosemary Sullivan. "An Interview with Dorothy Livesay." *Canadian Poetry: Studies, Documents, Reviews* 3 (Fall–Winter 1978):87–97.

Carlsen, Jørn. "Dorothy Livesay: Interview." *Kunapipi* (University of Aarhus, Denmark) 1, no. 1 (Summer 1979):130–34.

Lever, Bernice. "An Interview with Dorothy Livesay." *Canadian Forum* (September 1975):45–52.

Marshall, Joyce. "Dorothy Livesay: A Bluestocking Remembers." *Branching Out* 7, no. 1 (1980):18–21.

Meyer, Bruce, and Brian O'Riordan. "Dorothy Livesay: Unabashed Romantic." In their *In Their Words: Interviews with Fourteen Canadian Writers*. Toronto: Anansi, 1984.

Mintz, Helen, and Barbara Coward. "The Woman I am / is not what you see / move over love / make room for me." *Grape,* 9–22 May 1973, 10, 21. Rpt. as "Being a Writer in the Thirties: An Interview with Dorothy Livesay." *This Magazine* 7, no. 4 (January 1974):19–21.

Robertson, Heather. "Dorothy Livesay at 73—The Unquiet Thoughts of a Romantic Feminist." *Quill & Quire* 49, no. 3 (March 1983):4, 6.

Twigg, Alan. "Matrona." In his *For Openers: Conversations with 24 Canadian Writers.* Madiera Park, B.C.: Harbour, 1981.

Index

Acorn, Milton, 12, 123
Aix-en-Provence, 2, 20, 33, 109, 117, 128
Alexander, Mary, 131
Allan, Ted, 137
Amnesty International, 70
Atwood, Margaret, 126, 135, 146
Auden, W. H., 3, 36–37
Austen, Jane, 115
Avison, Margaret, 46, 147, 148

Bennett, R. B., 39
Birney, Earle, 60, 66, 126, 145, 147
Blake, William, 36
Brodie, Steve, 137
Brontë, Anne, Charlotte, and Emily, 115
Brown, E. K., 46
Browne, Sir Thomas, 109
Bruce, Charles, 2, 17, 24, 127
Buck, Tim, 39

CV/II, 14, 70, 86, 124, 125
Callaghan, Morley: *They Shall Inherit the Earth*, 137
Canadian Authors' Association, 125
Canadian Bookman, 37
Canadian Broadcasting Corporation (CBC), 6, 14, 55, 57, 119, 131, 132, 137, 146
Canadian Forum, 37
Canadian Poetry Magazine, 3, 37, 46
Canadian Press, 1, 127
Canadian Women's Press Club, 127
Carman, Bliss, 23, 143
Carr, Emily, 123
Cézanne, Paul, 90
Collin, W. E., 24, 147
Contemporary Verse, 4, 6, 14, 86, 87, 124
Crawford, Isabella Valancy, 12, 123–24, 126
Crawley, Alan, 4, 86–87, 123, 147
Crawley, Jean, 86

Day Lewis, Cecil, 3, 36–37; *A Hope for Poetry*, 36; *The Magnetic Mountain*, 49
de la Roche, Mazo, 123, 127
Dickinson, Emily, 135
Dudek, Louis, 123

Edel, Leon, 2
Eight Men Speak, 136
Eliot, T. S., 2, 22, 36, 63, 92
Ellis, Havelock, 83
Engel, Marian, 135
Engels, Frederich: *Family, Property and the State*, 33

Finch, Robert, 147
Frye, Northrop, 126, 146

Gallant, Mavis, 135
Geddes, Gary: *15 Canadian Poets*, 147
Gnarowski, Michael: *Selected Stories of Raymond Knister*, 123
Goldman, Emma, 33, 83
Griffin, Sean, 137
Gustafson, Ralph: *Penguin Book of Canadian Verse*, 147
Gwyn, Sandra: *The Private Capital*, 15

H. D., 143, 146
Halifax Star, 45
Hiatt, Mary, *The Way Women Write*, 140, 141
Hitler, 39, 52
Huxley, Aldous, 2

Imperial Press Conference (London, 1930), 128

Jameson, Storm: *Three Kingdoms*, 129
Jelinek, Estelle: "Female Autobiography and the Male Tradition," 138, 140–41
Juhasz, Suzanne, 141

Keats, John: "On Looking into Chapman's Homer," 87
Kennedy, Leo, 143, 147; "Direction for Canadian Poets," 137
Klein, A. M., 63, 95, 123, 143, 145, 147
Knister, Raymond, 2, 12, 17, 49, 117, 123, 124, 137, 147
Kroetsch, Robert, 126

Lampman, Archibald, 23, 47, 62, 126; "The City of the End of Things," 47

171

Lane, Pat, 123
Laurence, Margaret, 135
Lawrence, D. H., 83
Lawson, Lon, 136
Layton, Irving, 79, 95, 145, 147
League Against War and Fascism, 3
League of Canadian Poets, 121, 125
Lenchina, Alice, 65
Livesay, Dorothy: and sexuality, 8, 9, 25, 30, 78, 82–113; and Marxism, communism, 2–3, 24–25, 33–40, 51–52, 54, 61, 124; as teacher, 6, 7, 14, 66, 124, 125–26, 157n30; childhood, 1, 11, 16–17, 52–54, 114, 118, 119–20, 121; education, 1–2, 7, 33–34, 83, 88, 94; health, 3, 15, 82, 102–4; journalism, 3–5, 54, 59, 126–133, 136; literary influences on, 1–3, 7–8, 24, 33, 36–37, 62, 84, 87, 93, 94, 97, 98, 112, 115, 119, 135, 143, 145–46; on aging, 69, 78–81, 96–97, 104–105, 130; on Japanese Canadians, 5–6, 54, 57–59, 124, 130, 131; on native peoples, 5, 54–57, 74–76, 106, 124, 130, 145; on nuclear threat, peace issues, 60, 69–74, 106; on women, 69, 71, 78, 95, 96, 110–113, 124, 130, 134–42, 144, 145, 147–48; promoter of work of others, 12, 14, 15, 71, 123–25, 137; pseudonym "Daphne Wilson," 117; radio, 6, 55, 57, 119, 131–32, 136, 137, 146; social worker, 3, 6, 32, 34, 39, 54, 83, 117, 128, 136

WORKS: EDITED VOLUMES
Collected Poems of Raymond Knister, 123
40 Women Poets of Canada, 14, 78, 124
Woman's Eye: 12 B.C. Poets, 14, 78, 124–25

WORKS: POEMS, BOOKS OF
Beyond War: The Poetry, 12, 70
Call My People Home, 6, 65–66, 131
Collected Poems: The Two Seasons, 6, 8, 10, 19, 26, 28–31, 40–45, 55, 60, 62, 65, 67, 78, 83, 86, 88, 89, 92, 93, 94, 100
Colour of God's Face, The, 8, 64–65, 92, 94, 95
Day and Night, 4, 45–52, 65, 68, 86
Documentaries, The, 6, 9, 36, 65–67, 132
Feeling the Worlds, 12, 13–14, 70, 74, 76, 77–78, 79, 80–81, 108, 110–113, 144
Green Pitcher, 1–2, 17–20, 25, 90, 143
Ice Age, 10–11, 55, 67, 72–74, 77, 79–80, 104–106, 144
New Poems, 6–7
Nine Poems of Farewell, 1972–1973, 10, 79, 81, 104, 105
Phases of Love, The, 12–13, 74, 78, 106, 110, 144
Plainsongs, 9–10, 74, 78, 100–104, 144
Poems for People, 5, 59–62, 131
Raw Edges: Voices from Our Time, The, 12, 71–72, 106–107
Right Hand Left Hand, 3, 11–12, 28, 34, 35, 38, 39, 52, 63–64, 68, 78, 83, 116, 118, 128, 132–33, 134–42, 147
Selected Poems of Dorothy Livesay, The, 10, 26, 28, 40, 60, 62, 86, 87
Signpost, 2, 20–28, 50, 143
Unquiet Bed, The, 8, 9, 10, 28, 30, 65, 66, 78, 92, 95, 96–100, 107, 144
Woman I Am, The, 11, 67–69, 74–76, 77, 78, 106

WORKS: POEMS, INDIVIDUAL TITLES OF
"Abracadabra," 61
"Absences, The," 88–89
"After Grief," 89
"After Hiroshima," 63
"Again the fever: at last to see you!" 30, 83
"Aging," 79, 104, 105
"Amazement," 30
"And Even Now," 29
"And Give Us Our Trespasses," 99
"Arms and the Woman," 112
"Artefacts: West Coast, The," 74
"Articulate Defense," 90–91
"'Ask of the Winds,'" 27
"At Dawn," 101
"At English Bay: December, 1937," 44
"Auguries," 101–102
"Aunt Helen," 80
"Autumn in Wales," 62, 131
"Autumn: 1939," 44
"Ballad of Me," 82, 111
"Bartok and the Geranium," 6, 11
"Before Independence," 94. *See also:* "Zambia"
"Bellhouse Bay," 74
"Blindness," 27

Index

"Book of Charms, A," 97
"Bread and Circuses," 13
"Breathing," 110
"Broadcast from Berlin," 35
"Bus Trip," 74
"Cabbage, The," 79
"Call My People Home," 6, 9, 57–59, 65
"Canada to the Soviet Union," 35
"Canadiana," 53, 63, 74
"Carnival," 61
"Cassandra," 79
"Catalonia," 44
"Catechism, A," 79
"Caw," 29
"Cave, The," 101
"Centennial People," 63
"Child Looks Out, The," 4, 47–48
"Child on Steps, The," 93
"Chinese," 18
"City Wife," 20, 22, 23, 29
"Climax," 22–23, 27
"Collared," 12, 79
"Comrade," 68, 83–84
"Con Sequences," 101
"Conversation, A," 92
"Conversation Macabre," 77
"Dark Runner, The," 85
"Dawnings," 110
"Day and Night," 3, 4, 9, 46–47, 49, 65
"Deep Cove: Vancouver," 43
"Depression Suite," 42
"Dialectics of Acupuncture, The," 13
"Difference, The," 24
"Dominion Day at Regina," 43–44
"Down Beat," 104
"Dream" (*Plainsongs*: "Sudden / a sceptred bird"), 101
"Dream, The" (*The Unquiet Bed*: "I met a unicorn, one seldom seen"), 97
"Dream, The" (unpublished, 1959: "Who has not been a thief"), 91
"Dust," 26
"Easter Saturday," 100
"Editorial Notes," 75
"Emperor's Circus—for Alden Nowlan, The," 95
"Enchanted Isle: A Dialogue, The," 15, 108
"Epitaph," 13, 80–81, 113
"Epithalamium for Susan," 86
"Euthanasia," 80

"Everywoman Every Man," 80
"Eve," 95
"Evensong," 62
"Experience," 19
"FDR," 62
"F.R.L.," 80
"Fable: The Bare Necessities," 13
"Fallow Mind, The," 4
"Fantasia for Helena Coleman, Toronto Poet," 52
"Fire and Reason," 19
"Fireweed," 18
"Five Months Young (for Galen)," 109
"Five Poems for Marcia," 49
"For Abe Klein: Poet," 95
"For Rent," 79
"For Gwendolyn [MacEwen]," 95
"Forsaken, The," 18
"Four Songs," 96–97, 99
"From the husk of the old world," 46
"Gathering Oysters," 74
"Generation," 63
"Grandmother," 70, 79
"Great Divide, The," 29
"Green Rain," 11, 23
"Growing Up," 35
"Gun, The," 105–6
"Halloweens, The," 53
"Heritage," 101
"Hermit," 19
"Hola! the moon," 30
"Houdini Eliot," 92
"Husband, The," 86
"Hymn to Man," 63
"Hard core of love, The," 107
"I am merry; till I lie alone," 30, 83
"I Never Hear," 40
"I never knew much about silence," 30
"I see you trying on an idea," 111
"I think I have not learned," 30
"Ice Age," 72
"If I Awake," 29
"If It Were Easy," 29
"Immigrant, An," 41
"Immortals, The," 89
"Improvisations on an Old Theme," 60
"Impuissance," 20, 25
"In Green Solariums," 35, 84–85. Originally "A Girl Sees It!"
"In the Street," 27
"Incendiary, The," 95
"Indian Graveyard," 131
"Indian Summer," 19, 89

"Inheritance," 61
"Inheritors, The," 80
"Inter Rim," 13
"Interiors," 104–5
"Interrogation," 27
"Invincible, The," 18
"Invocation," 89
"Isolate," 95, 121
"It's true, philosophies," 30–31
"Journey," 28
"Journey East, The," 100, 102
"Lake, The," 18
"Lament," 7
"Last Letter," 105
"Legends," 79–80
"Les Anglais: Coming Out of Quebec," 76
"Letter, A," 96, 98
"Letter at Midnight," 86
"Letter from Prison," 13
"Lizard: October, 1939, The," 44–45
"London Revisited: 1946," 131
"Lorca," 3, 4, 49, 50–51
"Lullaby," 60
"Making the Poem—for Jack Spicer, before his death," 95
"March 26," 79
"Mathematics," 105
"Matins," 60, 131
"'Meet me at noon.' 'All right,'" 30
"Merger, The," 112–13
"Metal and the Flower, The," 63
"Moments," 29
"Mon Semblable Mon Frère," 76
"Monition," 25
"Morning After, The," 86
"Morning Rituals," 105, 109
"Mother, The," 61
"Moving Out," 99
"My Mother Myself," 80, 110
"Neighbourhood," 26
"New Jersey: 1935," 63
"News from Nootka," 74, 75
"Nocturne," 86, 87
"Northern Loon," 28
"Notations of Love, The," 98, 99
"Nothing is Private," 111
"Now I Am Free," 29
"Now it is done," 107–8
"Of Mourners," 62, 74
"Of Neighbours," 63
"Okanagan Pictures," 62
"Old Bawd, The," 79, 105, 111

"Old Man Dozing," 28
"Old Soldier," 80
"Old Song," 97
"Old Woman in the K Mart," 77, 79
"On Looking into Henry Moore," 87–88, 110, 112
"On Seeing 'The Day of the Dolphin,'" 74
"One Way Conversation," 106, 111
"Ontario Story," 9, 66
"Operation, The," 102–4
"Other Side of the Wall, The," 80
"Outrider, The," 4, 9, 49–50, 65
"Page One," 61
"Panic Syndrome, The," 13
"Partings," 13
"Perceptions," 95
"Persephone," 89
"Perversity," 27
"Pheasant," 62
"Photograph," 80
"Picasso Sketching," 92. Originally "The Clowning Art"
"Pied Piper of Edmonton, The," 74
"Pioneer," 28–29
"Poetry is Like Bread," 69
"Postscript to Phyllis Webb," 95
"Precautions," 77–78
"Prelude for Spring," 4, 52
"Preludium," 61
"Prince Edward Island," 23
"Prisoner, The," 29
"Prisoner of Time, The," 79
"Prophet of the New World," 5, 55–57, 59
"Quartet," 79
"Queen City," 41
"Reality," 18
"Reservations," 74, 75–76
"Roots," 9, 66, 95, 109
"Russell Square: Spring," 90
"Salute to Monty Python," 79
"Search for Wholes, The," 112
"Second Language (Suite), The," 92, 93–94
"Secret Doctrine of Women, The," 108
"September Equinox," 13, 113
"Serenade for Strings for Peter," 2, 109
"Seven Poems," 47
"Shape me to your will," 30
"She Replies to His Pleas," 91
"Shell burst in my mind, A," 49
"Shrouding, The," 19, 109

Index

"Signpost," 21–22, 50
"Skin of Time, The," 86, 87
"Small Fry," 61
"Soccer Game," 95
"Song for Solomon," 26
"Song from a Sequence," 18
"Song from The Multitude," 29
"Sonnet for Ontario," 22
"Sonnet: the rule I follow," 89, 91
"Sonnets for a Soldier," 62
"Sorcery," 100, 101
"Snow Girl's Ballad, The," 101
"Spain," 44
"Speak Through Me," 45
"Spring," 95
"Staccato," 23
"Step Beyond, The," 111
"Stoned Woman, The," 105
"Sun," 27, 109
"Sunfast," 95
"Sympathy," 19
"Takeover, The," 77
"Taming, The," 99–100
"These things are patient out of time," 30
"This day takes hold of me and lifts me up—," 30
"This Page my book," 111
"Three Emilys, The," 11, 129
"Thumbing A Ride," 77
"Time," 26
"Time tells us we are tall," 91
"To a Younger Post [Al Purdy]," 95
"To Be Or Not To Be," 80
"To turn the pages of my loves," 91
"Touching, The," 97–98, 111
"Towards a Love Poem," 110–11
"Town Topics," 77
"Two," 13
"Unbeliever, The," 26
"Unitas," 55
"Unquiet Bed, The," 9, 96
"Vigil, The," 98
"Vintage," 89
"V-J Day," 61
"Voyage Out, The," 89
"Walking in the Park," 79
"Weapons," 21, 25
"Wedding," 94
"Wedlock," 86
"West Coast: 1943," 4, 9, 49, 65
"When I got home," 111
"Where I Usually Sit," 102

"White Fingers," 28
"Whitepiece," 73
"Who Are the Exiles," 74–75
"Widow" [*Collected Poems*: "No longer any man needs me], 89, 93
"Widow" [*Ice Age*: "The woman remembering"], 105
"Widow-Woman," 18
"Windows," 105
"Wine from Cyprus," 63
"Winter Ascendant," 74. *See also* "Winter Ascending"
"Winter Ascending," 12
"Winter Song," 86
"Without Benefit of Tape," 95
"Woman, The," 102
"Words Before Battle," 44
"Wraith," 18
"Your honesty," 30
"Zambia," 8, 64–65, 92, 94, 95–96

WORKS: PROSE—DRAMA
"Flags for Canada," 131
"Joe Derry," 37–38
"Personal History," 54
"Struggle," 38, 39, 40
"'Times Were Different, The'?" 38–40, 54, 63
See also: "Call My People Home," 6, 9, 57–59, 65; "Prophet of the New World," 5, 55–57, 59

WORKS: PROSE—ESSAYS AND REVIEWS
"Documentary Poem: A Canadian Genre, The," 66–67, 126
"Hunters Twain, The," 124
"Livesay's Choice," 124
"Not on My Verandah," 63
"Prairie Sampler, A," 116
"Proletarianitis in Canada," 35–36
"Song and Dance," 7, 93
"Tennyson's Daughter or Wilderness Child? The Factual and Literary Background of Isabella Valancy Crawford," 124

WORKS: PROSE—JOURNALISM
"B.C.'s Imaginary Headache—the Japanese," 131
"Better Break for the Indian, A," 131
"Blairmore," 136

"Canada's Japanese Problem," 131
"Corbin: A Company Town Fights For Its Life," 136
"Fascism in Quebec," 36
"Greenwood," 131
"Indians at Caughnawaugha," 36, 136
"More Population—Less Penury: Japanese Pioneers Prove It," 131
"Will B.C. Let Bygones Be Bygones for the Japanese Canadian?" 131

WORKS: PROSE—NOVELS (complete and incomplete)
Beginnings: A Winnipeg Childhood, 1, 11, 78, 116, 117, 118, 121
Her Father's House, 117–18
Give My Love to London, 117
Husband, The, 117
Intruder, The (or *The Glass House*), 127
Pavane, 117

WORKS: PROSE—SHORT STORIES
"Anna," 119
"Apple-Dear," 114
"Autumn Day," 116
"Cage, The," 117
"Case Supervisor," 116
"Cup of Coffee, A," 116
"Father's Boy," 120
"First Crocus," 116
"First Trials," 53, 119
"Flight," 118
"Glass House," 6, 116, 118
"Guardian Angel, The," 119
"Herbie," 116
"Immigrant," 116
"Matt," 116, 119
"No More Hankies," 115
"Other Side of the Street, The," 116, 120–21. Originally entitled "See the World Clearly"
"Out West," 116
"Party, The," 120
"Preludes," 116
"Six Years," 116, 118
"Sparrows, The," 116
"Two Willies, The," 116, 120
"Two Women," 116
"Uprooting, The," 120
"Wedding, The," 116. Originally "The Mother-in-Law"

"Week in the Country, A," 120
"Zynchuk's Funeral," 116

Livesay, Florence Randal (mother), 1, 14–15, 16–17, 20–21, 52–53, 78, 82–83, 110, 114, 126, 127; *Savour of Salt*, 114
Livesay, J. F. B. (father), 1, 16–17, 20, 53, 83, 85, 101, 111, 114–115, 117, 121, 126–27, 128; "The High White Bed," 115; *The Making of a Canadian*, 115; *Peggy's Cove*, 115.
Livesay, John Gillett (grandfather), 126
Livesay, Sophie (sister), 1, 39, 83, 118
Los Canadienses, 138
Lowell, Amy, 146
Lowry, Malcolm, 5
Lowther, Pat, 12, 123

MacClelland, David, 141
McClung, Nellie, 127
McCullagh, Joan: *Alan Crawley and "Contemporary Verse"*, 87
MacEwen, Gwendolyn, 95
Macnair, Duncan Cameron (husband), 4, 7, 8, 85–86, 88, 89, 91, 128, 129, 136
Macnair, Marcia (daughter), 4, 7, 49, 52, 67, 90
Macnair, Peter (son), 4, 7, 52, 67
Macpherson, Jay, 6
Mansfield, Katherine, 121
Marlatt, Daphne, 126
Marriott, Anne, 12, 66, 123, 147, 148
Marshall, Tom: *Harsh and Lovely Land*, 144–45
Masses, 35, 37, 38, 83
Massey's Magazine, 127
Matthews, William, 134–35
Mayne, Seymour, 124
Moore, Henry, 87
Munro, Alice, 135

Nation, 128
New Frontier, 3, 4, 37, 124, 128, 136
New Provinces: Poems of Several Authors, 147
Nowlan, Alden, 95

Ottawa Journal, 127

Pacey, Desmond, 10
Page, P. K., 123, 147, 148
Paris, 2, 7, 24, 25, 31–32, 34, 63, 83, 89, 129

Index

Picasso, Pablo, 63, 90, 92
Pierce, Lorne, 17
Pomerleau, Cynthia, 134
Porter, Cole: "Night and Day," 47
Pratt, E. J., 3, 46, 66, 121, 126, 127, 143, 145, 147
Progressive Arts Club, 3, 34, 38
Purdy, Al, 95, 126

Reaney, James, 60
Regina Leader Post, 126
Riel, Louis, 5, 55–57
Roberts, Sir Charles G. D., 23, 127, 143, 147
Room of One's Own. Livesay issue, 15, 63, 78, 108
Roosevelt, Franklin Delano, 62
Ryerson, Stanley, 2

St. Hilda's Chronicle, 121
Sandwell, B. K., 131
Saturday Night, 37, 130
Scobie, Stephen, 145
Scott, Duncan Campbell, 23, 126
Scott, F. R., 143, 145
Shaw, George Bernard, 33; *Arms and the Man, Intelligent Woman's Guide to Socialism, Major Barbara*, 112
Sitwell, Edith and her brothers, 2, 22
Smith, A. J. M., 143, 147
Souchotte, Sandra, 137

Spender, Stephen, 3, 36–37
Spicer, Jack, 95

Thomas, Audrey, 135
Toronto Daily Star, 2, 129, 130–31
Trower, Peter, 12

Van der Sprenkel, Otto, 2, 33
Vancouver Province, 16, 37

Waddington, Miriam, 60, 123, 147, 148
Watts, Eugenia "Jim," 1, 33, 137, 139
Webb, Phyllis, 95, 147, 148
Wells, Henry H., 146
Whitman, Walt, 24, 36, 62, 93
Wilbur, Richard, 13
Wilkinson, Ann, 147, 148
Winnipeg Free Press, 127
Winnipeg Telegram, 1, 126–27
Winnipeg Tribune, 128
Woman I Am, The (documentary film), 9
Woolf, Virginia, 115
Wylie, Elinor, 143

Young Communist League, 3, 37

Zambia (Northern Rhodesia), 7–8, 15, 40, 63–65, 92, 93, 94–96, 109, 117, 132, 144, 146
Zynchuk, Nick, 39, 41